or absorbed. Paracelsus
use "Ens Nature," those
om psychological causes.
is often caused by a dis-
ind.

e is spiritual in origin:
, disordered thoughts or
on. Such psychological
produce physiological

fth and final cause of dis-
has been created during
ce that might be consid-
ype of ailment must be
priority since it may be
o be paid. A cure for this
l require much more
rmaceutical concoction.
be of service in these
ble to see into the
and ultimately the
himself.

that plants were the
ions of astral influences,
e qualities of the stars,
act the influences of the
are sympathetically
should be gathered at a
et to which it is related
its essence may be
it is fresh. It is equally
ts should be adminis-
ing the corresponding
l.

of Paracelsus have been
r almost 200 years.
all hamlet in the

also followed the diet
going so far as to attempt to turn base met-
als into gold.

With the dawn of a new millennium
upon us, perhaps we should re-evaluate his
teachings for practical applications in our
own time. Consider the charge that Paracelsus gave to his students: "Those who attempt
to cure the sick by means of what they learn
in books and without using their own judgment, are like the foolish virgins mentioned
in the Bible, who wasted the oil from their
lamps, and tried to borrow light from others.
Those whose minds are open for the reception of the truth, who are charitable to all,
who love their art for its own sake and seek
to do the will of God, they belong to my
school and are my disciples. They will be
taught by the light of wisdom, and God will
perform his miracles through their instru-
mentality." (De Virtute Medici)

---

*A bishop in the French Gnostic church, John
Cole conducts services for the Parish of Mary
Magdalene in Evansville. He can be reached at
812/425-4440, or through the parish Web site
at www.dynasty.net/users/merlin.*

*In the accompanying illustration, Paracelsus is
shown surrounded by various philosophical
symbols, including his famous sword. From
Paracelsus: Etliche Tractaten, zum ander
Mal in Truck auszgangen. Vom Podagra
und seinem Speciebus (Coln, 1567). Washington University Collection.*

---

*Photo of fleabane and friend (left) and milk-
weed (above) © Angela Herrmann.*

John Lilly, so far…

JOHN LILLY, so far...

by

Francis Jeffrey and John C. Lilly, M.D.

JEREMY P. TARCHER, INC.
Los Angeles

Excerpts from John Lilly's work have been used with permission of the following:

Anchor/Doubleday, 666 Fifth Ave., New York, NY 10103: *Man and Dolphin* (1961), *The Mind of the Dolphin* (1967), *Lilly on Dolphins* (1975).

Crown Publishers, Inc., 225 Park Ave., New York, NY 10003: *The Center of the Cyclone* (1972), *Programming and Metaprogamming the Human Biocomputer* (1972), *Communication between Man and Dolphin* (1978).

Ronin Publishing Inc., P.O. Box 1035, Berkeley, CA 94701: *The Scientist* (1988).

Simon and Schuster Inc., 1230 Avenue of the Americas, New York, NY 10020: *Simulations of God* (1975), *The Dyadic Cyclone* (1976), *Deep Self* (1977).

The University of California Press, 2120 Berkeley Way, Berkeley, CA 94720: *The Dolphin in History*.

Library of Congress Cataloging in Publication Data

Jeffrey, Francis.
    John Lilly, so far— / Francis Jeffrey & John C. Lilly.
    p.   cm.
    ISBN 0-87477-539-6
    1. Lilly, John Cunningham, 1915–   .   2. Psychiatrists—United
States—Biography.   I. Lilly, John Cunningham, 1915–   .
II. Title.
RC438.6.L54J44   1990
616.89′0092—dc20
    [B]   89-28512
                                                                 CIP

Jeremy P. Tarcher, Inc.
5858 Wilshire Blvd., Suite 200
Los Angeles, CA 90036

Design by Susan H. Hartman

Manufactured in the United States of America
10 9 8 7 6 5 4 3 2 1

First Edition

CONTENTS

"Dr. Lilly, many people have different ideas about who you are. Some think of you as a scientist, others as a mystic, still others as a spokesman for the dolphins. How would you describe yourself?"

"I'm a student of the unexpected."

"Do you know where you're going next?"

"No way! But I don't have to; it happens."

—From a recent interview

CHAPTER 1

ANGELS IN THE BEGINNING

January 1925, age 10.

Fire within. The little boy's skin is waxen pale, with a pink glow where the fever scorches it. His body is limp, hot, and dry. Inside, he is unaware of the world surrounding his insensate body.

Outside, they are afraid he will die.

Inside is a golden world. Inside the little boy has a fuzzy-warm teddybear body cuddled by the golden, feathery wings of angels. From the golden blaze of light reaching to eternity, a point of exceptional brilliance comes toward him. It grows into a being whom he recognizes as his Guardian Angel. The Being communicates:

"Do you want to go away with me to join the other Beings?"

"No, I want to stay here. I want to get well and play."

"Very well, you will stay here and be a little boy. But someday you will go away with me. Meanwhile, I will be here whenever you need me."

John awakens in his sick, weak body lying heavily abed. Mother is there, and Nurse. They are smiling. Mother is saying soft and endearing things. They are grateful that the worst is past, the fever is broken, and he is regaining strength. He rests in bed. In a month he asks for solid food, and is fed eggs and toast. . . .

Awesome electrical storms polarize the humid summer morning as John is allowed out of bed after six months of confinement. Soon he may play with the other boys. Then it's au-

1

tumn, and back to school. Life continues for the ten-year-old, just as the Being promised.

A CHILD, DEATHLY ill, experiences something awesome, something that reaches beyond the confines of ordinary reality. Perhaps more extraordinary is the continuing memory of that experience as the child becomes a man, John Cunningham Lilly, a scientist who dedicates himself to exploring the frontiers of mind and brain, of inner and outer realities.

To understand that man, we must start with the coincidence of a bicycle accident at the turn of the century. Donald Lilly, destined to become John Lilly's grandfather, was riding his bicycle across St. Paul, Minnesota, on a chilling winter morning.

The bicycle was a one-speed. It had fat, knobby tires and a black leather seat stuffed with springs. It had big, springy shock absorbers and those funny old-fashioned handlebars, as in "handlebar mustache."

The dawn was gray and the streets wet, and there was a damp and biting cold in the air. His tires threw up globs of icy water melted from the dirty, frozen slush. Cloth couldn't keep out this Minnesota winter cold. Going somewhere was like taking a swim in ice water: All you could do was get cold and keep going and hope to warm up when you got to where you were headed.

Born in Brockton, New York, on August 16, 1858, Donald William Lilly had started out as a paper boy in nearby Jamestown and learned the newspaperman's trade in all its particulars: reporting, editing, typesetting, composing, printing, and hawking the product. He had a brief stint as editor of his own little Sunday paper in Jamestown, where he also had met his true love, Kate Enright of the flaming red hair, at the church social group organized by Father Coyle.

Catherine Loretta Enright was born in London on January 10, 1865, fair daughter of Jack Enright, a tailor and Irish Republican revolutionary who had fled his native land as a man marked for hanging. From London the Enrights migrated to upstate New York. When Kate's family later moved west, Don Lilly set out in pursuit.

On his way, he worked briefly for the *Cleveland Plain Dealer*. In St. Paul he fell back on his typesetting skill and his way with machines. Don took a job as a Linotype operator at the

St. Paul newspaper so that he and Kate could marry in February 1884.

Now long-settled in St. Paul, he had a wife and six kids to support. Before him this winter morning lay a day of work at the keyboard and controls of the big, chugging, smoke-belching, lead-stamping behemoth of mechanical ingenuity—the Linotype—chunking out studs of lead stamped with words of the daily news. Words to be melted down the next day and poured as bubbling hot lead back into the Linotype, day after day, over and over. (But it was one heck of an improvement over setting type by hand.)

It was here on the little downhill stretch of red brick road that Lilly's long journey intersected with the big black coal truck of destiny. A dull thwack in the chest hurtled Don Lilly from his bicycle seat to the ground. He was snagged by a pole protruding from the passing coal bin and thrashed about the rib cage. Broken ribbed, battered, and deflated, he lay on the pavement in pain. A long convalescence lay before him.

Kate and the newly disabled Don could not make ends meet, so their eldest son, Richard Coyle Lilly, born November 4, 1884, would have to go to work. At sixteen, he found employment for a pittance as a timekeeper and later as a messenger boy for the Merchants' National Bank. Energetic, diligent, faithful, good-hearted though aggressive, Dick rose through the ranks. He became the fastest teller on either side of the Mississippi, which flowed, one-foot deep in summer, right through the middle of this frontier metropolis of Minneapolis and St. Paul. He won the money-counting contest hands down, besting all the other apprentice bankers. In banking, his native intelligence found a place to shine, and by 1912 he was working at the First National Bank of St. Paul—as president. He was only twenty-eight years old.

Thus the incident that landed Donald Lilly in bed catapulted his eldest son, Dick, on an awesome rise that brought his hand within reaching distance of Miss Rachel Cunningham, princess of the St. Paul stockyards family, owners of Cunningham & Haas Company.

Rachel Lenor Cunningham was the daughter of a U.S.-born Scottish cattle puncher and a German mother who came from a village in Hesse-Darmstadt on the Rhine. (From the same tiny Old German duchy came the family of Hermann Hesse, the Nobel Prize–winning writer of German lyricism and the inner adventures of the soul.) By the turn of the twentieth century, the Cunningham-Haas family owned the stockyards on the edge of town—at the heart of the thriving economy of this western-midwestern trading center.

Rachel, born in St. Paul in April, 1888, married Dick in September 1910. Their first child, Richard, Jr., arrived the following year.

Before long, the Lilly-Cunningham family owned the bank.

In 1915 a second son—John Cunningham Lilly—was born to Rachel and Dick. It was January 6th, a day called "Epiphany" in the Christian calendar. Epiphany, an ancient Greek word meaning "a supernatural appearance," is the holiday that commemorates the meeting of a baby called Jesus and three Magi, wizards from the East.

John's childhood was marked by several extraordinary incidents that would shape his interests as an adult. Some involved his contacts with the Beings of his inner reality, as in the illness at age ten. John had recognized the Being that time because they had met before.

Once, as a tot, he had nearly stumbled off a cliff. Jamey, the family dog, grabbed little John and pulled him from the brink. John did not realize that Jamey had just saved his life, and he felt a flash of anger against the dog for tearing his jacket and pinching his shoulder in its canine teeth. At that point, the Guardian Angel appeared to set things right. "You shouldn't be angry at Jamey," explained the Being, "because I made him pull you back from the brink. I did it to save your body from being badly damaged by the fall."

At the age of seven, when his tonsils were removed under ether, John lost touch with the outside world. In the inner world, he was enfolded in the wings of two angels who comforted the frightened little boy until the operation was over and the ether wore off.

Later that year, as he knelt alone before the altar of his Catholic church and as the shadowy darkness receded to infinity and candlelight flickered upon the marble columns, he passed out of this world and into another. The interior of the church disappeared, and he saw God on His throne, surrounded by angels. They were praising God, singing, basking in His central radiance, while God's love and His caring for His creation radiated outward through the angels to all human beings. The two angels held their little boy in their wings in the midst of the rapturous scene.

So by the time John was ten, and deathly ill with tuberculosis, he knew that the Beings who communicated with him in the space of the golden light were the angels talked about in Catholic school. When his Guardian Angel told him he would get well and return to play with the other boys, John knew this was the truth.

His relationship with this Being, his Guardian Angel, would continue. The Being was closer to John than anyone in his family. Somehow it was attached to him, perhaps inside him, a part of himself. There were two other Beings who provided guidance, but they seemed less directly identified with John.

There were other, less sublime events in this little boy's life. In one trauma, shared by many children, his exceptional genius for controlling his inner world made an early appearance.

At age three, he was weaned from his mother's breasts with their warm, comforting milk. He was replaced at her breasts by his newborn brother, Dave (David Maher Lilly, born June 14, 1917). Many years hence, during his psychoanalytic training, John was to recall a recurrent dream of this incident.

"Mother does not love me," the boy thought. "Mother loves this new baby. I hate him. I hate Mother."

The little boy was caught up in rage, in hatred against Mother and her milk, her love and caring, and her security.

In the darkness of a closet he hid with his anger and disappointment. Tears burned his face like fire. These feelings were unbearable. In this space of darkness and isolation, he made the first major decision of his life. He decided to turn it all off. He decided to feel nothing. Mother, nothing. Breasts, nothing. Little baby David, nothing.

He cut himself off from his feelings for others. He somehow told himself to cut the links which tied him to feelings of warmth, closeness, security, identification, and to the consequent feelings of separation, disappointment, rage, and hatred.

His mind obeyed these instructions. John had his first successful experience of *programming* himself. He changed, and his world changed. The world was no longer a part of him. He was no longer part of Mother's crooning, caring identification with Baby. That world was gone. At age three, he stopped being Mommy's Baby and became an individual.

In place of the old world, there was instantly a whole new

world. His bonds to the old world had been emotional and sensory in a simple way, and, as a tiny bundle of feelings, his Being had been hardly distinct from the boundless, boundaryless world of Mother's affection. The ties to the new world were perceptual. The new world was made up of separate objects which could be explored. One experienced the new world by acting on it and acting in it. It was an environment in which he could move and operate, in which he was somebody *up against* that world.

This attitude would dominate John's approach to life for years to come. It would set him up to be a scientific observer *par excellence,* and a dispassionate observer of people. It would give him an uncanny objectivity and the ability to interact with people—even to marry and raise children without being very involved.

John Lilly's father, Dick, was a man of supreme good fortune and commensurate humility. Like his parents before him, he was a practicing Catholic. From them he inherited the best of Christianity the belief in a merciful God, the certainty that Heaven awaited, and the conviction that while on Earth he was to help others less fortunate than himself. In the home, in the family, he never ceased to express gratitude "to the Father"— meaning God. In the street, he never ceased to be captivated by the faces of little children, whom he would pause to admire, bless, and greet. In church he never failed to tithe.

Dick had sharp, chiseled features and a sleek, slender look. His basic stance—detached, alert, waiting for some event on which he was needed to take action—reminded one of an eagle sitting on a branch. He was friendly without being gregarious, and he didn't talk much except of matters at hand. His education was entirely practical; he was not a "thinker."

Dick became a philanthropist, once he had the means. He sent money to widows whose bereavement he read about in the newspaper. As a banker, he wrote loans to folks down on their luck, bending the rules of money lending as conscience demanded, and as intuition—not credit ratings—dictated. He was generous and prosperous.

Dick was a methodical man, in love with detail and repetition and regularity. He would work every day at the bank and then play eighteen holes of golf—every day, eighteen holes. (He and Dick, Jr., became Minnesota state "father-and-son" golfing champions.) Dick and his whole family shared a tremendous memory for detail.

John's mother Rachel was a tall, shapely woman with a pleasant maternal plumpness and a soft smile. Although well-to-do, she devoted herself entirely to caring for her family and keeping house. She took delight in the three little boys she had managed to bring into the world, in spite of a tendency to miscarry.

A well-educated woman, Rachel expressed her erudition only in the personal tutoring of her children and in the cultured ambience of her home. She was a wonderful mother who provided John with a home rich in educational opportunities. An expert pianist, she brought an aura of poetic sensitivity to her home and provided an element of culture that Dick, with his more pragmatic education, lacked. She opened rich arenas of knowledge for John and represented for him an "inner," "higher" world in the midst of Father's practical, local reality of money, business, and civics.

Convent educated, Rachel had attended teacher's college and later enrolled in the Montessori training seminars for parents. Dr. Maria Montessori, M.D., author of *The Montessori Method,* had revolutionized education by insisting that children need freedom of movement and by observing that when children are free to explore their environment, they naturally enter periods of intense concentration and concentrated learning.

Through Rachel, John was a direct beneficiary of Dr. Montessori's work. The home was full of books little Johnny could dig through. These included Mom's old schoolbooks, such as the writings of the philosopher Immanuel Kant, as well as the eleventh edition of the *Encyclopaedia Britannica.* John spent many hours immersed in the thick, leather-bound volumes of the great encyclopedia, where he could read articles written by such great scientists as Einstein, Raleigh, and Helmholtz. Thus he was exposed at an early age to the thinking of the leading scientists themselves, as expressed in their own words.

When John was fifteen, Rachel took him on a Caribbean cruise. She bought him a 16-millimeter movie camera, in which he used some of the very first color film. (Later he would use this camera to film a documentary at prep school.)

To John, Rachel was always deep, mysterious, and beautiful. He would retain this image of her throughout his life.

As a little kid, John was frightened by the scary movies that played in the dark at the local theater, especially films about monsters and ghosts. At the scariest parts, he would cover his eyes with his hands and slump down protectively into his seat. Then one day he had a revelation: When those scary scenes were filmed, no matter what was happening on camera, just off camera there was always a movie crew filming and directing the action—a cameraman, a director, a script girl, and so forth. He realized that the movie was a *simulation*, and he could take the off-camera perspective whenever he wanted.

After that, John was never afraid of movies—or anything else. He had learned the observer's point of view. It was a kind of enlightenment that was actually the goal of many esoteric teachings: The one who experiences is actually above and beyond the action, no matter how frightening it may seem at the moment. In later life he would develop this point of view with great sophistication, along with the concept of simulation.

When John was twelve, the FBI entered his life. Real G-men came to the Lilly home in a shiny black car, clean snub-nosed guns in their shoulder holsters, shiny badges inside their coats, fingerprint kits in their bags, a spit shine on their shoes. They were here to help. It had all started when John's dad launched a personal crusade to clean up city hall.

It was becoming increasingly obvious that St. Paul, Minnesota, had a corrupt city administration. So corrupt that you couldn't do *any* official business without paying off the crooks. As one of St. Paul's leading citizens, and foreman of the county grand jury, Dick Lilly decided it was high time to act, and applied his considerable influence to cleaning up the town. In addition to working through official proceedings, he launched a private "intelligence" operation in conjunction with some other business leaders.

One of the members of this ad hoc vigilance committee was a pal of J. Edgar Hoover's. Through Hoover's referral they hired an off-duty FBI agent to conduct an investigation. This anti-crime crusader bugged the phones in city offices, and soon he had "the goods" on both the gangsters and the city officials fronting for them. The transcripts showed that the mayor and the police chief were on the take, and the district attorney, although himself honest, was helpless in this situation.

Dick discovered that the crooks were from the notorious Tooey Gang, based in Chicago. Events took an ominous turn when Bill Hamm, heir to the Hamm's Brewery fortune, was abducted right off the golf course, and ransomed for $50,000. With that the FBI moved in and alerted Dick that his family also might be targeted for kidnapping. Dick's chauffeur, Ralph, had to pack a pistol and serve as bodyguard. At one point, somebody dynamited the mailbox in front of the Lilly house.

Of course, all this was in the midst of the "Roaring Twenties," when so much of American society had been corrupted by the criminal opportunities created by Prohibition. The attempt by do-gooders to save people from the hazards of alcohol had spawned a national black market in booze. Vast networks of organized crime reached into city halls, police departments, state capitols, federal agencies, and even into the FBI. By 1927, most government agents were corrupt; the few cops who couldn't be bought were distinguished as "The Untouchables." The threat to the Lilly family at this point was probably quite serious.

The three FBI men who came to the Lilly house that afternoon advised John, his mother, and his little brother, Dave, on how to deal with kidnappers. They fingerprinted the whole family. And they told John that in case he was kidnapped, he should leave his fingerprints wherever he could—such as on the windows of cars—so that his trail and that of the kidnappers might be followed.

Dad settled the crisis in a nonviolent manner. He had the transcripts from the wire tap published as a serial in the *St. Paul Daily News*. With that, everybody in town knew what was going on at city hall. When the situation got too hot for the Tooey Gang, they packed up and returned to Chicago. The revelations in the newspaper so embarrassed the weak and corrupt city officials that they were all cleared out of office in the next election. And the county sheriff, who had made a deal with the Chicago crooks that St. Paul would be a safe haven for wanted men from other counties, was eventually busted by the FBI and jailed.

From his dramatic encounter with the FBI, and from his father's battle with the Tooey Gang, John extracted several lessons. First, the good guys, men of goodwill and good repute, banded together as the Establishment and, represented by the government, were an effective force with powerful means at their disposal in the battle against the bad guys. Second, no one was really safe in this world, not even innocent little kids like himself and his brother David. There was no such thing as security, not even in a prominent family like the Lillys of St. Paul. Third, sometimes people had to take chances to uphold the good and defeat the forces of evil, and even children like John could be recruited. And fourth, the news media could be a potent tool for exposing corruption and inducing reform.

John was really impressed with Dad's fight against crime. At the same time he was aware that Dad had a favorite bootlegger who kept the family supplied with an illegal drug, alcohol, throughout the dry years of Prohibition. Dad may have been righteous, but he was no goody-goody.

As John grew up, he drew many positive and negative lessons from his parents. Regarding sex—insofar as he understood sex at that point—he determined that he would never allow himself to be caught in the situation in which he saw his parents during his late childhood.

Rachel had borne four children. After Dick, John, and Dave, there was little sister Mary Catherine, who was born in June of 1920 and died in infancy.

At least five other potential siblings conceived by Dick and Rachel were stillborn or spontaneously aborted. As a small boy, John had observed one of his stillborn siblings buried secretively in the backyard. He watched as Mother's belly repeatedly would grow to various stages of pregnancy and then abruptly return to its normal, nonpregnant shape. Little John watched his mother decline in health and vivacity, worn out by these many pregnancies.

In the beginning, Dick and Rachel desired children. They had heard the biblical admonishment, "Be fruitful and multiply," and they took it seriously. Every live-born child was an addition to God's happy family. Every unsuccessful pregnancy was regarded as a loss; but they would try and try again.

There was also the matter of Catholicism and the teachings of the popes, right down to that of the current incumbent, Pius XI, all forbidding contraception. John's parents, as members of a traditional Catholic community, did not practice birth control—at least until they decided one day to practice it in the old-fashioned, approved Catholic way: They moved into separate bedrooms.

There ensued the predictable alienation of affection, as John observed his father paying closer attention to other women. Although he did not understand the full implications of these digressions, he nonetheless felt something to be amiss. In fact (as he later surmised), his father was having sexual liaisons with several prominent local women. While relatively discreet, Dick was no hypocrite about it; he introduced these glamorous women to John as "lady friends" whenever the occasion arose.

John wondered how they could go on as Mother and Father in this warm, family way, while at the same time Father had something going on the side. He could not comprehend the rationale behind his parents' behavior. But he did sense something deeply wrong from the estrangement he observed, that no one ever forthrightly acknowledged or explained. In this respect at least, he resolved he would not follow his parents' model in his own future married life. Little did he know what lay ahead.

At ten John fell in love with a girl named Margaret Vance, who attended the same Catholic school. She was beautiful, with long brown hair and a La Giaconda smile. They were photographed together with their Catholic confirmation class, and he had his first premonitions of sex in the form of fantasies of "exchanging urine" with her.

Yet when he discovered orgasm at twelve, it involved angels and an exercise machine instead of a girl. The machine was one of those big gadgets with a belt worn around your belly or rump and a powerful electric motor on a stand to make the belt vibrate. Located in Dad's bedroom, it was part of his physical fitness regimen. With his parents away one afternoon, John decided to give it a try.

All the vibration stimulated his erogenous zones; he had the feeling that the world around him disappeared. It was a religious experience that sent John and his Guardian Angel flying for heaven. Enrapt in the vibrating belt, he went through orgasm and ejaculation and superconsciousness, and collapsed into a state of moist-eyed, wet-crotched postorgasmic bliss, in which his returning parents found him slumped on the floor.

After that, he learned about "masturbation," first from his father and mother, then from the family doctor, then from a Catholic priest. Evidently, the world at large already had well-formed ideas about this phenomenon John had only just discovered. According to Mother and Father, it was terribly embarrassing and cause for parental concern. According to the family doctor, Dr. Brunhal, it was a potential health hazard, called "abusing yourself," and too much of it could drive you insane. According to John's Catholic father-confessor, it was a "mortal sin" (referred to in lurid undertones as "jacking off") which all growing boys were apparently expected to commit. This sin led to confession, contrition, penance, and repentance, thus carrying out the divine plan of salvation as designed by the Catholic church.

"If this is religion," young John thought, "then I want nothing of it." After his first orgasm, John couldn't accept the idea that sexual pleasure was a mortal sin. The bliss, the divine ecstasy he'd experienced, just couldn't be wrong. In fact, it must be close and akin to God. After all, hadn't it lifted him into the realm of angels?

If religion didn't agree with his own experience, then religion itself must be wrong.

With this brilliant deduction, the child untutored in science conceived the embryo of scientific thinking: Ideas that conflict with experience must be abandoned. In the face of reality, in the face of actual experience, John threw the complicated system of ideas associated with Catholicism overboard.

These ideas were expressed in the Latin mass, which he had memorized as an altar boy. Religion was a creed which he had learned in catechism class: "I believe such and such . . . I believe in so and so . . ."

So, he reasoned, to reject religion, you simply reversed the formula: "I disbelieve such and such . . . I do not believe in so and so . . ." In this way John systematically renounced the religion he had been taught, because it conflicted with his physical and spiritual experience.

But there is more to religion than a system of ideas, a verbalized creed of beliefs. There is also the reverence, the sense of wonder experienced by the innocent mind encountering the awesome experiences of life and the awe-inspiring appearances of nature. All this stayed with the boy and became for him the emotional roots of the science he would embrace, whose intellectual creed he did not yet know.

And one other remnant of religious education survived his renunciation of the creed: deeply ingrained and preconscious reactions of guilt, and feelings of sinfulness. The emotional imprint from Catholicism survived far longer than the mental indoctrination. The context and tone of his religious education encouraged profound ignorance and practiced unconsciousness of the realities of sex between people.

This background would hobble John as he bumbled into and through his first marriage, and beyond. What his Catholic background effectively worked against is beautifully summed up in the term *carnal knowledge*—not sex per se, but a conscious, voluntary, intelligent, knowledgeable, self-determined approach to sexuality.

In discovering the experiential connection between the sensual and the spiritual domains so abruptly, through his first encounter with sexual ecstasy, John had stumbled into the very center of one of the prickliest conflicts in the history of human culture on Planet Earth. The spiritual-mental nature and the sensual-sexual nature were said to be opposed. The sexual dimension of being was devalued by Catholicism. Ideally, one was supposed to shun the animal world of sex in order to become a totally spiritual being—a saint. (Short of that, you were urged to become sexual with as little sensuality as possible—just enough to breed in the confines of a Christian marriage.)

As a child, John was neither fully sensual nor fully spiritual. After discovering the connection, he felt that he must now strive to be both—fully sexual and fully spiritual. It was a matter of both/and, not a question of either/or. But nevertheless, the two proclivities often seemed to pull one in opposite directions.

And John extracted one more intellectual lesson from this episode: Big organizations and prominent, respectable persons often believe in and promulgate irrational ideas and behavior that may be profoundly antithetical to the interests of the individual. Yet individuals are induced to believe in these notions, which support the agenda of the institution.

It did not escape John's notice that his family religion offered so many opportunities for sin and confession.

When John was thirteen, his family bought a 160-acre spread on the outskirts of town called Paradise Farm. Dave and John and Dick, Jr., got used to country ways.

John, the budding scientist, excavated for fossils and spent his spare time observing snakes, frogs, and bugs. He studied the night sky and wondered about distant stars. He gazed in awe at the aurora borealis.

He got hooked on amateur radio, thanks to a neighbor's kid, Jack Galt. John and Jack and Harry Morton (a young man who worked for Northwest Airways as a radio operator) built a short-wave radio station. At their "ham" station W9HRB, they spent their time with glowing vacuum tubes, telegraph keys, and antenna wires. They had conversations with people as far away as Buenos Aires, Argentina and Sydney, Australia. John learned that he could communicate with distant minds using science and technology, his consciousness no longer stuck in St. Paul, Minnesota. He became a global citizen of what would one day be called the electronic village.

This power of communication made a big impression on John. In future years he would rarely be found without an antenna or two.

Meanwhile, Dick, Jr., now seventeen, had obtained a horse, a car, a girlfriend named Alice Kline, and a gun. He began "feeling his oats," and getting into trouble regularly. Once his father had to bail him out of jail for drunk driving. On another occasion, he was beaten for taking shots at John with his rifle.

In June 1928, young Dick went out riding with Alice, who lived across the valley. On his way home in the dark and late for dinner, he was thrown from his horse. When the animal came home alone, Dick, Sr., went out and found his eldest son lying unconscious in the muck where his horse had tripped while crossing the brook.

An ambulance came and took Dick, Jr., to the hospital. He languished in a coma for three days, and then the surgeon decided to operate. Dick's liver hemorrhaged and the boy died on the operating table. John guessed that the doctor had acted incorrectly out of ignorance, an analysis later confirmed by his own medical education. John vowed to become a doctor and save lives by improving medical techniques.

In his new stature as eldest son, John felt an expanded sense of responsibility and became an enthusiastic scholar. At fourteen, he left Catholic school for the St. Paul Academy and its brilliant faculty, including many graduates of Harvard University.

John then began spending time himself with Alice Kline, several years his senior. Tall and athletic with long blond hair, she dressed in riding clothes, western style. She seemed highly intelligent to John, a quality that impelled him to idealize her. In his thoughts she became his image of a romantic heroine, a strong, smart woman, his muse. For the first time he experienced the natural cohesion of love and sexual desire, but he didn't get to express it. Beautiful and sweet, she refused to get sexy—at least with John. Alice appreciated John for his scientific knowledge and a shared interest in poetry.

After Alice, he approached other girls closer to his own age, but still got nowhere. He went through a string of infatuations with teenage girls who didn't reciprocate, even though John was a big, strong, energetic young man with a natural talent for athletics. (At prep school he starred in football, before losing interest. He practiced shooting and became an expert marksman.) The young women he pursued seemed to be meant for different kinds of boys—more extroverted and aggressive and rambunctious and "normal," less intellectual and more socially engaged in all of life's ordinary rituals and local tomfoolery. Young men already marked for the conventional future that lay before them—unlike John Lilly.

Following the 1929 stock market crash, American working folks were facing the hard times of the Great Depression. Those who still had any money were suddenly way ahead of those who lost it and couldn't find paying jobs. The Lilly family was fortunate to remain above the general distress. Their bank was one of the few that did not fail. Their money was suddenly worth *more*, in contrast to the depressed economy. In 1930, Dick Lilly built the largest building in town as a new home for his bank.

And Dad's name was even on the money! Take the 1929 $10 bill, for example. It bore the signatures of W.O. Woods, treasurer of the United States; E.E. Jones, registrar of the Treasury; H.R. Fairchild, cashier; and R.C. Lilly, president of the Federal District Bank.

Charles A. Lindbergh was the hero of the day. His 1927 solo

flight across the Atlantic thrilled the world and brought the continents closer together. Travel by air became the model for the emerging future. Lindbergh was destined to remain the unequaled American hero until the 1962 orbital space flight by astronaut John Glenn.

In St. Paul, John's father took control of Northwest Airways through his banking activities and became its president. This small firm, a commercial-aviation pioneer, would become the huge Northwest Orient Airlines. In 1930, the company was occupied with mail runs for the U.S. Post Office. Their bread and butter was getting the new "air mail" through on time. Working under economic pressure, time pressure, and the proverbial postman's ethic about rain, sleet, and so on, only the brave or foolhardy took the job of flying the early biplanes, trimotors, and Hamiltons at all hours and under the worst of conditions. It was deadly dangerous work.

John met the pilots, some of them daredevils left over from the Great War for Democracy, and they took him up on practice runs. John got to know the whole staff of this company. Within three years, twenty-five of the pilots were killed in various accidents. Mail planes would plow into dark mountainsides in the middle of the night. New models delivered from Lockheed would explode mysteriously in midair, killing the whole crew. It was a wonder the airline stayed in business.

Passenger service was started using Ford trimotors. Air travel was considered a health hazard, and the first stewardesses were required to be registered nurses.

At fifteen, John signed on for ground work with the manager, Colonel Britton. He spent a miserable summer retrofitting electrical wiring in sweltering aircraft fuselages on the sun-baked airfield, collecting fifty dollars per month for hard, productive work. He surmised from this experience that the workaday world where most people spend their lives consisted of boring, repetitious slavery.

Even his father, a millionaire, who was head of the bank and the airline, was doomed to spending most of his life sitting at a desk pushing paper.

To young John Lilly, the danger and adventure of the pilots' lives seemed bright and appealing by comparison.

CHAPTER 2

"EINSTEIN, JR."

May 1928, age 13.

Mother is in the kitchen making pies. Dick, Jr., and his pals are playing football on the lawn.

John is crouched over a washtub filled with chemicals in the basement. He has access to the biggest chemistry set in St. Paul, in the form of Mr. Dickson's drugstore. Mr. Dickson is a pharmacist eager to share his chemical magic with the bright lad. As a result, John's secret basement laboratory includes a book on how to make chemical reactions, a large collection of chemical species scavenged from Mr. Dickson's inventory, and an impressive array of equipment. With these resources, he has already undertaken several successful experiments, including an explosion in a cauldron and a firewood bomb—which he exploded in a snow bank one previously calm evening as his father was attempting to relax with the evening news before the family fireplace.

A Coke bottle full of magic powders in his hand, John leaves the basement and approaches Dick, Jr., and his friends in the yard. "Hey, guys, look at this!"

John shakes up the Coke bottle which grips the boys' attention and drops in a match.

Blammo! The gunpowder explodes. The boys scatter, terrorized, peppered with glass fragments and bleeding.

John is unscathed.

HIS FASCINATION WITH science began with magic.

The magic of metal sodium melting on the surface of water

and skittering about under its own power . . . the magic of potassium bursting into a violet flame . . . the magic of chemicals mixing together to make an explosion. The magic of electricity, which can make a compass needle turn and little motors move and buzzers sound. It can make sparks fly, and if you put it into your body, it can make your muscles twitch.

And then he learned that behind the magic was science. In the 1920s, the boy John Lilly was catching on to an idea yet to take hold in the world at large: that a sufficiently advanced technology appears as magic to those who do not understand how it operates. Magic is merely the outward appearance of science.

John loved to experiment. He loved the noise and smoke and flashes of light and smell and brilliant colors. He loved the danger and became hooked on its thrill. He connected being scared with exhilaration, power, triumph—the same juxtaposition of feelings found in warriors, the same sensation as the thrill of combat. John was preparing for his future battles and adventures in science.

No experiment is a failure, he was destined to write many years later as a distinguished senior scientist. No experiment is a failure—no matter what happens, no matter how unexpected the results or how shocking the outcome. (Unless it kills you—and even then it is sure to yield new information.) What matters is that you perform the experiment and experience something new.

For young John, science was about excitement and participation and revelation. It was the moment of discovery that mattered—the awesome moment of revelation. It was the wonder of seeing Nature reveal Herself. (And, perhaps, to see God reveal Himself through Nature?)

This excitement and wonder characterized the formative experiences of John the Scientist. More sophistication would come when John left his parochial school at age fourteen and entered prep school. Here he encountered a more practical and intellectual understanding:

Science is about finding answers to questions.

Around this time John read *The Mysterious Universe* by Sir James Jeans, the astronomer. Deeply impressed by the magnitude of the physical universe, he realized how little people really know about the world around them. He realized that our knowledge is tiny compared with reality, and our ignorance vast in comparison with our knowledge. John felt that it would be futile to try to expand knowledge to encompass reality; but at least one could hope to chip away at the colossus of man's ignorance. This endeavor required discovering pieces of that ignorance—in the form of the right questions.

In St. Paul, all the boys could tell that John Lilly was not an ordinary kid on his way to prep school. They called him "Einstein, Jr."

At the St. Paul Academy, John had some fine teachers. Science instructor Russell Varney encouraged him to do experiments for himself, and allowed John to stay after hours to use the science lab. Varney, a trim and fit-looking man who always wore glasses and a uniform, was also the military instructor at this semi-military academy. Varney expanded John's understanding of science as a matter of firsthand experience and experimentation, as opposed to abstract information found only in books.

Another teacher who heavily influenced John was Herbert Tibbetts, master of English and Latin. A charming man with a lopsided smile, he listened carefully to students, displaying an endearing openness and camaraderie unusual for teachers. Mr. Tibbetts encouraged John to tackle the great philosophers, including Immanuel Kant, some of whose works John had already read at home.

From Kant's *Critique of Pure Reason,* John discovered that you can prove anything you want by using logic and language. Never mind whether it has any relation to reality! Kant would prove one thing, then turn around and proved the opposite, his two antithetical arguments laid out side by side on the page.

Philosophy was thus very different from science, where ideas are tested in direct confrontation with the reality of experience. John concluded that science is therefore *greater than* philosophy. In science, you philosophize all you want but then test your ideas against the real world. Although science *includes* philosophy, it is more complete because it includes experimentation as well as abstract thought. It was this idealized view of science that John took away with him from St. Paul to Caltech and his subsequent career. It was an approach he would frequently test against the real world of scientific institutions, where he would find that science as actually practiced by organized groups often fell short of this ideal.

Kant also helped to finish off Catholic dogma for John once

and for all. He finally realized that the doctrinaire teachings of the church were arbitrary. One could just as well make up a different set of beliefs! The real point was *the act of believing.* The decision to believe or to disbelieve is a powerful action with enormous consequences—as the pervasive impact of various common religious beliefs on individual lives and on human culture powerfully demonstrates.

Mr. Tibbetts encouraged John to write an essay on the meaning of "Reality." During weeks of intellectual searching, he hit on the central issues of *brain versus mind,* and *objective versus subjective,* which he developed along the following lines:

The brain, as the physical organ located in the head, is physically real and can be objectively observed. The mind, on the other hand, is the activity of the brain. Its presence in another person can only be inferred through that person's conduct, but the mind can be observed subjectively in oneself. Therefore, the mystery of reality lies in the relationships between the brain and the mind, between the objective and the subjective, between the outer and the inner, between the public and private reality.

It was an stunning piece of work for a sixteen-year-old.

Reality

by John C. Lilly

—1931—

. . . Today reality may be said (in its less involved meanings) to possess the same attributes as the original meaning of *res* [Latin: a law court]. First it expresses that which is completely objective as opposed to anything subjective. By objective we mean existing without the mind, outside it, and wholly independent of it. Subjective, on the other hand, takes the meaning of that which is in the mind. For instance, consider the case of a small child who has its fingers stepped on for the first time. The child perceives through its sense of sight that a thing has caused a sensation of pain, also that this was not under control of his mind therefore it is objective. The sensation of pain passing to the child's brain forms a thought of fear, or anger directed towards the cause of the sensation. This thought is subjective.

Let us consider the two cases, one of a genius working on an original problem, . . . and one of a young man intensely in love for the first time. The genius concentrates on his

problem to such an extent that he entirely forgets . . . his
environment. The only real existence this man now has is in
his mind. It is practically the same in the situation of the
young man. He is so perfectly under the influence of the
captivation of the girl that he thrusts aside everything but the
thoughts of her; he undergoes stresses that he has never met
with in objective reality. He is controlled, not by outside
means, but by his own state of mind. He can hardly eat or
sleep; he doesn't pay attention to anything exterior to his
thoughts. This great emotional stress is so predominant that
it is now his only existence and reality.

. . . How can the mind render itself sufficiently objective
to study itself? In other words, how are we able to use the
mind to ponder on the mind? It is perfectly feasible for the
intellect to grasp the fact that the physiological changes of the
brain occur simultaneously with thought, but it cannot conceive of the connection between its own thoughts and these
changes. The difficulties of the precise relation between the
two have caused many controversies as to which is the more
real, the objective or the subjective reality. . . .

A man is alone on a barren island with no sign of life
on it. After a period this man begins to see the stark barren-
ness of objective reality; he perceives that there is nothing for
him in the world but his own thoughts. The question now
arises—Is this reality the man experiences really subjective,
that is, does it exist solely in his mind, or has it an external
existence?

. . . Reality, then, resolves itself into more of a study of
the intellect than of objectivity.

The essay was a big hit with Mr. Tibbetts, and was published in the school magazine, *Now and Then,* on May 7, 1931. It
also set John's brain-mind on one of the great themes to govern
his future life and career: the search for Reality. The search for
the elusive relationship between the brain that can be observed,
and the activities of the brain that can be experienced, between
the outer realities and the inner realities.

The process of writing the "Reality" paper provoked some
deeply disturbing thoughts in John, avenues of speculation that he
chose not to develop fully in the essay itself but would return to
in later life.

Theologian and philosopher George Berkeley had suggested that in order for anything to exist, it must exist in someone's mind—either a person's mind, or the mind of God. From this idea, John went on in his essay to the unsettlingly profound thought that his personal, *subjective* ideas might not be his alone; rather they might be contained in some greater mind, such as the "mind of God," and thus have an independent existence—and hence, in some sense, they would be *objective.* With this leap of philosophical imagination, John pounced upon the concept (not stated in the essay) of a universal *network of mind,* Mind with a big M, of which each individual mind is only a small compartment.

If this universal Mind exists, then scientific "discovery" is actually a process of revelation in which the larger Mind transfers some of its knowledge into an individual mind. The exercises of experimental science are then no longer seen as procedures for programming the physical conditions of experiments; rather, they are viewed as methods for preparing the individual mind to receive the revelation by focusing it on the pertinent questions.

These ideas were so unconventional that John did not dare to touch on them in his writings for some thirty years, until *Man and Dolphin* in 1961. But all the while such notions hovered in the background, urging skepticism about the very meaning of the scientific enterprises in which he was engaged throughout that period.

Proudly, John showed his "Reality" essay to his parents. Mother read it with great interest, grasped its meaning, and showed appreciation for its depth. Father said he didn't get it at all. He read it straight through as though it was a business plan or a newspaper—but he couldn't find any numbers in it, or any news. The issue of what constitutes Reality escaped him completely.

For Dick Lilly, reality was what happened at the bank and on Main Street. Reality was what you read about in the papers. Reality was feeding and clothing and housing your family. For Dick Lilly, there was no question about Reality, or any room for such a question in his view of life.

About this time, John and his father sat down for a man-to-man discussion about John's future—by which Dick meant John's choice of a future career. Their talk took place at the bank in

Dick's huge corner office on the mezzanine level. Dad was seated at his big oak president's desk, a vantage point from which the meaning of reality appeared perfectly clear, neatly arrayed in his stacks of business papers.

For Dick Lilly, the obvious next step for John was to go into banking, after attending the best Ivy League college for the sort of education that Dick had missed. "With your top grades, you'll have no trouble getting into Harvard. And after that, there will be a place for you here at the bank. After you've had some experience, I'll set you up in a business of your own." (This program was later followed by brother Dave who, after a distinguished career in business and government service, ended up quite wealthy, creating the TORO brand of lawnmowers, among his other accomplishments.)

From his less powerful position in a leather side chair, John told his father unequivocally, "I don't want to spend my life pushing paper around the top of a desk!" For John, this world of the "paper reality" lacked both the sensory immediacy of real physical work and the exciting uncertainty of intellectual, scientific exploration. While he did not yet fully appreciate the power inherent in all the paper-pushing operations his father performed, young John was certain they were not for him.

From his desk, Dick could look out through the wide-framed windows of his citadel at the crossroads of St. Paul, this thriving metropolis where his influence was shaping the external reality of buildings, factories, and concert halls, as well as the lives of the people who lived there. He could scarcely imagine a more meaningful life. His position in this no-nonsense reality was solid. He had learned the reality of business from the school of hard knocks. Along the way he also earned a law degree, studying part-time at a local business college. He had risen through the ranks by his own indomitable efforts. In his desk he kept a small notebook in which he had recorded how much he was paid from the time he joined the bank at age sixteen to the present. This was his reality—a story of remarkable success achieved by focusing on the matter at hand.

And yet from his position as civic kingpin, as president of the premier bank, as a director of the Great Northern Railway, the Minnesota Mining Company (later called 3M), Northwest Airways and Archer Daniels Midland, and as cofounder of the country club—in all this Dick Lilly may have sensed a certain emptiness, a lack of depth. Perhaps it was an intimation of a deeper, inner reality into which his son was now moving after Dick had done the pick-and-shovel work of making the family rich. Perhaps it was an inkling of a genetic trait in his own constitution that was more fully expressed in his son. Perhaps it was the next step in a man's development, at which he would arrive only very late in his own life. In this respect, the child was far ahead of his father.

In later life, Dick would become profoundly bored with his polished performance as a business wizard, and his consciousness would pass its days in an inchoate inner absorption, as his body continued going through the expert motions of managing the financial life of his family and community. And much later, in the late 1950s, Dick would finally acknowledge to John that his own life, from its business machinations to its Catholic code of morals, had long since become merely pro forma.

Dick and John did not resolve the issue of John's future for some time after their conversation at the bank. But perhaps it was these early intimations of this emptiness, which later became so poignant, that prompted Dick finally to acquiesce to John's wishes.

Back at school, Mr. Tibbetts encouraged John to explore the communications media. With two buddies, John made an hour-long documentary movie about life at the St. Paul Academy. They shot many hours of 16-millimeter black-and-white film, and edited it into an effective presentation. The film highlighted social problems at the campus, such as hazing and bullying. Headmaster John de Quadville Briggs, fearing it would portray the Academy in a bad light, attempted to censor it. But John and his colleagues stood firm, the film was shown, and it had the effect of prompting the headmaster and the board of trustees to institute reforms. These events convinced young John of the impact of recorded events, the power of the media over people and organizations, which he had first seen during his father's successful campaign against city corruption.

In his senior year at St. Paul, John was accepted at the Massachusetts Institute of Technology, but Mr. Varney persuaded him to apply to the California Institute of Technology as well. John took the special Caltech entrance exam, and his efforts were rewarded.

A letter arrived from Caltech: "We are pleased to inform you that your grades on our entrance examinations were high enough that we wish to offer you a scholarship. . . ." It was a full scholarship, covering tuition and all expenses. (Little did the school know that John Lilly was a "rich kid." And little did John know that being a rich kid could become a problem at Caltech later.)

This inviting offer prompted a fierce joy in young John Lilly. All at once he was independent from both Father and his money. After a family argument, in which Dick pressured him to go to MIT, all expenses paid, and Rachel took John's side, it was decided that he could go where he wanted. And so at the appointed time, John took a big diesel train to the quiet little town of Pasadena, California—where, coincidentally, his parents had spent their honeymoon in 1910.

CHAPTER 3

THE EDUCATION OF THE SCIENTIST

September 1933, age 18.

John's parents drive him to the railroad station. He is literally leaving home for the first time. He is eighteen years old and facing a future in which he will only occasionally return to his childhood home in Minnesota.

The train travels through Iowa, Nebraska, Wyoming, Utah, and Nevada before arriving in Pasadena three days later. During those three days John gradually develops a sense of his aloneness, of a future in which his family and his old friends will be less and less important to him inside his own being, even though they will remain important to him in terms of his survival on the planet.

OUT WEST JOHN Lilly threw himself headlong into the world of Caltech, an exclusive school for boys devoted to a life of science and engineering; to burning the midnight oil and wearing down the stubs of pencils. There was something of a monastic or fanatic spirit here; true believers, devoted to the life of the mind, forming a new Masonic brotherhood to serve the age of science and technology.

John was installed in the freshman wing of Blacker House, a thick-walled labyrinth of tiny cells at the eastern end of Caltech's cloister of low, utilitarian, Moorish buildings. Presiding over Blacker was Professor Harvey Eagleson, the resident faculty man *in loco parentis*. With his old tweed coat and his few surviving strands of hair protruding from his head at random, Doc

Eagleson was a gentle bundle of ticks and mannerisms, frequently removing his thick, gold-rimmed eye glasses to fidget with them. Eagleson was a confirmed bachelor: After the tragic death of his one true love in an auto accident many years before, he could not imagine he would ever love again. He had a passion for English literature, a collection of Japanese prints, and a fascination with Freud and psychoanalysis—which he was inclined to apply to all the students. Teas with Doc in his rooms were considered a special treat.

Dinner at the home of Robert Andrews Millikan, chairman of Caltech, and his gracious wife, Greta, was another special occasion for the hundred newly arrived freshmen. Dr. Millikan, the winner of the 1923 Nobel Prize in physics, was, ten years later, the greatest living American physicist. Pudgy, prim, with thinning grey hair, an understated manner, and a restrained sense of humor, Dr. Millikan looked more like a successful banker in his trim five-button suitcoats than a giant of science. John noticed that Millikan never sat down while working; he always stood at a table, whether at home or at his office, where he worked like a scientist at a laboratory bench—or a bank teller at his counter.

There were other intellectual giants at Caltech, including such Nobel Laureates as particle physicist Paul Dirac, who had predicted a particle called the positron, and Carl Anderson, who had recently confirmed its existence. Edwin P. Hubel, father of the expanding universe theory, was on the faculty. Sir James Jeans, whose book John had read in prep school, visited Caltech and inspired him with titanic visions of the nature of the universe. The astronomy department on campus was busy grinding the mirrors for the Hale Telescope, destined to sit atop Mount Palomar. For decades it would be the world's most powerful instrument for seeing far into the skies and deep into the past. Caltech engineers had also constructed the world's most sensitive seismometer, so precise that it could detect the gravitational difference caused by the presence of nearby mountains. In the Kellog Lab, they had a transformer that generated over one million volts, making the room crackle with artificial lightning.

The young man from St. Paul was suddenly in the company of men responsible for determining the fundamental values of Reality, insofar as physics had anything to say about it. He decided to become a physicist himself. In the company of like-minded devotees of the search for Reality along the path of sci-

BIOGRAPHY

ROBERT A. MILLIKAN (1868–1953) was born in Morrison, Illinois, and took his doctorate in physics at Columbia University in 1895. After studying at Berlin and Gottingen, where he was exposed to the founders of the theory of quantum mechanics, he joined the faculty of the University of Chicago in 1896, moving to Caltech in 1921.

Millikan received the 1923 Nobel Prize in physics for his work, which included the experimental determination of the charge of the electron, and of Planck's constant, two of the most fundamental and significant numbers in physics. The famous *Millikan oil drop experiment* strengthened the foundations of quantum mechanics by establishing that the particles measured by physicists are fundamental units, rather than statistical averages. He wrote a number of books, including *The Electron* (1924), *Cosmic Rays* (1939), and his autobiography (1950).

At Caltech, Millikan headed the Norman Bridge Laboratory of Physics and served as chairman of the college. From 1922 to 1932 he represented the United States on the League of Nations committee for intellectual cooperation.

---

ence, and with the guidance and inspiration of acknowledged trailblazers of this path, he plunged into the study of physics with great zeal, directing all his energies toward this noble enterprise over the next two years—until his fateful meeting with Mary Louise Crouch in the autumn of 1935.

After John completed his first year at Caltech in 1934, Doc Eagleson called him in for a most awkward meeting. The scholarship committee had caught on to the fact that John was from a wealthy family. They expected him to stop drawing his scholarship money. Furthermore, they wished to invite Dick Lilly to become an "associate" of Caltech, contributing at least $10,000 to the school annually. This was devastating news to John. It undermined the sense of independence and self-sufficiency which he had gained by winning the scholarship.

Eagleson bluntly told John that his views of the economics of science were naive. He advised a closer reading of Machiavelli's handbook of practical politics, *The Prince*, and a course in economics. As a scientist, John would have to depend on his father's money for his own research, and he would need to develop the political skills necessary to get further support. If he chose to continue to accept the scholarship money, the faculty would judge him prejudicially and limit his future chances.

When John reacted with anger and rage, threatening not to return to Caltech, Eagleson told him, "You have an admirable independence of mind; however, this can be a liability as well as an asset. . . . The reality [is] interdependence with other humans. You must study this interdependence even as you study your physics, your biology, your chemistry. Eventually you will realize that there is no such thing as an independently operating human being; there is only the illusion of independence."

This incident also gave John his first exposure to psychoanalysis in action. Doc Eagleson had initially encouraged him to read the works of Sigmund Freud. Eagleson was something of an amateur psychoanalyst, as were many highly educated people in the 1930s, when Freudian psychoanalysis was intellectually fashionable.

As an armchair analyst, Eagleson suggested that John was projecting a hostile model of his father onto Caltech, his future supporters, and Eagleson himself. He thought John might need psychoanalysis later to "straighten this out." He cited what he called Freud's Reality Principle: Social reality requires us to compromise our natural impulses and personal desires, to postpone pleasure until such time as it is safe to enjoy it.

Wrapping this odiously practical package in pat psychoanalytic clichés made John's capitulation into a farther step in his personal growth. John's current anger at Caltech was read as leftover childhood anger against his father and warmed-over adolescent rebellion. John's angry *reaction* to the situation was interpreted as the *cause* of his problem. His acquiescence became the "cure." In this instance, psychoanalysis worked. John gave in.

Through this first pragmatic introduction to psychoanalytic interpretation, John gained insight into the complicated and devious logic sophisticated people used in order to operate in society. He began to see how they smooth over the rough edges of individual preference, and persuade, compromise, and acquiesce for the sake of social expediency.

When John returned to St. Paul that summer, he presented

the issue to his father in pragmatic terms. Dick Lilly, grasping the situation quickly, agreed to set up a trust fund to cover John's expenses at Caltech. (Later it would be expanded to cover John's expenses throughout his education and scientific career. In 1937, management of the fund was transferred to a trust company, in order to relieve the father-son relationship from the pressures of filial dependence and parental control.)

John wrote to Caltech relinquishing his scholarship money. With his father's money flowing, the faculty was happy with him again. Eventually, Dick Lilly did become a Caltech benefactor.

Much later, John discovered that his real independence from the economic realities of the world came precisely because of his dependence on family money. Had his short-lived independence persisted, he would have had to compete in the economic world for salary and grant money. Its conflicting demands would have seriously interfered with his self-directed search for Reality.

But for now, the loss of even symbolic independence created a painful sense of vulnerability.

In the study of science, John was in for a few shocks. From Professor Fritz Zwicky, astrophysicist, John learned that supernova explosions occur with sufficient frequency in our part of the galaxy that any day now one such explosion might wipe out all life on Earth without warning. Science could calculate the probability of such a catastrophe, but there was nothing that scientists could do about it.

This cataclysmic revelation shocked John out of any sense of complacency about the familiar reality of the human world. "If all this can be destroyed in an instant," he reflected, "then how real is any of it?" John was thrust into the mental space shared by such ancient philosophers as Plato and the Buddha, who had also glimpsed the transience of all things in the flow of time. This scientific knowledge brought real poignancy to Shakespeare's observation that "Life's time's fool, and time that makes a survey of all the world, must have a stop."

From botany professor Fritz Went, John learned that practically all life, including human life, is dependent on a single chemical reaction, photosynthesis. In the future, the supply of food and energy for an expanding population might depend on the ability of scientists to harness and control that reaction with greater efficiency.

From chemistry instructor Arnold O. Beckman, John learned that science and technology go hand in hand. The rate of scientific progress is limited by the availability of laboratory instruments for conducting the next crucial experiment; thus, creating new instruments is an essential part of the scientist's work. This made so deep an impression that John would eventually become preeminent in his scientific field for pioneering the development of new and improved instrumentation.

From physicist Ernest Wätson, John learned that an overemphasis on statistical analysis goes hand in hand with poor experimental design. A scientist is free to design his experiment to cleanly answer a crucial question. Little statistical analysis is necessary after a well-designed, well-thought-out experiment. Excessive use of statistical analysis in a scientific paper suggests imprecision—either in the way the experiment has been set up or in the way the original question has been conceived and framed. As a scientist John Lilly would meticulously design his experiments for clean results and, failing that, would draw some new and unexpected lesson even from a "failed" experiment. No experiment was really a failure.

In 1934, John read Aldous Huxley's 1932 novel, *Brave New World,* with great excitement. This novel proved to be a pivotal influence, refocussing John's interest from physics to biology. The shift was from physical particles and what moves and influences them to human organisms and what controls and motivates their behavior. *Brave New World* depicts a future society in which science and technology are used to manufacture human beings and shape them into "ideal citizens" with preassigned social roles. This is accomplished by genetic engineering, deep conditioning and learned limitations; the result is consummate specialization—every citizen mentally and physically designed to fit their social role.

These concepts opened a grand vision for John, suggesting how human behavior and consciousness are determined by physiology; how this relationship might be studied, and how the limitations which physiology imposes on personal reality might be overcome by a sufficiently advanced scientific technology.

John would have the chance to discuss these ideas with Aldous Huxley personally in 1956.

BIOGRAPHY

ARNOLD O. BECKMAN (1900–   ), a native of Cullom, Illinois, took his Ph.D. in chemistry in 1928 at Caltech, where he taught for a number of years in the chemistry department. A pioneer in the development of high-tech instruments for scientific research and medicine, he founded several enterprises, including Beckman Instruments, which began in his Pasadena garage with his 1939 invention of the pH meter, an electrical device for measuring the acidity of liquids.

With his business success, Beckman became a major patron of Caltech. He also served on the boards of a prodigious number of corporations and professional and civic organizations, including a term as president of the California Chamber of Commerce. In retirement he has devoted his time and sizable fortune to scientific philanthropy.

Back at Caltech after summer break, in the autumn of 1934, John's focus now shifted to biology. He came under the influence of Professor Thomas Hunt Morgan, a pioneer in genetics and embryology, who had received a Nobel Prize for his efforts. Charismatic, with a warm sense of humor, Morgan was much loved by his students. He liked to open his lectures with pranks. On the first day of his introductory biology course for science students, he began by projecting the picture of an embryo on the screen: "Ah, this is the embryo of a pig . . . no, I'm mistaken! It's the embryo of a human . . . I'm not certain what it is, but it doesn't matter—at this stage of development there's no difference."

In the company of biochemistry professor Henry Borsook, John's interest in biology narrowed to human physiology. His courses with professors Wersma and Van Harenveld further narrowed his focus to neurophysiology—the study of brains, nerves, and the cells that make them up, the neurons. He decided that this was the field in which he could best pursue his research for Reality. It was, after all, the puzzling relationship between brain and mind that had catalyzed his first insights into the deeper questions of Reality. With neurophysiology, John was in for life.

BIOGRAPHY

THOMAS HUNT MORGAN (1866–1945), born in Lexington, Kentucky, took his doctorate in zoology at Johns Hopkins University in 1890. At Columbia University he established the foundations of the modern theory of genetics, working with his students Muller and Bridges, who coauthored *Mechanism of Mendellian Heredity* (1915). In *The Theory of the Gene* (1926), Morgan summarized the chromosome theory of genetic inheritance. In 1933 he received the Nobel Prize in medicine.

Morgan moved to Caltech in 1928, where he established the Kerckhoff Laboratories of Biological Sciences, which became the world's leading center for genetics research. Here his interests turned to the processes that governed the expression of genes in the developing organism. He served as president of the National Academy of Sciences and of the American Association for the Advancement of Science.

It was the beginning of his junior year at Caltech. John still didn't date much, but on this rare occasion he was visiting a girl from San Diego who interested him. While there, he met the young woman whom *her* brother was dating—Mary Crouch, child of a family of lawyers in San Diego, who studied art at Scripps College, near Pasadena.

John's first impression of Mary was that she was lovely and highly intelligent. Indeed, Mary was a beautiful young woman—cultivated, artistic, educated.

At this age, all John's sexual and romantic motivations were unconscious and unexamined. At a subconscious level, then, the following connections were made: Due to her intelligence and other attractive qualities, Mary was a suitable love object—someone whom he might wed. She was, therefore, someone with whom he might have sex.

He was immediately captivated, enraptured, and entranced. Young, virginal John Lilly, with absolutely no knowledge of the realities of sex and intimate relationships with another person, was driven into rampant idealization by his profound ignorance of his own sexuality. He projected every conceivable virtue onto the object of his fascination. Clearly, it was true love at first sight, storybook stuff.

They were both 20. Several months later, on his 21st birthday, John proposed marriage and Mary accepted. They both believed in premarital chastity as a matter of civilized ethics. John had rejected Catholic precepts, but Catholic moral conditioning continued to exert an unseen power.

Long overworked from the frenetic pace of his scientific studies, John was suddenly facing the vast unknowns of marriage, sex, and fatherhood, three areas in which he was totally unprepared. The mysterious impending events created enormous pressure. He lost interest in his studies and suddenly found himself unable to concentrate on the physiology of the brain. In February, he fell into a state of "nervous exhaustion," according to his physician, who prescribed a break. John got away from Caltech, got away from Mary, and got a job in the Pacific Northwest cutting brush for a lumber company survey party. Here he buried an axe in his foot and got to experience the current state of medical treatment firsthand. Impressed by the pain and suffering all around him in the hospital trauma ward, he renewed his resolve to become a man of medical science and offer help for pain. He buried himself in a copy of Gray's *Anatomy* during his recuperation.

Meanwhile, back in St. Paul, and in San Diego, the two great families constructed their plans for the wedding. The Crouches of San Diego, like the Lillys of St. Paul, were in banking. A Southern California power, the family had migrated from Iowa at the turn of the century and made it big in the expanding, young economy of the Golden State. Mary's father Charles had run for District Attorney of San Diego County. His and Mary's two uncles were among the founders and directors of Union Bank, later known in California as "The Business Bank." Mary's aunt was a lawyer with the firm of Crouch and Crouch, which had a lucrative practice in San Diego and Los Angeles.

The religious union of these two twenty-one-year-old virgins was thus a marriage between two clans of power—at least as the families saw it. It was a big formal affair at the Catholic cathedral in Altadena, near Caltech. The Crouch wedding party came by motorcar from San Diego; the Lilly contingent came by airplane from St. Paul, their family priest in tow. They all converged on the cathedral in the picturesque formal attire of that era: for the men, morning coats with tails, top hats, and gray ascots, suitable for the coronation of a king or the inauguration of a president; the ladies, their necks strung with pearls, wore elegant gowns tailored for the occasion.

Married July 16, 1936, John and Mary began living together in a small white house near the campus. John became the only married undergraduate at Caltech. Mary Crouch Lilly continued her art studies at Scripps College.

On their nuptial evening, they were amazed at how simple and straightforward sex was. "Is this all there is to it?" said Mary, pleasantly surprised. John thought there *must* be more to it. He decided he had better learn all he could about sex, in a big hurry. True to his scholarly ways, he went straight to Vroman's Book Store, informed the clerk he was newly married, and asked for sex manuals. The clerk nodded solemnly and took him to a safe in the back room, where such incendiary materials were kept under lock. John bought and studied Van de Velde's *Ideal Marriage* and several other early classics in sex education and sexual culture around the world. He read and read and read, accumulating knowledge that he could not use, for Mary showed no interest in developing the art of sexual relations beyond the basics.

Just as he had promptly mastered every other topic his mind had tackled, John had now become very sophisticated sexually— on an intellectual level. Mentally, John was what the argot of a later era would call "sexually liberated"; in practice, however, he had no experience to match his knowledge. Shortly after being introduced to the reality of sexual relations, John found himself frustrated by a partner whose drive to explore and learn was nowhere near his own. This exciting, recently discovered area of experience was quickly reduced to an uninspired routine. Instead of a vast sexual wilderness open for exploration, he found a little suburban housing tract of domesticated sex. John's interests quickly returned to the life of the mind at Caltech.

"Safely married," John plunged into the study of neurophysiology, glimpsing in this immature science the Grail of his quest for Reality. "It is perfectly feasible for the intellect to grasp the fact that the physiological changes of the brain occur simultaneously with thought, but it cannot conceive of the connection between its own thoughts and these changes," he had written at age sixteen. Now he was beginning his fledgling efforts to study that connection scientifically.

In a 1937 course with Professor van Harenveld, he imagined a possible method of recording the physiological changes in the brain by registering electrical activity over the entire brain surface simultaneously. John shared his ideas with van Harenveld, a skinny Dutchman, whose thatched blond hair resembled a pup tent or a haystack. This nervous neuroscientist seemed the very personification of a nerve cell, always jumping with pulses.

Van Harenveld pointed John to a paper by Edgar Adrian, "The Spread of Electrical Activity in the Cerebral Cortex," which encouraged the young scientist to pursue his inspiration. It would be a long haul, leading to the first working "bavatron" device in 1950.

But according to Professor Henry Borsook, the biochemist with whom John studied at Caltech, medical school would be a necessity. John took this sage advice from his scientific mentor seriously and began shopping around for a medical school.

Dick Lilly set up a meeting for John with Dr. Will Mayo, head of the famous Mayo Clinic in Rochester, Minnesota, where Dick was a trustee and patron. In the summer of 1937, John took an overnight train to Rochester. He promptly fell asleep while waiting in Dr. Mayo's outer office.

Roused from slumber by the great doctor himself, John was embarrassed and overawed. At first this figure reminded him of a successful banker, with his perfectly tailored blue three-piece suit and neat gray hair. Observing more closely, John formed a second impression: Dr. Mayo's gray eyes twinkled with the special gleam of a man who views the universe as a cosmic comedy.

This was John's first encounter with what he would later identify as the archetypal successful doctor. Time and again, such a person has seen everything that transpires in human bodies and human lives—birth, death, and the infinity between—and in the process developed an attitude of amused, compassionate detachment toward the human drama.

John was equally impressed by Mayo's peremptory prescription of Dartmouth. It was, according to the great surgeon, the only medical school where a fellow could get a proper course in anatomy—the bedrock discipline of medical science. Armed with a strong letter of introduction to the head of Dartmouth's Medi-

BIOGRAPHY

WILLIAM JAMES MAYO (1861–1939), born at Le Sueur, Minnesota, graduated from the University of Michigan as a medical doctor in 1883. With his father and brother, he practiced surgery in Rochester, Minnesota, where, in 1889, they established the Mayo Clinic. With its unprecedented record of successful surgery, this clinic became famous throughout the world as the preferred center for surgical treatment.

Dr. Mayo served as president of the American Medical Association and was a founder of the American College of Surgeons. During the First World War, he was head of surgery for the United States Army.

---

cal School, a friend and colleague of Mayo's, John applied for admission.

Dartmouth accepted his application, a privilege rarely attained by anyone outside Dartmouth College's own graduating class. From this John understood that one could follow Mayo's prescriptions with confidence—he tended to *make* his prognoses and predictions come true.

John would shortly become friends with Mayo's son Chuck, himself an innovative and masterful surgeon, who would set a splendid example and influence John during his forthcoming medical education.

Within two months of the Lilly-Crouch marriage, Mary was pregnant. The pregnancy drove them farther apart. Mary did not want to be a mother so soon—she wanted to be an art student and an artist first, and therefore decided to have an abortion. This John would not permit.

And then it turned out to be a problem pregnancy. After Mary injured her back in a fall, it was discovered that she had *spondylolysis,* a genetic defect in which the bones of her lumbar spine were incompletely formed. This probably became a critical issue as a consequence of calcium draining from her own bones into the fetus. In the advanced stages of the pregnancy, she traveled to St. Paul to be cared for by John's parents, while John completed his education at Caltech.

So while John took the final exams of his junior year in Pasadena, his child was born in St. Paul on June 2, 1937. He was named John C. Lilly, Jr. John met his son when Mary returned to Pasadena. He was deeply moved. He was grateful they had kept the embryo that would grow up to be a brilliant, fascinating man of science and culture.

Reunited in Pasadena, things improved for the Lilly family. Unable to complete her college education for the time being, Mary adapted to the life of a young mother and wife. John and Mary enjoyed outdoor activities together; here at last they found something in common. In the summer they went camping on Mount Lassen, beside the "Grandmother Trail" John liked to ski in winter. Mary loved the outdoor way of living. John liked the high altitude because it made him feel "a little crazy"—it reminded him of those childhood episodes when he had gotten out of his body and out of this world.

During John's last year at Caltech, Mary did manage to continue her own education, part-time, at Pasadena City College.

That senior year at Caltech, John got an urgent call from home. While returning late at night from a party in Minneapolis, Dick had driven his big Chrysler off the High Bridge across the Mississippi, crashing onto an embankment one hundred feet below and ending up in a hospital bed in a coma. That he had survived at all was miraculous.

Nobody in St. Paul really expected Dick to recover fully; they thought his brain must be scrambled beyond repair after the damage he should have sustained by falling such a great distance. But Dick surprised them.

A specially assigned Northwest Orient airplane picked John up at the Burbank Airport and flew him straight to St. Paul. It was a wild ride through stormy skies. John was the only passenger.

He was with his father when Dick Lilly emerged from his three-week coma and began to recover normal functioning. When Dick came to, his mind was right in the middle of a discussion he had had with John a few days before the accident. The topic involved which medical school John should attend. Dick's first words as he emerged from coma: "You're going to Harvard!"

"No, Dad, I'm going to Dartmouth. Welcome back!"

T wo things particularly impressed John about this incident. For one, he observed that while in coma, the brain was just like a machine that had been switched off in the middle of some action. Once switched back on, it continued the action from where it had left off. Today, we'd compare it to a tape recorder that you stop and then restart later, but there were no tape recorders in 1938.

The other significant aspect was the unusual sequence of coincidences that saved Dick's life. The chances of plunging one hundred feet in a car, hitting the ground, and surviving are actually quite small. The day before the accident, a mechanic had worked on Dick's car, welding the front seat to the floor. Apparently John's younger brother Dave had noticed that the seat was rattling and had taken the initiative to have it fixed. When the car landed at the foot of the bridge, the tail end hit first and collapsed, absorbing the impact of the fall. Because it had been welded in place, the front seat did not tear loose. Instead, it stayed in place and supported Dick's body like a shelf. He landed just right, with his entire body lying lengthwise on the seat's back. Medical help arrived promptly. If any of these events had happened in even a slightly different way, he certainly would not have survived.

In later years, when John Lilly found himself in the midst of some death-defying stunt, he would reflect on his father's accident as his first intuition that some higher power can arrange coincidences very precisely. You are almost killed, you're sure you're going to die, but miraculously you survive.

After Dick recovered and was ready to go back to work at the bank, his board of directors questioned his fitness on the grounds that he may have suffered brain damage. John was able to come to his father's support with all the credibility provided by his recent education in neurophysiology from Caltech. All the bank directors gathered at the Lilly house, where John confidently told them that his examination of his father had indicated there was no brain damage—and if they had any doubts, he'd be happy to bring in Dr. Will Mayo to confirm that diagnosis. That did it. The bankers had little choice but to declare themselves convinced, in the face of so much medical expertise. So Dick returned to work, where he remained until his retirement in 1955.

Years later, toward the end of Dick's life, after Rachel had died, the Catholic Archbishop of St. Paul visited Dick at Paradise

Farm. The bishop suggested that Dick might consider bequeath-
ing the farm to the church, implying that such a decision would
credit Dick spiritually in the afterlife. According to one of his
grandsons, who was listening from behind a curtain, Dick responded: "Father, I agree it might be appropriate if I were going
to go through purgatory. But in fact I already went through purgatory when I drove off the High Bridge. I was saved by a miracle,
and I do not feel that I am in spiritual need of making this be-
quest."

John received his Bachelor of Science degree from Caltech
on June 10, 1938. It was signed by R.A. Millikan and bears the art
nouveau sigil of the California Institute of Technology, depicting
heroic nude male and female figures walking on clouds, aspiring
to heaven.

The inscription reads: THE TRUTH SHALL MAKE YOU
FREE.

CHAPTER 4

THE HUMAN BODY

September 1938, age 22.
John walks into the classroom for his first instruction in
human pathology at Dartmouth. Lying on a table is a cadaver
covered with a sheet. Beside it, Professor Frederick Lord be-
gins his introduction: "There are many things to learn if
you're going to be a pathologist. One of the first is the differ-
ence between a dead body and a living person. The body on
the table is at the end of its social career."
He pulls off the sheet. Half the class faints. It's their be-
loved professor of music from Dartmouth College. It's the first
they have heard of his dying.

JOHN AND MARY and infant Johnny traveled to Dartmouth by
car through a country still recovering from the stock market crash
and the big hangover left by Prohibition.

Traveling great distances by automobile in 1937 was an uncertain adventure. They were hulking contraptions then, like
giant beetles with curved fenders, big round bumps, flat wind-
shields, stiff steering, tight clutches, grinding gears, bumpy sus-
pensions, and radiators that boiled over at the slightest provocation. Roads were narrow, winding, and rough; maps were an
absolute necessity. It took careful, strategic planning to be sure
that the end of a day's driving would coincide with the appearance of one of those little roadside bungalows frequented less by
real travelers than by trysting couples from the next county. In

the great 1930s, outback, rural America was an underdeveloped country.

They took the northern route, stopping off in Chicago for a few days to visit John's college chum George Tooby. An industrial engineer, he was working for the Campbell Soup Company, setting up a huge vegetable processing factory. Tooby had thought up a better way of making powdered milk, which he explained to John and Mary.

When Tooby was finished, John said, "My father sometimes takes a flyer in a speculative venture such as your invention. Why don't you go up to St. Paul and talk to him?" Tooby followed John's advice, and soon after Dick Lilly set up a business with him, providing capital and connections. Their partnership grew into the Lilly Dried Milk Company at Okonomowak, Wisconsin, which supplied powdered milk to the U.S. Army during World War II.

The great drive continued. East of Chicago, the roads were smoother and amenities far more frequent. Somehow, they made it through. One day, as the sun was setting, they motored into Hanover, New Hampshire.

In Hanover, the young family lived in a little rented apartment not far from campus. David Lilly, John's younger brother, was already an undergraduate student at Dartmouth College. (Dave would eventually graduate, then serve in the army as an aide to General Douglas MacArthur in the Pacific.)

At Dartmouth Medical School, John cut his way into human anatomy. Under the tutelage of Dr. Frederick Lord, anatomy consisted of spending hundreds of hours with cadavers. Lord had a special talent for exhibiting the principles he was teaching by building models of human anatomy out of odds and ends, and by contriving dramatic demonstrations.

While at Dartmouth, John worked on thirty-two cadavers. During the long hours in chilly rooms reeking of formaldehyde, John dissected all the organs and tissues of human flesh, becoming intimately versed in the intricate details of the human body.

One day, John cut out an entire intestinal tract. When Professor Syvertsen, dean of the medical school, walked in, he was shocked to see the intestine stretched all the way across the length of the dissecting room. He gave John a stern lecture about the respect due a cadaver. John replied, "Well, it says in this book that the intestine is twenty-eight feet long, and I want to find out if that is true."

For John, the real prize was the human brain, reached by carefully sawing off the top of the skull after meticulously cutting away the scalp and all its blood vessels, peripheral nerves, muscles, and facia. The brain: the organ of mystery whose obscure relationship to the mind was so crucial to John's search for Reality.

In his gloved hands, John held the brain of a body whose name he did not know. It had once been the "numinous loom" described so poetically by the neurologist Lashley, in which thoughts, feelings, and a sense of being someone had flickered as the living brain tissues pulsed with life-blood and sparkled with electricity. Now, in death, hardened by formaldehyde, a palpable physical object with the consistency of a soft rubber eraser—or a stale piece of cooked liver sitting in the refrigerator. Gray on the outside, whitish deeper inside, the drained blood vessels accentuated with red dye. If this was the seat and center of the human mind, there was damn little here to show it.

John dissected the brain and identified all the inner structures as discovered and named by distinguished anatomists who had come before him, geographers and geologists of the bumpy planetoid within the cranial orb. Like so many terrestrial explorers and map makers of yore, they had left their names on its topography, labeling every little feature they discovered or thought they had seen in this *terra incognita* inside the head: the Fissure of Roland, the Sulcus of Sylvius, and so forth. Before they were through, anatomists had affixed hundreds of names to different places in the brain, creating a nightmare for later generations of medical school students who had to memorize them.

The map makers of the brain spilled much blood and ink, and yet their diligent work shed practically no light on how anything actually worked. Nowhere else in the human body is the physiology—the relationship between structure and function—so obscure and incomprehensible as in the brain. The first scientific anatomists, the classical Greeks, denied that the brain had anything to do with the mind; they believed it to be a radiator for cooling the blood, or an organ for producing mucus. Despite technical advances, when John Lilly first dissected a human brain in 1939 there was still no hint as to how the brain really functioned.

Some basics were known. First visible is the *cerebral cortex* (tree bark)—the gray matter on the outside, its surface convoluted into intricate swirls and rills, like an eroded landscape viewed from an airplane. Beneath and within lie the *corpus callosum* and the *commisures,* tense bundles of fibers interconnecting the east and west hemispheres. Other fibers connect the surface to inner nuclei with picturesque names. The *thalamus* (named for a Greek hareem, or wedding chamber). The *fornix* (a Roman arch, or brothel). The *hippocampus* (a horse of the plains, or seahorse). The *cerebral aqueduct.* The *red nucleus.* The *striata negra.*

Then come the portals on the underside where the world rushes in: the cranial nerve tracks and the spinal medulla. Knots and bumps on the underbelly serve as signposts for anatomists, and as relay stations for messages from the outside world. Extending into the bottom of the brain from the nose, eyes, ears, tongue, and other locations are the all-important cranial nerves: olfactory, optic, occulomotor, trochlear, trigeminal, abducens, facial, vestibulo-cochlear, glosso-pharyngeal, vagus, accessory, hypoglossial.

Or, abbreviated:

O-O-O-T-T-A-F-V-G-V-A-H

In the sophomoric, mnemonic chant of the mostly male neuroanatomy students:

Oh oh oh,

to touch a

(formerly virginal)

girl's vagina.

Ah heaven!

The naming of all the parts, however, told nothing about the brain's operations. If there was any story about the mind that the cadavers of Dartmouth could tell, it was not to be detected by the naked eye gazing at the dead brain or at the pieces dissected from it. Most organs of the body do something observable. Every tissue is exquisitely formed and streamlined to perform its specific function. A muscle pulls. A bone withstands. A gland exudes some kind of fluid. But the gross anatomy of the brain revealed nothing beyond which part of the brain is connected to which part of the body. Even living brains, which John saw while observing surgical operations in which the skull was opened, revealed nothing of the organ's secret mission.

In the brain, the real message is inscribed by Nature, or Nature's God, in miniscule glyphs discernable solely through a microscope. And it was in gazing upon these microscopic details of the brain that John Lilly experienced real wonder. He made slender slices of brain tissue, stained them, and beheld the glory in his microscope. His inspiration from these intricate evolutionary etchings was akin to the rapture he felt as a child in St. Paul, gazing at the wonders of nature around him.

He puzzled over the intricacy of individual cells and the complexity of their interconnections. He learned that these cells belonged to different types—different "families." A cell of one type was usually accompanied by cells of several different types. He realized that each individual cell must be a significant player in this game played by the living brain—*whatever that game might be.*

During that first year at Dartmouth, Mary's spinal problem grew more severe. The pain worsened, radiating down both her legs. It made walking agonizing and almost impossible. John, through Will Mayo, found the top orthopedic surgeon in the country to treat Mary. Spinal fusion surgery was required, which left her locked in a full body cast for three months. At the end of the school year, a recuperating Mary took Johnny with her to Hawaii on vacation, where she continued to study painting.

Meanwhile, John returned to Caltech for the summer to do some research with his erstwhile professor, Dr. Borsook. A pioneer in the field of nutritional science, Borsook headed the U.S. government panel responsible for determining the RDA—recommended daily allowance of essential vitamins and minerals. He also designed the diets for the first U.S. team to climb Mount Everest. Borsook was short, stocky, and in good shape, with a hearty personality and an extrovert's proclivity for athletics. John taught him to ski, and the two became buddies, as well as scientific collaborators.

Borsook was absorbed in the study of glycocyamine, the principal source of muscle power in the human body. He wanted to find out where it comes from and how it is produced in the body. His theory was that it could be produced in the body only from the two amino acids, glycine and arginine. To test this hypothesis, John went on a completely protein-free diet for six weeks. He took measured doses of arginine solution ("tastes like shit") and glycine ("way too sweet"). Mixed together, the two chemicals tasted like coconut milk. He drew blood samples from his veins forty times per day and analyzed them himself for the presence of glycocyamine. This was quite a feat. He was becoming increasingly weak, almost delirious, and could think only of meat.

Toward the end of the six weeks, he knew he was in trouble when he saw a pretty girl in short-shorts coming down a flight of stairs, and, instead of thinking about sex, all he could think of was ripping off her thigh and devouring it.

The blood analyses indicated that increased blood levels of glycocyamine closely followed the ingestion of glycine and arginine in the predicted proportion. The experiment thus proved Borsook's hypothesis. John published his first scientific paper with Borsook in 1941, based on this research. John's name came sixth on the list of authors, one of only two instances in his scientific career that his name would not come first, as principal researcher.

Something of a public relations flap ensued. The manufacturers of Jell-O gelatin got wind of the glycocyamine research and began citing it in their advertising as proof that Jell-O and gelatin are a pure source of "muscle energy." (Gelatin, which is derived from the connective tissues of cattle, consists almost entirely of the two amino acids, glycine and arginine; but eating it won't significantly increase your store of muscle energy, because the amino acids are inefficiently absorbed and utilized in the absence of balanced protein.)

John learned three principles from this research and the consequent Jell-O incident that would prove to be significant in his later career: First, in the interests of scientific progress, people sometimes make personal sacrifices and do unpleasant things to themselves. Second, the state of the body and mind are very tightly dependent on what chemical substances—foods and drugs—are ingested. Third, scientific discoveries can have immediate economic and social consequences.

Back at Dartmouth for his second year of medical school, John continued to engage in extracurricular research beyond his studies of medicine and anatomy. John pursued his project to invent a new method for identifying drugs by precisely measuring the melting points of minute samples viewed under a microscope.

There was only one other medical student in his class, Fred Worden, who shared this interest in research. The two formed a close friendship that was destined to affect John's life in significant ways from time to time in the future. John also acquired a passion for skiing while at Dartmouth. This habit became more important in the future, when he discovered that by skiing to excess, by skiing to distraction, by making skiing a full-time preoccupation, he could avert the periodic migraine attacks that had tormented him since childhood and that resisted all available medical treatment.

Most of the med students at Dartmouth were looking forward to careers in therapeutic practice. After two years of absorbing the anatomy curriculum, John was ready to move on to a school with more research opportunities and greater enthusiasm for medical research. Following the advice of Dean Syvertsen, the new dean of the med school, John chose and was accepted at the University of Pennsylvania. John and Mary and their child moved to a small rented apartment close to the Philadelphia campus.

As a med school junior at Penn, John learned about a professor named Bazett, who reportedly held very advanced views about medical research. John decided to drop in on the professor, and immediately recognized him as one of those truly great teachers who can create turning points in the lives of their students. Similarly, Dr. H. Cuthbert Bazett took one look at John Lilly and knew immediately that here was an unusually brilliant young man.

Professor Bazett, a short man in his fifties with gray, close-cropped hair, sat in his office during this first meeting with John, chain-smoking as usual. As one cigarette burned down to a stub, Bazett would flick out another from his pack and light it from its predecessor. He talked continuously, pausing only long enough to gauge by John's gestures that he was following each point, but not long enough for John to actually say anything.

Bazett had been the protégé of the noted British physiologist J.B.S. Haldane, who studied the human respiratory system. Haldane did most of his experiments on his own body, and had instilled in Bazett the belief that this was, ethically and scientifically, the correct thing to do. Following this tradition in his study of sensory nerves, Bazett had experimented on the foreskin of his own penis. He had marked the nerve endings with permanent dyes, then had himself circumcised so he could study the patterns under the microscope. When Bazett wanted to know the temperature inside the brain, he attached a thermocouple probe on the end of a catheter and threaded it through his blood vessels, right into his own brain.

"Unless a medical scientist experiments on his own body first, he has no idea what he might be subjecting his patients or volunteers to," Bazett emphasized. "And what does it say of a man of science, if he is willing to do to other human beings what he is not prepared to do to himself?"

Finally it was John's turn to speak, and he told Bazett he wanted to do research in physiology. Bazett immediately offered John a laboratory of his own, in Bazett's part of the building. John was thrilled to have his first real lab.

Here John would work on a pet project of Bazett's. Bazett wanted a method of measuring blood pressure that could be used on test pilots and volunteers undergoing simulated stresses and hazards of high-altitude flight under combat conditions. John's solution to this puzzle would be the electrical capacitance diaphragm manometer, his first published invention in medical instrumentation.

Deciding that the methods traditionally applied to this type of measurement were woefully inadequate to provide the degrees of sensitivity, stability, and reliability that Bazett required for the stressful conditions he was investigating, John drew on his fascination with physics, always a close second for him after his interest in brain physiology. He decided that the solution must come from an area that hardly anyone had considered in connection with research on the human body: the high-frequency electronics used in radios. This was an especially bold direction in view of the primitive state of electronics in 1941. There were no components available "off the shelf" in those days, so John would have to design, engineer, and build all the basic gadgets he needed to carry out his plan. Falling back on his Caltech physics courses and his "ham" radio background, he built a quartz crystal high-frequency oscillator, a DC amplifier, and a specialized cathode ray oscilloscope.

The idea was brilliantly elementary in its conception. A hypodermic needle would insert a probe into a blood vessel. The probe was connected through a tube to a tiny electrical capacitor. Blood pressure would compress a stainless steel diaphragm on one side of this capacitor, thus increasing the amount of electricity the capacitor could store. That, in turn, would lower the frequency of the oscillator to which the capacitor was connected. This oscillator was initially set at 14 megahertz because the high frequency was necessary in order to sense such minute movements in such a tiny capacitor.

John had to build the electronic instruments needed to measure these changes and give a readout in terms of blood pressure. When he ran into technical difficulties, Bazett sent him to Britton Chance, right down the hall in the E.R. Johnson Foundation, an endowed research institute within the School of Medicine.

John walked into Britt Chance's office and found the wizard in the midst of a smoothly flowing ballet of continuous productivity. Here was a man who could do three things at once, without even raising a ripple. He was simultaneously doing his own work, instructing his secretary, and now, without missing a beat, getting to know his visitor, and John's technical problem. A short man with an enigmatic smile, only a few years older than John, Chance was starting to lose his prematurely graying hair. A biologist, physicist, and electrical engineer with two Ph.D.s, Chance was responsible for designing most of the radar then in use in America.

John explained his problem, and Britt responded with just two words: "negative feedback." John returned to his lab and added some negative feedback to his circuits by connecting a resistor. That solved the first problem, but created a second problem: higher-frequency oscillations were introduced. Back to Chance. Britt had the answer in one sentence: "At high frequencies, resistors start to look like little coils, introducing positive

BIOGRAPHY

BRITTON CHANCE (1913–   ), born in Wilkes Barre, Pennsylvania, took two Ph.D.s, at the University of Pennsylvania in 1940 and at Cambridge in 1942. He was a key player in the development of the new science of biophysics, a boundry-jumping discipline that applies the analyses of physics to the problems of biology. An electrical engineer of exceptional genius, Chance patented inventions in cybernetic devices and radar circuitry that played a crucial role in World War II. His work was conducted principally at the University of Pennsylvania and at M.I.T., and he had numerous foreign appointments. Chance served on the President's Science Advisory Committee and received the Presidential Certificate of Merit, among many other awards. He was a member of the most prestigious national and international scientific organizations, including the Royal Swedish Academy of Sciences (which awards the Nobel Prize). A fellow of the IEEE, the AAAS, and the American Physical Society, he took the gold medal in yachting at the 1952 Olympics.

---

feedback." John caught on, added some small capacitors in his feedback path to decouple the inductors—and the darn thing worked! In the space of a single day, two engineering problems were solved.

By what? By rapid feedback.

This sequence of events made an impression on all concerned. John's teachers—now suddenly his "colleagues"—were convinced that this was one heck of a smart fellow. "Got a problem? Call Lilly! He'll come up with a brilliant solution."

John was impressed with how quickly and efficiently things could be done—in the right company. In such company there was, perhaps, no limit to what one could accomplish. The key was to place oneself in the midst of intelligent and effective people who had among them all the requisite expert knowledge. And the Johnson Foundation at Penn seemed like just the right place.

John continued his research and development of physiological instruments under the patronage of Bazett and with the advice of Chance. From Chance he first got wind of the "electronic brains" that were being developed—the first computers. Chance gave him a brilliantly concise description of the essentials of computing and computer design. These powerful, cutting-edge ideas made a lasting impression. Chance also introduced John to biophysics researcher Detlev Bronk, destined to be his boss at the Johnson Foundation.

From Bazett, John absorbed the Haldane-Bazett ethic for human medical research: *"Do first to yourself whatever you would propose doing to other humans. Unless you are willing to expose yourself to an experimental procedure, do not expose another human being to it."* In the future he would apply this principle to his own research with electrodes in the brain, with sensory isolation, with LSD, with anesthetics. Many years later John would sum up this principle more succinctly: "My body is my laboratory."

John developed variations on his manometer intended for different research situations. Eventually he perfected instruments for measuring rapid changes in air pressure, the rate of air flow in respiration, and the amounts of nitrogen or oxygen present in air. These devices were applied to research for the air force. Through the Johnson Foundation, John became involved with these projects as a medical scientist, after his graduation from medical school.

Like Chance, he also learned to do two or more things at once. Concurrent with his research and invention, he continued his clinical studies as a junior and then as a senior medical student. He experienced firsthand the real human consequences of medical research, and of the absence or deficiencies of such research in certain areas. What doctors can do for people is directly determined by their knowledge of how the body works. Whether a patient lives or dies, gets well or gets worse, feels relief or remains in horrible pain depends on the presence or absence of the doctor's accurate and adequate knowledge.

John took a lesson from Chuck Mayo, M.D., Will Mayo's son. The younger Mayo was a surgeon who really understood what surgery is all about. As he put it, "surgery represents the failure of medical science to cure diseases by medicine." Given a sufficiently advanced medical science, surgery would be needed only to repair traumatic injuries. Mayo recognized that all surgery constituted a traumatic injury to the body. Therefore the surgeon should make the smallest possible incisions so as to minimize pain, promote recovery, and speed healing. John would put this lesson to work in his own future research in neurophysiology.

All the while, John was building up a network of friends and admirers in the medical research establishment. He was also learning how to move and maneuver in this exclusive club.

As John was wrapping up his medical school education at Penn, his mother Rachel's health was beginning to unravel back in Minnesota. Malignant lumps were detected in her breast, and she underwent a mastectomy. But by that time, the cancerous tissue had spread into other parts of her body, and further problems were inevitable.

On a visit home to St. Paul, John made a disturbing discovery. One afternoon his mother said to him, "Johnny, I think I have a brain tumor." John performed a cursory examination, and had a talk with her in her sunny bedroom. He found no superficial signs of a neurological problem, but she elaborated: "I know something is different, because those trees I see outside my window right now I *know* aren't there. Those are the trees that are outside the window of the old house on Summit Avenue."

Then John realized that something was terribly wrong with his mother's brain. He had missed an important sign several months earlier. Rachel had mentioned that her sense of smell wasn't working. Immediately, John arranged for her to visit the Mayo Clinic. In Rochester, the staff confirmed the diagnosis of brain tumor, but brain surgery was not their specialty.

John consulted Dr. Wilder Penfield, the eminent brain surgeon with whom he had recently become acquainted through his growing personal network among medical researchers. They also shared a mutual interest in EEG (brain wave recordings). Penfield, a tall, slender gentleman with an ascetic appearance and kindly presence, had delicate, skillful hands, seemingly with a life of their own. They poised in midair, as if awaiting their next act of surgical artistry.

John took Rachel to Dr. Penfield's hospital in Montreal, a leading center for brain surgery. Penfield examined her and decided that surgery was indeed indicated—immediately.

In the green-tiled operating room, scented with ether, oxygen, and disinfectant, John stood by in his sterile surgical gown as Dr. Penfield and his assistants carried out the procedure of entering Rachel's head. His mother lay on the table in a deep coma induced by the anesthetic, her head shaved. Penfield's assistant drew his scalpel across the skin of her forehead in a graceful semicircular incision. Next they sawed through her skull and lifted off the top like a trap door, secured by a wide flap of skin in back. In the brilliant focus of the shadow-free lamps, before John's incredulous eyes there lay his mother's brain, pulsing beneath its dura sheath. At this revelation, he had to turn away, unable to watch the rest of the operation up close. But from a distance he watched Penfield's slender, artistic hands fly through the sensitive, intricate movements of removing a tumor from the most delicate and sacred organ of the human body. The surgeon, absorbed in a calm ecstasy of dedicated concentration, worked in unison with his skillful assistants.

Penfield found a solid tumor the size of a walnut, right behind the center of Rachel's forehead. It had been crushing her olfactory nerve, which accounted for her loss of the sense of smell. It was also evident that this tumor had exerted pressure on the frontal lobes of her brain, impairing circulation and causing the lobes to atrophy. The tumor had, in effect, given her a frontal lobotomy.

John reflected how remarkably little his mother's mind had been impaired, considering the extensive damage she had sustained to that part of the brain associated with foresight, the sense of time, and the "higher faculties" of the mind. She had remained sufficiently lucid to be aware of the "hallucinatory" nature of the visual scenes her brain had concocted under pressure from the tumor.

The surgery was a stunning success. Rachel made a rapid recovery and went home, where she continued her life as before. The operation prolonged her life by seven years. During this time, complications from the progressive, metastasized cancer occasionally occurred. Through the years, John used his own medical expertise and his personal connections to the medical establishment to find the most advanced care available for Rachel. Meanwhile, she continued to host garden parties, maintain her prominent status in Twin Cities society, and enjoy her children and grandchildren, occasionally even going swimming with the kids.

Much of Rachel's long illness was like graceful, though rapid, aging. For this woman of faith, charity, insight, and gentle pragmatism, only the last year, from 1952 to 1953, was truly horrid.

After the brain operation, John realized the depth of his admiration for Wilder Penfield. Both a pioneer in brain research and a surgical savior, he had not only restored John's mother but also performed life-saving surgery on his own sister. Penfield had applied his new diagnostic technique of electrical brain stimulation as she lay conscious on the operating table, her brain naked before him. In the medical literature he had reported the vivid, lifelike experiences of his unanesthetized surgical patients when their brains were gently stimulated with electricity in specific locations. Many of these experiences remarkably resembled the visual scenes Rachel had experienced from the pressure of the tumor on her brain.

Penfield's work was attracting wide attention in the scientific world and beyond. Popular commentators, including Aldous Huxley, were not slow to grasp the philosophical implications: Human experience could be generated right there in the brain, by electrically activating specific networks of neurons. Such generated experiences were relatively independent of anything going on in the current time and space of the external reality. The brain, not the outside world, really was the immediate source of human experience. For John Lilly, this idea would eventually lead him to the theory of "internal realities."

During the war, John took a class at Penn on "How to Build an Atomic Bomb." The students got together and turned the notes from this class into a book of the same title. General Groves, director of the huge, secretive Manhattan Project, found out about this project and attempted to suppress publication on the grounds of "military secrecy." But the students were able to overcome this censorship because none of the information in the book had come from the secret government project; it was just a group of college physicists speculating on how a bomb *might* be built, based on publicly known physics. This episode was John's first encounter with the military drive for secrecy, in its competition with the open exchange of information that is the ideal of science.

It was 1942, and the war was in its most desperate hours. After graduating from medical school, John accepted an invitation to stay on at Penn as a member of the faculty. As a researcher in the biophysics laboratory of Dr. Detlev Bronk, he would be engaged in top-priority war research for the air force under a program run by the Johnson Foundation. (John would continue working at Johnson until 1953.) He found himself laboring side by side with a sturdy crew that included Glenn Millikan (son of Dr. Robert Millikan, chairman of Caltech in John's undergraduate days), with whom he would coauthor a 1945 paper on respiration. Meanwhile, Mary got a job as a volunteer nurse at Swarthmore Hospital.

CHAPTER 5

INNER AND OUTER REALITIES

July 1942, age 27.

At Wright Airfield near Columbus, Ohio, in the aeromedical lab, the entire cabin of a P-28 aircraft is placed inside a huge high-altitude chamber. Inside the cabin, the air pressure is equivalent to that found at an altitude of 8,000 feet. Outside the cabin, the thin atmosphere of the chamber replicates conditions at 42,000 feet. John is strapped into the pilot's seat, and dangling from his body are the physiological sensors he'd invented—nitrogen and oxygen meters, inhalation volume and velocity sensors. Catheters he designed to register blood pressure are stuck into his blood vessels like IVs.

Three . . . two . . . one . . . WHOOOMP! A thin diaphragm is torn, opening a gaping hole in the cabin. Air is sucked out to the larger void. From 8,000 feet to 42,000 feet in one millisecond—explosive decompression. It feels like being slapped on the back by the hands of some monstrous giant—it literally takes your breath away. The pressure change is enough to make your eyes bug out.

Then the wind rushes in. It takes a minute to get back up to full atmospheric pressure. John is feeling woozy, headed toward passing out. He breathes some pure oxygen from the mask and gets his mind back.

This research is making significant impressions on John:

The human organism is vulnerable, but with special techniques and discipline it can survive extreme conditions. Normal consciousness depends on maintaining a rather narrow range of conditions in the physical environment. Changes in those physical parameters produce different states of consciousness.

Furthermore, a scientist can knowledgeably experiment on himself, even in dangerous situations, and survive. This impression, formed during his war research, will lay the groundwork for the potentially life-threatening yet path-breaking experiments John performs on his own body in later years, in his single-minded, single-handed search for Reality.

WITH DETLEV BRONK, Glenn Millikan, and others at the Johnson Foundation, John studied the perils awaiting military aviators: explosive decompression, oxygen starvation (anoxia), and nitrogen boiling in the blood (the bends). He designed instruments to measure changes in the atmosphere, and physiological changes in airmen undergoing the consequent stress. In this work he gained firsthand knowledge by subjecting his own body and mind to the painful and dangerous conditions faced by flyers whose aircraft were punctured by enemy antiaircraft guns, who crash dove to "bail out" with their engines belching flames, or who flew so high that their muscles knotted and their vision "blacked out."

This was a military operation. In the military, a man could exercise command only if he had the respect of his subordinates. If he was to lead men into combat, he would have to "earn his stripes" by first going through combat experience himself. At the Wright Field Altitude Lab, John worked under the command of an air force captain who was a combat veteran and a test pilot, a man who insisted on putting himself through every experiment before calling on his subordinates or volunteers.

Here, medical research ethics and the military approach converged, as they had so splendidly in the case of Walter Reed, the legendary army doctor, and his committee of "microbe hunters" who tracked down the cause of the dread yellow fever in Cuba. For John, the captain's policy only reinforced the research ethic he had learned from Professor Bazett at Penn, which Bazett had received from his mentor, Haldane: *Don't try it on any other human unless you are prepared to try it yourself.* And, by implication: *Design your experiments very carefully, with the reality of the human subject in mind.*

John subscribed to this tradition. He subjected himself to

every physiological hazard a U.S. Airman could face in the cock-
pit of his plane, short of taking a 40-millimeter slug in his own
chest, crashing into a mountain, or exploding in a ball of flame.
He took his place on the tilt tables and in the centrifuges, experiencing a 3-G turn that drained the blood from his brain and
contorted his face.

John learned that being a flyer involved a kind of athletics.
It entailed a rare, disciplined coordination of mind and body that
tested the limits of both. It "stretched the envelope" of a human
being. To survive, you had to practice special physical skills, like
the "grunt," in which a pilot tenses every muscle in his body and
compresses air in his lungs to keep from blacking out under
G-force accelerations. To do that, you have to be conscious and
alert. To remain conscious and alert, you have to keep the blood
from draining out of your brain. And to do that, you must practice
the grunt—it's circular!

The body and the mind are inextricably yoked together in a
loop of interdependence that John began to glimpse under these
extreme conditions. For the first time, John felt he was making
some real progress in his search for Reality, as he had first enun-
ciated it at the age of sixteen. This was daring, adventurous, and
dangerous, but it yielded knowledge he couldn't get in any other
way. *It was physically risky, and it was rewarding.* There was
something of the thrill of combat, mixed with the exhilaration of
scientific discovery. He was marked for the future.

Throughout this period, John recorded what was happening
on two levels. With his instruments, he recorded the physiological stresses and changes in his body, while in his own brain he
recorded the personal experiences that accompanied them.

He was proud of his work for the air force, and he hoped to
help win the war by finding ways to reduce casualties. It was the
least he could do in a world where other men were actually flying
those fragile crates into combat, loaded with TNT and gasoline.
It was good, honest work for a doctor.

And, through this work at the high-altitude research laboratory, John Lilly was beginning to think of his body as a crash test
dummy, to be used in the service of the noble cause.

The end of the war finally appeared imminent. Det Bronk
told John that he planned to return to the work he had been

pursuing before the war set different priorities. He wanted to start a major research project on the properties of individual neurons. He invited John to join him as his chief collaborator, working in a new lab under his direction. He also invited John to ask his wealthy father to donate the new lab.

But John also had a pet project interrupted by the war. He had an idea for a device, which he called the "bavatron," that would sense electrical activity over large areas of the brain's surface and project an image of this activity onto a televisionlike screen. And so he declined Bronk's offer.

It was as scary for John to voice this decision as it was disappointing for Det to hear it. By going his own way and following his own real interest, John was rejecting the wisdom of his scientific mentor and immediate boss. Det responded coolly that John was welcome to do what he wanted in Bronk's lab, but would have to find his own funding.

Thus began a pattern in which John would give up the full support of his superiors and their scientific institutions in favor of setting his own priorities. In the war, his research priorities had been set by the military and by the exigencies of wartime. But in peacetime, the research priorities of institutions were set by funding agencies and by senior scientists such as Det Bronk. If John wished to call the tune, then he would have to pay the piper. He did this by persuading his father to give the lab $10,000. In addition, John agreed to draw from the Johnson Foundation only a token salary of $4,000 per year.

Thus he used his impressive credentials and position in the institute to secure the benefits of working in an academic research environment, while he used his private income to escape from the control and obligations which usually accompany such a position. He created extraordinary leverage for himself, enabling him to set his own course in his scientific search for Reality.

John put his full energies into the bavatron, an instrument he had conceived at Caltech, and in short order he had it working (a paper on the subject was published in 1950). He could place an array of twenty-five electrode sensors on the surface of the living brain of a cat or monkey and, on his display screen, see the moving patterns of wavelike electrical activity that spread over the cortex of the brain. The patterns would vary with what the animal was doing, seeing, or hearing at the moment.

BIOGRAPHY

DETLEV BRONK (1897–1975), born in New York City, graduated from Swarthmore College and took his Ph.D. at the University of Michigan in 1926. From 1918 to 1919 he served in the U.S. Naval Aviation Corps, and much of his subsequent research activity was related to aviation medicine. His numerous awards include the Presidential Medal of Freedom, the Order of the British Empire, and the National Science Medal. From 1929 to 1949, Bronk was director of the Johnson Research Foundation at the University of Pennsylvania. He served at various times as president of the National Academy of Sciences and the American Association for the Advancement of Science, as chairman of both the National Science Foundation and the National Research Council, as member of the President's Science Advisory Committee, and as president of Johns Hopkins University.

John studied his screen and the patterns of light flickering and moving against a dark background, thrilled to be watching the activity of a living brain, however imprecisely portrayed. Was this the objective trace of an experience? Was he seeing the mind in this record of brain activity? He set up a special movie camera (operating at 128 frames per second) to record the pattern's movements over time. In this way, he was recording more pieces of information simultaneously than any neuroscientist in history. In the future, he anticipated, the movie camera could be replaced by one of the new electronic digital computers just then being developed.

Later this approach would be expanded by others in this country to reach arrays of 1,000 electrodes, while researchers in Canada increased that number to 4,000 electrodes, and scientists in the USSR managed 10,000. Much later, in the 1980s, new techniques using powerful computers and superconduction technology would allow viewing of brain activity in even greater detail.

In 1967, in *The Human Biocomputer,* John would further develop this concept into a proposed experiment to record the brain's electrical activity in minute detail, and then play the recording back into the brain. The 1980 movie *Brainstorm,* starring Natalie Wood, would feature a version of this idea: brain activity recorded during an experience could be played back into the brain to reproduce the original experience.

In the summer of John's high-altitude research, he and Mary discovered she was pregnant again. On January 9, 1943, their second son, Charles R. Lilly, was born. At this time they lived on Cedar Lane in Swarthmore.

Later they moved to Wallingford, and in 1945, John, Mary, and their two sons moved to a large rural house in Rose Valley that they rented from Earl Harrison, dean of the Law School at Penn. The driveway was lined with apple trees, and the yard backed up onto a creek. It was a good place for children.

In this huge house, John and Mary rented out several rooms to interesting characters from the university. One of them was Leonard Schiff, a physicist just returning from the New Mexico desert, where he had worked as J. Robert Oppenheimer's assistant on the Manhattan Project. Schiff would later become head of physics at Stanford and was the man who rounded up the funds to build the Stanford Linear Accelerator Center (SLAC), one of the world's leading centers for the study of elementary particles.

In 1948, the Lilly family bought their first home, a narrow, three-story brick row house dating from 1880. It was on Regent Street in West Philadelphia, next to Clark's Park and just a few blocks from the Penn campus.

Various circumstances had continually come between John and Mary. As soon as they'd become engaged, John had gone away to work off his "nervous exhaustion" in the Pacific Northwest. Within two months of marriage, Mary had become pregnant, and didn't want to be. She wound up being nursed through this difficult pregnancy by John's parents, 2,000 miles from Caltech. While babies are often thought to bring people closer, the pregnancy had pushed John and Mary farther apart.

Then there was Mary's fractured spine. While John was starting out in medical school, Mary was in a body cast. And, with the war effort, John's research required him to spend long stretches far from home.

By 1942, domestic life with Mary had settled into an uneventful routine for John, punctuated by infrequent acts of sex. Things never really clicked between them sexually, even though it was the quest for sex that had motivated him—unconsciously given his lack of experience or understanding—to idealize Mary and, while in that state of entrancement, to propose marriage.

A few years after the wedding, John might well have thought he had chosen an unsuitable mate. But by then his energies were directed elsewhere, and he was too busy with his work even to consider the matter fully.

Predictably enough, the result of all this was that during the war, John experienced his first extramarital liaison, which he later characterized as his first real love affair. It was with a woman named Kacy, who lived next door. With her, he discovered real sexual intimacy, conscious passion, and all the tender feelings this kind of relationship can induce. Kacy was inventive and experimental, a voluptuous woman with a conspicuous freedom from the inhibitions and disinterest Mary had demonstrated regarding sex. Their bodies fit well together, and this full sexual expression drove John wild. It was physical-chemical magic, a sensual heaven with mind-blowing, consciousness-raising orgasmic blasts that brought him to a realm where he could sense (but not quite see) the angels he had known as a child.

They carried on like this for a year, whenever they could steal some time together. All the while John went through the familiar motions of family life with Mary and the kids, as if that life took place in a parallel universe. But both of John's lives were in the same physical universe—not to mention the same block— and the neighbors started talking. Of course, Mary found out. Enraged, she demanded that he break it off.

John acquiesced. Kacy, devastated, went into a deep depression. Feeling trapped, helpless, and thoroughly hating what he was doing, John tried to console her: "You will have one chapter in my history that no one else will have. I will never again be as deeply in love as I have been with you."

Nevertheless, John continued to have sexual relations outside his marriage—occasional flings he managed to conceal from Mary for some time. But she finally caught on. This time Mary told John's mother, Rachel, who had nursed her through that first difficult pregnancy in 1937, and Rachel told Dick. Dick reacted as if he were furious, called his errant son on the phone for a dressing down, reminded him of the family's moral code, and threatened to disinherit him. He even arranged for a Catholic priest to call on John and lecture him about morals.

John knew the threats were hollow, a mere formality. He recalled his father's discreet affairs during his childhood and adolescence, and became deeply disturbed that Dick now saw fit to censure his behavior.

So this, apparently, was the deal: Father, who had made all that money, could do as he pleased, as long as he observed certain niceties; while John, who was drawing on that money, was to follow orders. It didn't really count for much that he was a grown man who had earned both a degree in medicine and the respect of his colleagues, nor did it matter that he was devoting his professional life to the improvement of the human condition.

By 1949, some thirteen years into his marriage, John simply wanted out. As a growing child and teenager, John had watched his parents hold their marriage together while passion withered, leaving in its wake fondness and propriety mixed with sexual wandering and frustration. Although he had resolved then never to let himself be caught in the same situation, here he was. The life of an adult was not as easily managed as the child had imagined.

The marriage had come to feel like a trap from which he yearned to escape, but now he was restrained by the same "Reality Principle" Doc Eagleson had cited to him at Caltech: that social reality requires compromise of natural impulses and personal desires, that one must delay gratification until there would be appropriate time and safety to enjoy it.

Reality was complicated. There were the two children, one still quite young. There were John's parents, with their Catholic belief system that marriage was for keeps. And there was Mary, who had grown dependent on her position as Mrs. Dr. Lilly, wife and mother. John couldn't buck it all—that independent he wasn't.

For a brief time, in college, he had felt independent. But his encounter with Doc Eagleson and Dr. Freud had convinced him that his position in the world was closely tied to his family and was not simply a function of his own individual merits and personal efforts. From that point on, he felt stuck. He had yet to understand how the family money had actually given him the independence to pursue his own scientific research and exploration of Reality; for now he felt only the burden of the dependence on his parents which that money entailed. In this context of sexual frustration and the reassertion of parental control over him, he felt humiliated and childish.

So, bowing to family pressure, John accepted his "guilt" and played the part of a wrongdoer in a game he really didn't believe in—conventional sexual morality.

According to this game, John had broken one of the cardinal rules: he had committed adultery. Since he was playing this game, he now had to concoct an explanation for his sin. He was led into this transgression, he surmised, by his own "excessive" sex drive, and by a male "instinct" to impregnate as many females as possible. This was a lurid, cynical, and derogatory interpretation of his own wishes to explore, experiment, and grow in directions that seemed blocked within his marriage.

Having accepted a negative and humiliating self-interpretation of this incident, the mental conditions were set for a bad time ahead.

John shortly experienced what he later described in *The Scientist* as "three weeks of paranoid fear in which everyone was talking about me and in which I was terrified that something or someone would kill me. I stayed in my office and did not allow myself to go out. When I did go out, I felt that they were all against me and were planning to somehow do me in. I felt this way about my director, my scientific colleagues, about my wife—anyone and everyone. I spent most of my time isolated, fearing, crying, and going in and out of this paranoid state."

In later psychoanalysis, he linked this event to the rage and hatred he had felt toward his mother and younger brother when he was weaned, feelings he had cut off in the isolation of that dark closet at the age of three, during his first attempt to "reprogram" his feelings.

Whatever the best explanation for this paranoid episode may be, it coincided with that period in his life when he was beginning to focus on his *internal reality,* the inner arenas of his own brain and mind. His severely disturbed state was somehow related to the early phases of this process.

John confided in no one except an old med-school chum, Mike Hayward, who recommended psychoanalysis. He referred John to Dr. John Nathanael Rosen, a therapist in New York City who pioneered the "direct analysis" technique. The idea was for the therapist to reflect back to the patient the same "basic" language that the patient used in talking about his problem. The use of "obscene" or "gut level" language was supposed to excite the patient's "primary process" of basic feelings, prior to the intellectual interpretation and censorship that Freud had described.

With many patients direct analysis worked splendidly, but John, with his elaborately worked out system of ideas about the brain, the mind, and his own behavior, was too sophisticated. They tried to get to the root of whatever was bothering John for several sessions, but without success.

Dr. Rosen finally concluded, "You are uniquely crazy, and need an analyst who is both a scientist and an analyst."

Through Rosen, John found Dr. Robert Waelder, analyst extraordinaire. Waelder had been analyzed by Freud himself, as well as by his daughter Anna Freud. Since John was a medical doctor, he was allowed to take a "training analysis"—an analysis which would also train him to practice psychoanalysis. Though he was not a psychiatrist, he qualified under the rules of the American Psychoanalytic Society in those days. And Dr. Waelder was a physicist, and thus was allowed to practice only with other analysts and M.D.s aspiring to be analysts. John, who was a nonpracticing M.D., and Waelder, who was a not a medical doctor although he practiced psychoanalysis, got on splendidly.

Dr. Robert Waelder was a consummate intellectual who seemed to have little contact with his physical body. He was quite overweight and smoked heavily—big Cuban cigars. As he listened he seemed to inhale everything that John said, along with the smoke. He said little during their early psychoanalytic hours together. He just listened, and smoked.

Waelder, whom John called Dr. Robert, would sit in his big leather chair while John reclined on the traditional couch. As John lay on the couch and talked, Dr. Robert would slouch in his seat, listening and smoking. He'd offer a comment or analysis only when John entered a "negative transference"—meaning that he was projecting his negative feelings for someone else onto Waelder:

John: What am I doing here? How can someone like you, who eats too much and is overweight, and smokes cigars which raise his blood pressure, possibly analyze me? You and I both know that you're going to kill yourself with a heart attack.

Dr. Robert: Remember that I did not have the benefit of being analyzed by an analyst as clever as your analyst!

John loved analysis. He plunged into it with fascination and passion—passion deflected from his sexually unsatisfying marriage. When John decided to try to patch things up with Mary, he insisted that she too go into analysis.

In the Lilly household, the lingo of neurophysiology became seasoned with the jargon of psychoanalysis. John would be self-analytical over dinner, sharing with Mary and the kids all the methods he learned in psychoanalysis—free association, interpreting dreams, reading metaphors, analyzing projections and transferences, uncovering evasions.

While John thrived on analysis, Mary hated it. For Mary it was an uncomfortable medical procedure she submitted to only because it was prescribed by John, as the only way to save their marriage. He was in analysis, and how could they be close if she did not share the same world?

As John got deeper into psychoanalysis and learned to interpret his own metaphors, symbols, and the meaning of his loose words and minor deeds, he began applying the same techniques on Mary. Based on the history of how she had suffered in their marriage, he inferred that she must harbor deep resentment against him.

Mary tolerated psychoanalysis for over three years and then dropped out, despite the threats to the continuity of their marriage.

John talked with Mary's analyst after she quit. The analyst related that he had never seen a case like Mary's. She had been angry during every single analytical hour she had attended—every one, five days a week, for years. Nothing but angry.

Through psychoanalysis, for the first time John became conscious of what he himself was all about. He came to realize what his own real priorities were and how they were in conflict with his way of life. He discovered within himself what Freudians called the "superego," a mass of inculcated moral rules, an authority figure resident in one's own mind, a disciplinarian personified vaguely as a parental figure.

In spite of the eccentricity of both patient and analyst, for John psychoanalysis proceeded along very classical lines, as drawn by Sigmund Freud. Moreover, considerable progress was made. And what exactly did that mean? Simply put, successful psychoanalysis "cures" the patient of his superego. The ego then becomes a consummate game player, free of internalized rules, limited only by the actual constraints of the world outside.

Psychoanalysis thus helped John to become less inhibited. He became increasingly free to do what he wanted, in a carefully planned, fully conscious, and effective way. Over time he became freer to experiment sexually and have affairs without getting caught and creating a scandal. He was free, some years later, to get divorced without suffering internal conflicts.

Eventually, after three years of analysis, John was certified by the Philadelphia Psychoanalytic Association, and the Washington-Baltimore Psychoanalytic Institute, where he completed his training as an analyst. (In *The Scientist* John would reconstruct several of his sessions with Dr. Waelder.)

Through psychoanalysis John also became acquainted with Dr. Lawrence Kubie, and they became friends. Kubie was keenly aware that psychoanalysis and psychiatry as practiced in those days, loosely based on the pioneering directions taken by Freud at the turn of the century, must evolve to incorporate growing knowledge about the brain. John returned to the study of Freud's writings, which he had first encountered at Caltech. He also discovered the works of Carl Jung, Freud's renegade protégé, who vastly expanded the concept of the unconscious.

As a result of analysis, John turned his attention toward the mind, which, in contrast to the brain, he had increasingly neglected while burying himself in neurophysiology research. In 1931, when John wrote his "Reality" essay, he was very much aware that the brain and the mind were two perspectives on the same thing. But *in what way* they were the same thing—just how they were connected—was something which, as a sixteen-year-old, he could not figure out. Nor could anyone else in Western civilization, as far as he could discern.

Now, as a thirty-four-year-old medical doctor, he realized he was only slightly closer. He had become an expert on the brain, but its connection with the mind was still as obscure as ever. Nearly all that neurophysiology and medicine had to offer was the observation that if you hit somebody over the head hard enough, the mind of that person seemed to disappear. More sophisticated methods, and less overwhelming insults to the organ of cognition, seemed to diminish the mind in certain specific ways. Evidently, the mind was the activity of the brain, in the same sense that movement was the activity of muscles. Injury to the brain interfered with the activity of the mind, but beyond that, the connection remained a mystery.

Now, his involvement with psychoanalysis returned John's focus to the mind. This brought the two parts of the brain/mind equation back into balance. At his office in the university, he worked on brains for eight, ten, or twelve hours per day; and at Waelder's office, John worked on his own mind for an hour every day. Everything to follow in John's scientific career stemmed from this returned focus on the mind.

At age three, the child in the closet had learned that he could consciously program his mind; that his mind would follow orders; and that this programming was powerful enough to override the most deep-seated and primitive emotions. In this respect, the very young John was highly exceptional. For most children this knowledge and power develops slowly and incompletely over the course of many years; in some it does not develop at all.

Human society and social reality is a reality of, by, and for the vast majority of humans. Society's inherent conservatism and its fixed rules of conduct—*morality*—reflect the relatively fixed emotional structure of the average human, as a representative of the species at its present evolutionary stage. Against this background of the normal and moral, John Lilly was a prodigy and an oddity. He was gifted with exceptional inner freedom.

John learned that inner programming could maximize his degrees of freedom within the fixed structures of the emotional and social world. He was, for example, capable of withdrawing his energy almost entirely from a marital relationship, to channel it into his scientific work or into psychoanalysis. But at the same time, the fixed structures continued operating—in society, in other people, and in his own mind. John ran into these constraints as he tested the limits of his freedom from social constraints.

The two tracks operated concurrently, in parallel with each other. While he was increasingly free in the self-programmed reality of his own creation, the conflict with the other reality grew. He was pinned to external reality by the corresponding structures of his own brain—the parts he could not fully master by programming with conscious intention. For example, hunger drove him to seek food. His physiological need for sustenance entailed an interdependent relationship with other people and established social institutions (money, work, commerce, government, and so on). Similarly, his sexual drives, and more subtle emotional inclinations, led to entanglements with women, children, and parental responsibilities. The human body, and its guiding brain, imposed definite limits on the freedom of the human mind.

To resolve that basic conflict, and to escape its grip, he would have to go deeper within—deeper into the mind with psychoanalysis, and deeper into the brain itself.

Throughout his research career, John Lilly found that his unrelenting quest for Reality drove existing scientific methods, technology, and worldview to the breaking point. He repeatedly found himself on the cutting edge of technological development, stretching the latest breakthroughs from other areas of science to get the instruments he needed for his unprecedented probing of the brain.

In those days, most neurophysiologists were using equipment that could be described as crude at best. With such instruments, they could only know that they were stimulating nerves. They didn't have any clear idea of what signals were really going in or coming out. Most of them underestimated the technical difficulties of getting meaningful data from electrical exploration of the brain.

With his background in physics and his fanaticism for detail, John knew that to get anywhere he would have to apply the best gadgets and the best thinking available. He was an eager and early pioneer in the fledgling disciplines of biophysics and cybernetics. From Britt Chance he had learned the technology of vacuum tubes, magnetic amplifiers, and radar transformers. Using the latter he had produced the first Lilly Waveform, an electrical pulse that stimulates the brain tissue without injuring it (first published in 1955).

His physiological sensing amplifiers pushed the technology of vacuum tubes to its operational limits. To assure their stability, he tested tubes for three months before using them in his apparatus. He was something of a marvel to his colleagues, with his ever-present racks of glowing vacuum tubes lining his laboratory walls.

Once adequate electrodes are in position at exactly the right spots in the brain, the problem becomes twofold: first, how to precisely control the stimulation of the nerves; and second, how to accurately read out what's going on in there. The first task requires switches capable of clean, split-second timing of electrical pulses. The second requires amplifiers capable of picking up minute signals in the brain and amplifying them, with high fidelity, to the level where they can be seen or heard.

It was with some enthusiasm, therefore, that John tried out the latest breakthrough. In 1947, his technological trail-blazing had led him to electronics pioneer William Bradford Shockley, inventor of the transistor. Shockley had come to John's lab with some of the very first transistors constructed at Bell Labs. John tried out these early models and found they were too noisy to use as pulse switches or physiological amplifiers.

From time to time thereafter, Shockley would send over samples from his latest batch of transistors, as he gradually improved his fabrication techniques. It took about five years to develop transistors good enough to match wits with nerve cells.

At Penn, John's principal research collaborator and co-author of many publications was his student, Ruth Cherry.

In 1953 John was invited to join the National Institutes of Health at the invitation of Seymour Kety, a medical-school acquaintance from the University of Pennsylvania who had become the director of NIH that year. Kety promised John a free hand to pursue whatever research agenda interested him most. John brought his bavatron, used to view electrical activity over an area on the surface of the cerebral cortex, to the NIH campus at Bethesda, Maryland. The Lilly family moved to nearby Chevy Chase.

At NIH John set up a larger neurophysiology lab to continue his research on animal brains. His interest was shifting to the deeper structures of the brain, which could only be reached by inserting long electrodes. He was also eager to explore the deeper structures of his own mind. Through psychoanalysis, he had found, he could approach these structures—but only approximately. A deeper, fuller exploration ("inploration," he would call it) awaited the development of new techniques.

CHAPTER 6

PHYSICIAN, PROBE THYSELF!

December 1953, age 38.
It's a strange sort of dream world.
The laboratory at the the National Institutes of Health is
lined with benches covered with gadgets. In a special cubicle,
a monkey is strapped into a chair with wires dangling from
the top of its head. He is jerking on a lever frenetically, then
shrieking and trembling in the throes of electrically stimu-
lated sexual rapture. In one corner of the lab, the Scientist
has begun the procedure of driving a stainless steel spike into
the top of his own head.
He begins by positioning a metal frame over a chair and
assembling some instruments on an adjacent table tray: a
modified stainless steel syringe needle, a shiny new claw
hammer, a dentist's mirror. He takes his place in the seat and
clamps his head into the aluminum stereotaxic frame. A bite-
bar, coated with a plastic gum similar to what dentists use to
take dental impressions, goes into his mouth. He bites down
on the gum, making an impression of his upper and lower
teeth, to assure that his skull will not shift from the initial po-
sition. He slides blunt aluminum bars that lock into the open-
ings of his ears on both sides, and he tightens the wing nuts
that secure these in place. Then he fastens a strap behind his
head and another one under his chin. This arrangement will
hold his head firmly in place to assure that he is on target
when he takes aim for a specific spot in his brain. (It's ap-
proximately the same assembly that he uses on the monkeys
when implanting electrodes in their brains.) He has shaved off

a small patch of hair on top of his head, just to the right of the midline, and drawn a red X.

Meanwhile, the monkey is continuing his electrical self-stimulation. After about ten pulls on the lever, he squeals in delight, trembles, and falls into a torpor with an ecstatic grimace on his face. A couple of minutes later, he's back at the lever, working for his next jolt to the orgasm center in his diminutive brain. This pattern usually repeats for about twenty hours per day, after which the monkey sleeps for about four. Occasionally he sips some water from a feeder tube, or nibbles a little food from a tray without much interest. The pattern continues day after day, demonstrating that an animal who can stimulate his own brain has no interest in and little need for the outside world.

The Scientist readies himself for the first blow. Watching his moves in a pair of mirrors, he inserts the needle into a slot in a precision micrometer holder and positions the assembly over his head. With his left hand he turns a knob on the micropositioner, moving the needle until its tip is exactly over the designated spot. He slides the modified needle down in its holder until the blunt, tubular end, two millimeters in diameter, contacts the scalp. After a final check on position, he raises the claw hammer in his right hand and prepares to strike the top of the spike.

Bham! On the first strike, he cringes from the excruciating pain, straining involuntarily against the metal clamps holding his skull. He did not expect it to hurt this much. But the needle is right on target. It has pierced his scalp and its tip now rests on the periostium of the bone of his skull. Somewhat dismayed from the jarring pain of the first blow, he proceeds more cautiously. Just a light tap, this time.

The impact of the hammer on the spike and the spike on the skull sounds like a bomb going off in his brain; then, a split second later, he registers the overwhelming pain of impact. Number two is even worse than number one.

He pauses to check the depth-measuring scale: A scant two millimeters of progress has cost him two moments of incredible agony. . . .

John Lilly awakens from his dream, rubbing the top of his head. He is lying on the living room couch in his house out-

*side Baltimore. In the rooms upstairs, Mary and the children
are asleep in their beds.*
   *Quite a dream! Extraordinary detail—very convincing.
Even the pain seemed real!*

AS JOHN SAT up on the couch and collected himself, he recalled
how many times he had performed the kind of procedure he'd
dreamt about doing on himself on the skulls of his laboratory
animals. Following the rules for humane treatment, he would first
put the creature under general anesthesia; then he'd inject some
novocaine into the scalp, before driving in the tube. One good
blow with the hammer, and it would be through the scalp and the
skull. Another little tap, and the tube would be right where he
wanted it, clean through the skull and its tip resting just outside
the dura sheath, the tough and flexible inner membrane surrounding the brain.
   When the animal awoke from anesthesia, he would insert
the electrode itself through this little stainless steel tube. The
barrel of the needle would provide a passageway through the
skull that could be used again and again. The scalp would rapidly
heal around the exposed end of the tube, and the monkey or
chimp would behave as if nothing were unusual; but from that
moment on, the animal's brain would be open for probing by the
Scientist.
   When John had first tried this tube-and-hammer procedure
on the dried skulls of dead animals, the tube had cracked the
skulls or knocked small, irregular chunks of bone from its path.
It was entirely different with the moist and living bone of a live
animal. On impact, the bone would stretch and compress around
the tube as it entered, rather like driving a nail into green wood.
It would never crack, split, or shatter.
   Many of these needles could be driven into the skull of a
single animal at different angles, providing tubular guides for
electrodes into different parts of the brain. Electrodes could be
slid into these tubes and inserted through the dura, the arachnia,
and the pia—the three flexible linings covering the brain inside
the skull. Then it was simply a matter of cranking the electrode
down into the cortex or deeper parts of the brain, using a precision micrometer drive.

Maps of the brain—"the brain atlas"—provided general guidance, but the exact positioning of the tip of the electrode was a trial-and-error process. The electrode itself was a thin wire of tungsten, an extremely tough and inflexible metal. The length of the electrode was coated with insulation; only the very tip of its exquisitely sharp point was exposed. The other end of the electrode, outside the skull, was connected to a device that delivered electrical pulses. These signals would stimulate the surrounding nerve cells in the brain, wherever the tip of the electrode was lodged. From the animal's response to this stimulation, John could figure out where in the brain his electrode was. (Back at Penn he'd worked all this out with Macaque monkeys and published his results, which were groundbreaking at the time.)

With a monkey, any location stimulated in the cortex would either make one of the animal's muscles move or cause the animal to behave as if it had seen, heard, or smelled something. In the cortex of a chimpanzee, on the other hand, there were a few places in the very front that seemed to produce no response at all. John knew that several neurosurgeons had electrically stimulated the surface of the human cortex during surgical operations, and found similar, seemingly nonresponsive areas in the frontal cortex and elsewhere. These places were named the "silent areas." When the patients could talk about their experiences, they sometimes reported vague and complicated impressions from electrical stimulation of these areas.

At NIH, John probed deeper in the brain, where he located the "primitive" areas related to basic animal urges and instincts. These centers represented pure forms of pleasure, pain, and other basic drives—hunger, thirst, aggression, sex, and so forth. There was a particular spot that would cause a male monkey to have an erection of the penis. Stimulating a different, nearby area would cause ejaculation. A third location would cause orgasm in either gender. Yet another would trigger the full sequence of erection, orgasm, and ejaculation. A chimp with an electrode positioned in its orgasm center, and a lever it could operate to switch on the stimulation pulses, would turn on the current whenever it got a chance. It would stimulate itself to orgasm, rest a few minutes, and then do it again and again, all day long. It would sleep a little and then repeat the process on the next day, and the next, and the next. . . . It would seem happy and healthy for weeks or months at a stretch, even if restrained in a chair.

John was haunted by an urge to perform these kinds of experiments on himself, which gave rise to his extraordinarily vivid dream. He not only wanted to stimulate the pleasure centers but to probe all the mysteries of the human brain. He had wondered since childhood how the mind and the brain were related. He wanted to find out the precise nature of the connection between conscious mental experience and physical-electrical events in the tissues of the brain. He wondered what would happen if he could record the electrical activity in his brain while he was having a particular thought or some other experience and then play the signal from the recording back into his brain. Would he then have the same experience, the same thought he had recorded?

The Scientist had first considered these ideas as a sixteen-year-old schoolboy in St. Paul. He remembered the words from his essay, "Reality," penned in a small school notebook for his philosophy class:

How can the mind render itself sufficiently objective to study itself? In other words, how are we able to use the mind to ponder on the mind? It is perfectly feasible for the intellect to grasp the fact that the physiological changes of the brain occur simultaneously with thought, but it cannot conceive of the connection between its own thoughts and these changes.

Perfectly feasible, yes; but hardly easy. Writing those words, he had first considered the idea that reality was actually much more than what most people meant when they used the word. Reality was multiple—actually, it was plural: *realities.* There were outer realities and inner realities, "objective" physical realities and "subjective" personal realities, private realities and public realities. It was the human brain that put them all together. John now clearly realized that ever since his school days in Minnesota he had been pursuing the search for Reality and for the role played by the human brain in the nature of that Reality. Not simply "the brain" in the abstract, but his own brain in particular. He had stalked the mystery through two decades of education and research; now he was gripped by the desire to drive a probe into his own head in search of the answer.

Contemplating his dream, he was troubled by a question: Would the answer provided by such an experiment refer only to the *physical* reality? Perhaps it would leave him without any new understanding about the other reality—the reality of the mind. He closed his eyes. What came to him was the image of Jesus on the cross.

He was back in childhood, before his scientific career had started, before prep school, before writing that pivotal essay. He was an altar boy kneeling in his Catholic church, gazing at the icon of the crucifixion in the flickering candlelight. What was the meaning of that awe-inspiring and pathetic image? *Had the body been crucified to reveal something about the soul?* What was the connection between body and soul, between soul and mind, between religion and science?

As he mingled childhood revery with adult speculation, he realized the meaning of his vision of the church altar and the dream about the stereotaxic frame: *He was bent on crucifying himself.* The stereotaxic frame was his cross; the probe was his lance. The body was to be nailed to the crucifix and mortified to reveal its connection with the spirit; the brain was to be locked in the stereotaxic frame and penetrated to reveal its connection with the mind. He was both crucifier and crucified.

Could this gory icon from childhood really have been driving his scientific quest for all these years?

John imagined a map of the brain in cross-section, showing the physical structures of the brain against a rectangular grid of coordinates. From this data, and readings on the micrometer knobs of the stereotaxic frame, the neuroanatomist could get a pretty good idea of where the tip of a probe in the brain of a monkey would be relative to the known physiological structures of human brains.

The X and Y axes of his coordinate system formed a cross! The sign of the cross was the secret sign of science. Nature drawn and quartered, stretched over the quadrants of the scientist's coordinate cross to expose its secrets. *Quantification* to reduce the mystery to numbers and physical reality. *Reduction* to fit the living reality to a precisely limited description of it.

And crucifixion was the ultimate test of the brain/mind relationship—the ultimate in "destructive testing" of the human organism. The body faced death, and the mind faced death along with it—*or did it?* Was it only the *experience* of death that the mind faced and, if so, what experience would come next? The Scientist had returned to his basic problem: the relationship between the brain and the mind. Was the mind confined to space and time in the brain, doomed to die with it? After all, if the mind was nothing more than the activity of the brain, wouldn't it vanish when those activities ceased? After centuries of scientific progress, this rational distillation of the ancient riddle of body and soul was still an open question.

John was pursuing this mystery from both sides. In addition to his work in the neurophysiology laboratory, he had also completed three years of training to be a psychoanalyst. Nothing had been left out. Dr. Robert Waelder was himself a scientist, a man John could level with, the only man that John had ever met with such total objectivity. In recent sessions, they had talked about John's plans, or fantasies, to probe his own brain with thousands of electrodes.

On the occasions when John had discussed his plans for self-experimentation with brain electrodes, Dr. Robert had always urged him to examine his own motivations for wanting to do this. The analyst was consummately neutral, nonjudgmental, and objective. He guided John skillfully through the maze of rationalizations, assisting him to identify his real motives and reach his own conclusions about the wisdom of his plans. Many years later, in *The Scientist,* John would reconstruct one of his sessions on the subject:

Waelder: So you want to hook your brain up to a recording system, and then play that recording back into your own brain. Is this correct?

John: Yes, I visualize ten thousand electrodes inserted through my skull into my own brain, hooked up to an adequate recording system. The records would be made while I am actively doing something. At a later time they would be played back through the same electrodes. I would then be able to tell if I went through the same actions, also recorded on motion-picture film, that I had gone through originally. I would also be able to see whether I had the same inner experience that I had during the original recording.

Waelder: I can see that this raises a number of intriguing questions scientifically. . . . However, here we must analyze your motivations for doing such experiments on yourself. What are the dangers to you of such experiments? . . . You admit, then, that the present techniques are far too damaging to be used on yourself. Correct? You reported that at age sixteen you wanted methods for correlating the activities of the brain and mind. You saw the possibilities of doing this in 1937 at age twenty-two. . . . However, I am a bit skeptical about your wish to do this on your own brain.

John: My motivations are not self-damaging, suicidal, or masochistic. At least they are not consciously so.

Waelder: Well, as you have learned in this analysis, you do have strong components underlying your conscious motivation which could lead in the direction of self-damage. It seems to me you've picked the ultimate in self-damage by means of tens of thousands of brain electrodes.

John: It could be. . . . Yes, unconsciously maybe I do want to eliminate myself from the human competitive sphere. But I also detect a tendency to want to be a hero to other humans. A hero takes risks. A hero may end up damaging himself. A hero can fail and become . . . a martyr.

John's secrecy with his colleagues concerning these ideas was unfortunate, but necessary. Science should be a domain like psychoanalysis, one in which anything could be openly discussed. Nothing scientific should be shocking to one's colleagues. Unfortunately, the reality of organized, institutional, funded science was not like that. A word of this to any of his colleagues at the institute and he would be out on his ear—branded as a lunatic, a maniac, an unscientific, nonobjective, outcast. He would surely be drummed out of the elite corp of grant-supported scientists. There was no way he could ask a colleague or assistant to hammer probes into his head, and there was no way he could safely do it himself.

With his credentials he probably could have gotten a research grant from the government to insert electrodes into the brains of institutionalized neuropsychiatric patients, on the pretext that it might be "for their own good," or "for the good of society." But that would not be permissible under John's own ethics. Dr. Bazett had given him what became for John a kind of scientific Golden Rule: *Do not do unto others what you would not be willing to have done unto yourself.* While a risky, new research procedure could be perfected on laboratory animals, the researcher himself was the obvious first guinea pig before attempting it on another human volunteer. The researcher himself must know how it feels and what it does to consciousness before seriously proposing to do something to another human, whether an experimental surgical procedure or a new experimental drug.

By and large, the medical profession tended to overlook this ethic. They reasoned that whatever the doctor did to the patient was, after all, intended for the patient's benefit, since it was the patient, not the doctor, who needed the procedure.

The option of brain electrode experimentation, whether on himself or others, was therefore closed to John. He would have to devise alternative, if equally novel, means to explore the relationship between the brain and the mind.

In 1953 John's mother Rachel died. She had suffered intensely from her illness in the last year of her life. John watched the attending physician perform euthanasia by injecting a drug which released her from her body's struggle for survival. John was relieved that her pain was finally over.

After his neurophysiology lab was up and running at NIH with several assistants, John turned his attention to an extraordinary invention whose purpose was to observe the brain and mind, which rendered the scientific observer totally isolated from the outside world's input. That invention was the isolation tank, and it would profoundly affect John's search for Reality.

CHAPTER 7

THE DEEPER AND DEEPER SELF

September 1954, age 39.

From underwater, he inhales deeply through his breathing tube, the lifeline that connects him to the surface. He is totally surrounded by tepid liquid. It is completely dark—not a single photon of light enters the tank. There is not a whisper of sound, except the monotonous pulsing of his heart and the soft whoosh of air through the breathing tube, through his nose and mouth, larynx, trachea, bronchii, and into the tiny air sacks, the alveoli lining his lungs. He breathes slowly and regularly, more and more deeply.

Suddenly, he is inside an anatomy lesson from med school. He is within one of the alveoli, looking out through the translucent, pinkish maze of a lung. Blue veins and red arteries pulse around him, meeting in tiny purple capillaries where fresh oxygen enters and carbon dioxide is discharged.

Outside, beyond the layers of pink tissue, he sees the towering figure of a young man pointing a scalpel toward him. It is John Lilly, a medical student at Dartmouth, dissecting the lung of a cadaver. The air is sharp with the smell of formaldehyde.

He takes a deep breath and realizes the air in his breathing tube is fresh—not laden with the stench of formaldehyde. He remembers that he is in the tank, and the scene dissolves into a whirlpool.

He whirls and swirls into Mother's bedroom. She is reclining on her couch in a white gown, looking much younger

*than when he last saw her, before her death the previous
year.*

*"Johnny, why did you keep me alive all those months? It
was so miserable and so pointless. I felt the presence of death
the whole time. It was such a relief when it finally came. The
last moment was no worse than all the others. I guess you
did it because you love me. Or maybe because you feel
guilty. . . ."*

*"What does she mean?" John cries, caught in the under-
tow of conflicting emotions evoked by the scene.*

*"This is your analysis, not mine," retorts Dr. Waelder in
his good-natured way. Now John is lying on the couch in the
office of his former analyst. "I'm here merely to point out to
you the questions you might have overlooked," Waelder continues. "I'm not here to answer them for you."*

*Then Dr. Waelder is gone and John remembers he is
floating in a large volume of warm water in a big tank in a
secluded building called T-2, on the campus of the National
Institutes of Health in Bethesda, Maryland. John laughs in-
wardly at having put one over on himself yet again. It all
seemed so real!*

*He feels a glow over all his skin and a craving for physi-
cal contact. But there is no one present to caress. His penis
becomes erect and feels as if it's about to burst from internal
pressure. He touches his penis, his whole body shivers, and
the scene changes.*

*He is clasped in the embrace of a translucent goddess of
sex. She dances all around him and makes love to him at the
same time. The image is shattered by an orgasm more intense
than he has ever experienced before. He is blasted into a
space of scintillating golden light, and there are angels singing everywhere.*

MANY SCIENTISTS HAD wondered what would happen if a
person were cut off from all sensory stimulation and from interaction with the world outside. There were two competing hypothe-
ses, advanced by two different groups. One group, heavily influenced by the psychological school called behaviorism, thought
of the brain as an organ that reacts to stimuli. They predicted that

if all outside stimuli were cut off, the brain would cease its activity. The resultant condition would resemble coma, or dreamless sleep.

To John, the behaviorist perspective was totally implausible. The behaviorists had no acceptable explanation for the activity of dreams. After all, when you sleep and dream, the outside stimuli are normally darkness and quiet. Your dreams are usually not related to what's going on around you. To take the behaviorist hypothesis seriously, one would have to suppose that in dreaming, the brain is "reacting to stimuli," in some manner quite unrelated to the nature of the stimuli themselves. Certainly, in dreaming, a person can have the most outrageous experiences, while actually in the most sedate circumstances.

A different perspective was offered by a group that included most modern neurophysiologists and neuropsychiatrists, those who had actually studied the physiological activity of the brain. They were aware of autorhythmic processes occurring in the nervous system, in which a nerve cell or a group of cells can stimulate itself or one another in a circular feedback, generating and maintaining a level of automatic activity—somewhat analogous to natural pacemakers that keep the heart beating regularly. Their hypothesis suggested that in a state of profound isolation from stimuli and interaction with the world, the brain would continue operating and generating experiences.

A few scientists had performed experiments aimed at drastically reducing the level of stimulation for prolonged periods. This approach was called "sensory deprivation," or SD. (Government agencies, such as the CIA and military intelligence services, were intrigued with SD because of its possible implications for brainwashing and interrogation.) Most of the sensory deprivation experiments had been flawed; they did not eliminate all sources of stimulation, such as skin pressure, and they introduced stress through uncomfortable confinement of the body in fixed positions.

John Lilly set out to perfect the design of such experiments. He wanted to attenuate stimulation to the minimum possible level and to remove sources of discomfort and stress. His isolation tank design approached this ideal as closely as possible when working with a human body under the pervasive gravity found on the surface of planet Earth.

During 1953 and 1954, in building T-2 at NIH, John con-

John, with big brother Dick (R.C. Lilly, Jr.) and little brother Dave (David M. Lilly), in St. Paul, about 1922. *Photo: Courtesy of Lilly family.*

John and Mary camping by Lasen Glacier circa 1937.

John C. Lilly, M.D., with the U.S. Air Force in World War II. Working with uniformed officers at the Air Force Laboratory of Aviation Physiology, Wright Field, Ohio, he monitors a volunteer in a decompression chamber, using physiological and electronic instruments he designed. *Photo: Old film found and developed in 1984 by Jay B. Dean at Ohio State University, courtesy of American Physiological Society.*

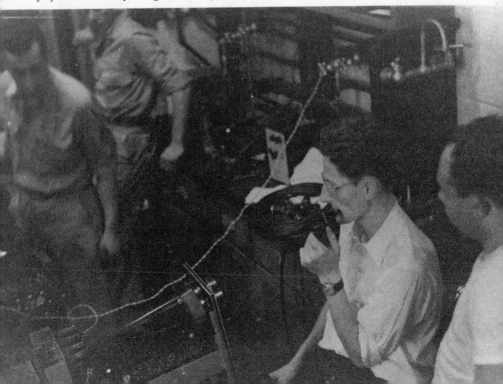

Laura and Aldous Huxley in Italy, 1960. *Photo: La Stampa.*

John and Elisabeth arrive at Marineland i 1961. *Photo: Alice Miller, courtesy John Lill*

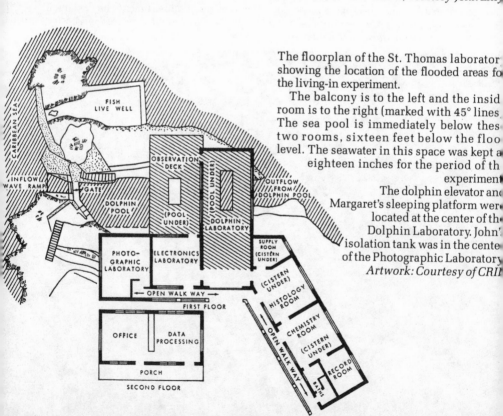

The floorplan of the St. Thomas laborator showing the location of the flooded areas fo the living-in experiment.

The balcony is to the left and the insid room is to the right (marked with 45° lines The sea pool is immediately below thes two rooms, sixteen feet below the floo level. The seawater in this space was kept a eighteen inches for the period of th experimen

The dolphin elevator and Margaret's sleeping platform wer located at the center of th Dolphin Laboratory. John' isolation tank was in the cente of the Photographic Laboratory *Artwork: Courtesy of CRI*

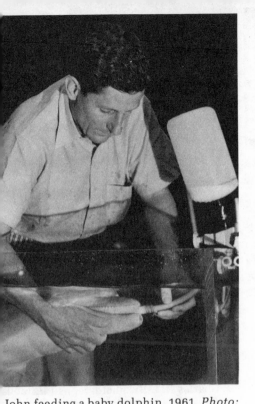

John feeding a baby dolphin, 1961. *Photo: CRII, courtesy of John Lilly.*

Tolva presents her flipper for Alice Miller to scratch. *Photo: CRII.*

Interspecies communication pioneers: At the CRII Dolphin Point Lab in 1964, Margaret Howe plays with Peter or Sissy in the deep pool. *Photo: Jon Lovett, courtesy of CRII.*

Nina, Toni's daughter, at a party in 1974. *Photo: Courtesy of Lilly family.*

Charles R. Lilly, photographed in 1969. *Photo: Brooks Studios, courtesy of Charles R. Lilly.*

CRII, about 1962: John's younger son Charles, and Pamela, Elisabeth's daughter, whom John adopted. *Photo: CRII, courtesy of John Lilly.*

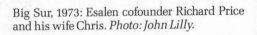

Malibu, 1973: John poses with Toni and neighbor Douglas Campbell and friend beside his new isolation tank, hatch open. *Photo: Nate Cutler.*

Big Sur, 1973: Esalen cofounder Richard Price and his wife Chris. *Photo: John Lilly.*

Balancing an egg on Ram Dass's head. *Photo: Toni Lilly, courtesy of Lilly family.*

John and Toni, about 1975. *Photo: Courtesy of Lilly family.*

John, suffering from a migraine, is cared for by Craig Enright, M.D. *Photo: Courtesy of John Lilly.*

John and Toni on an airline in the mid-seventies, about the time of Comet Kohoutek and the encounter with the Solid State Intelligence. *Photo: United States Travel Bureau, North Hollywood.*

Leading a seminar at Esalen Institute, where the custom is to sit on the floor. *Photo: Courtesy of John Lilly.*

Esalen, mid-seventies: Heinz von Foerster at one of the seminars he co-led with Gregory Bateson, Lois Bateson, John and Toni Lilly. To his right is his friend, philanthropist Jean Taupin, who sponsored many scientific meetings on the subject of consciousness). *Photo: Toni Lilly, courtesy of Lilly family.*

With Gregory Bateson at Esalen. *Photo: Courtesy of John Lilly.*

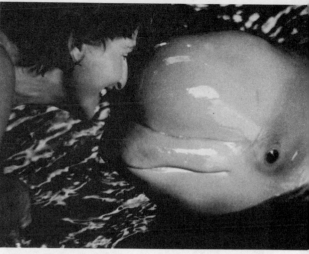

Toni meets a beluga whale (a large type of dolphin with a huge brain), in 1977 at Dr. Bill Evans's research institute on Mission Bay, San Diego. *Photo: Paul Gaer, courtesy of John Lilly.*

John at the controls of JANUS instrumentation.

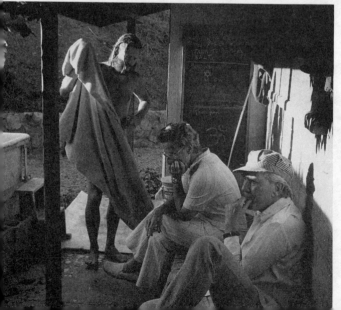

Malibu, 1978: John and Burgess Meredith ponder the future of human-dolphin communication research, sitting beside John's isolation laboratory building. (Jeff Bridges is in the background, having recently emerged from the isolation tank inside.) *Photo: John Bryson.*

structed and refined the first isolation tank. It took him the better part of a year to get the bugs out of this invention. The trickiest part was the air supply. Applying his knowledge of respiration instrumentation from the war years, he came up with a latex rubber mask that stretched to fit tightly around the head. From the area of the nose and mouth protruded a wide-bore breathing tube that led above the surface of the water. The top end of the breathing tube was clipped to a support that kept it safely above water level.

The tank was a soundproof and lightproof room. He floated reclining, with his head just below the surface of the water. His feet, the least buoyant part of the body, rested on a rubber strap. Other than this strap, he had no contact with anything even remotely solid. The air he breathed, about the same temperature as the water, flowed in and out through the tube without resistance. His chest was close enough to the surface that there was no noticeable water pressure against its expansion as he breathed.

Getting in was a bit tricky, since he had to pull the eyeless mask over his head, climb a ladder, turn out the lights, and then lower his body into the water with confidence that he was not about to drown himself. Once inside, he could totally relax and remain in that condition for hours. It was permissible to urinate, because old water was continuously replaced with fresh. The only limits on the time he could spend in the tank were created by the need for food and the demands of his schedule in the outside world.

By the end of 1954, the first isolation tank was up and running, and it worked well. Floating in the still water at 93.5° F felt like nothing at all.

Then the flights of thoughts and images began. The experience of being in the tank resembled free association in psychoanalysis—only much more vivid and sensory. It was far more "real" than the passing words and thoughts or the fleeting images behind closed eyes with which John was familiar. The images in the isolation tank had a life of their own. They marched in a realistic parade which would continue as long as he allowed it. And he could allow himself to be convinced that these experiences were real—but never for long.

In this respect, being in the tank was like dreaming. In dreams, events seem to be real, unless your sleepy consciousness somehow becomes aware that you are dreaming. In such "lucid dreams," you may even be able to control what happens in the dream or the part you play in it. In the isolation tank, John found that he could relax his mind and dream, but his consciousness was always there, ready to take charge. He could choose to relax and let things happen, in which case the images would free-associate, moving as if randomly from one to the next. Or he could choose to program what would happen, in a process similar to lucid dreaming, but with an even greater degree of control. He could invent a scenario ahead of time with his consciousness fully focused, and then relax and let his brain carry out the program.

In these experiences lay an important discovery. Somewhere, deep within the brain, was a mechanism capable of generating internal experiences completely independent of the outside world.

John was thus able to settle the issue of what happens in profound physical isolation. In the absence of stimulation and interaction with the external world, with total relaxation of the body and voluntary suspension of movement, the mind does not pass into unconsciousness. The brain does not shut down. Instead, it constructs experience out of stored impressions and memories. The isolated mind becomes highly active and creative. This was the principal discovery that John reported in his first three scientific papers on the isolation tank research, published in 1956, 1957, and 1958.

Privately, John had always considered the question of whether or not brain activity and experience would continue in profound isolation fairly obvious. This question had merely given him an acceptable agenda that he could present publicly to his scientific colleagues in the 1950s in order to justify the isolation tank work. But John had a deeper agenda, his own set of questions to explore with the help of the tank.

These questions were the natural extension of his search for Reality, begun as a teenager. Foremost among them was: how to use the mind to study the mind?

This issue formed the basis of the first of his private objectives in his isolation tank experimentation: to study the properties of the scientific observer (himself) in isolation. Second, John wanted to use the tank to continue his own psychoanalysis, begun with Dr. Waelder. The analytic process that Waelder had taught him was now internalized. It operated within him constantly. Third, John used the tank to escape from the social pressures of interaction with his family and scientific colleagues. In the tank, John found access to a state of deep rest in which, without distractions or interruptions, he could think and solve problems at high speed.

This experimental separation of self and environment stimulated John to rethink ideas about the relationship between the mind and the brain, the cornerstone of his search for Reality. The self, or the "ego" as the Freudians called it, had usually been considered in relationship to reality, implicitly, *external* reality—the world *outside*. The behaviorists, the predominant school of psychology at the time, had carried that idea to the extreme. They denied that there was anything in the head except what had been learned through interaction with the environment.

John found that by cutting off the environment he could examine the self in stark relief, from a perspective that simply wasn't available to those who were continually involved with the demands of the outside world. From this point of view, it became clear to John that if the self is dependent on anything, it is not the external, but the *internal* environment—the interior milieu of the brain. In the dark and silent void of the tank, it seemed as if it were the brain that generated the self, created the mind, or whatever each of us calls "me." John began to think of himself as generated by his brain. His brain no longer belonged to him; he belonged to his brain.

In the isolation tank at NIH, John found a whole world inside his own brain. Eventually he was driven to conclude that an *internal reality* exists within the confines of the human brain, alongside and in parallel with the external reality defined by contact with the world outside.

By working from the inside, he found everything that he had previously found by working from the outside with neurophysiological techniques. There were systems of pleasure and pain that, though they exerted a commanding influence over the whole, could be mastered and controlled with practice. There were incredible energies that shaped the development of human life and individual personality. There were all the problems of his individual life that he'd struggled with in psychoanalysis. There were vast reserves of intellectual power and resorts of inner peace. There were untapped realms of imagination. In fact, all the things men and women strive for, and all the things they fear, were right there, inside the brain.

John allowed a few other scientists to float in his isolation tank, and he compared their experiences with his own. One such carefully selected individual was Ed Evers, a psychiatrist moving into neurophysiology, who spent several hours in the tank, experienced "nothing," and dismissed the tank as uninteresting. A more promising reaction came from Dr. Jay T. Shirley, a physiologist who took to this experimental medium in a big way. (In 1961, John and Shirley would coauthor a major article on the isolation tank work. After John left NIH, Shirley continued isolation tank research independently. When he later moved to the Department of Psychiatry at the University of Oklahoma Medical School, he built a new tank there.)

From his own experiences and those of others, John drew some fascinating conclusions that stimulated the development of much of his subsequent thinking, including many far-reaching, radical, and unorthodox ideas he would not express in print for years to come.

One example involved the idea of extrasensory perception, telepathy, for example, and culminated in some surprising conclusions about the role of beliefs in psychiatric diagnosis. In profound isolation, one may have the experience that other people are present, or that one is receiving communications from sources outside the tank. What one makes of these experiences depends on one's beliefs. A person who believes in telepathy is likely to conclude that the messages are actually coming from someone or something at a distance from the tank. Within such a belief system, the experience will be perceived as real. On the other hand, someone who does not believe in telepathy, having the same basic experience, will perceive the experience as unreal, perhaps calling it an "hallucination."

A behaviorist, usually the most skeptical and hard-boiled sort of psychologist, might enter the tank with the belief that nothing can happen in the brain without some external stimulus as the cause. Should an experience occur which appears to come from a source outside his own head, but with no such possible source nearby, such a person might then be forced to adopt a belief in telepathy in order to explain it. Within the belief system of the behaviorist, this becomes the only acceptable explanation for such phenomena in a framework that does not allow for any inner experience or even hallucinations. Paradoxically, then, a person who does not even believe in the psyche may end up believing in "psychic communication." The apparent dilemma is not generated by the experience itself, but by the prior belief system within which the experience is interpreted.

A person who believes that the mind is contained within the brain will interpret such an experience as a phenomenon originating in his own brain. For such an individual, the experience is perceived *as if* real; no matter how vivid it may seem, it never acquires a convincing sense of reality. "As if real" is quite different from *real*.

Someone who can accept neither the hypothesis of telepathy nor the hypothesis of internally generated experience is completely stumped in the face of an experience of this type. His belief system may prevent him from ever having such an experience. If, in spite of his beliefs, he nonetheless has such an experience, it would probably be dismissed as a "mere hallucination."

This sort of correlation between experiences and beliefs led John to conclude that what psychiatrists choose to characterize as "hallucination" or "psychosis" depends strongly on the prior belief system of the person who undergoes the experience. The psychiatric dogma of that time held that hallucinations were a sign of psychosis, a more-or-less permanent state of disease in which voluntary control of one's own mind or brain was lost. In the context of psychiatric thinking, John recognized, such reasoning was compelling. Even today, this view remains prevalent among psychiatrists.

Any normal, healthy person could have unusual experiences that would seem real *if he believed in them*. If he did not believe in them, the experiences would seem *unreal*. When such a person believes in the reality of the experience and communicates this belief to a psychiatrist, the psychiatrist would conclude that the individual was hallucinating and might be psychotic. However, if the person reported having an unusual experience they believed to be unreal, the psychiatrist might be less inclined to assume mental pathology. Thus the psychiatric diagnosis would be based on the patient's beliefs or opinions about his experience, not on the experience itself. Note that it is the *patient's* belief or disbelief in the experience that matters most, not the doctor's.

The irony of this situation is that the beliefs that led to the diagnosis were in place before the experience. And, in fact, these beliefs may be no different than those of people considered mentally healthy—indeed, no different from the beliefs of the psychiatrist himself! A normal person, even a psychiatrist, can have experiences of something which is not actually present. A normal person can reasonably believe that what he or she experiences is real. Now, put a normal person, an acceptable belief system, and a certain category of experience together, and you have, in the opinion of the psychiatrist, "a crazy person" who is having hallucinations.

And yet, from his own experiments in the isolation tank, John knew that hallucinations could be voluntary and controlled. One could allow oneself to have these experiences, or one could decide to stop them. There was no loss of voluntary control, no loss of consciousness or "ego functions." Instead there was a continuum of states of experience, ranging from fleeting images to vivid scenes full of action, meaning, and involvement. One could choose a position along this continuum, and venture into it more or less deeply. One could choose to get out at any point, and return to a state of peaceful quiescence or intellectual activity. There was no threshold which, if crossed, plunged a person into an abyss of psychosis and a morass of uncontrollable hallucinations.

John drew the conclusion that the term *hallucination* is rather meaningless, a trash heap for a wide variety of potentially significant experiences that are not acceptable according to established systems of belief. In the light of this line of reasoning, psychiatry begins to appear startlingly unscientific.

John became sensitive to the necessity of being very cautious about what he chose to reveal of his experiments to his colleagues, many of whom were psychiatrists. In his scientific papers of this period, John carefully articulated his observations in a manner and in a language that he thought would appeal to his psychiatric and psychoanalytic colleagues, without directly challenging the current dogma. His private thinking would have been threatening to them; if it became popular, it would place much of the intellectual foundations of psychiatry on dangerously shifting sand.

Although he never explicitly stated his thinking on the matter until years later, it became clear to John that beliefs determine experiences as well as the interpretation of experiences. The isolation tank studies made John abundantly aware of the power of beliefs, and of the importance of beliefs in formulating a truly scientific theory of the mind. His early exposure to the philosopher Kant had introduced him to the role of arbitrary belief systems in religion and philosophy; now it was beginning to appear that beliefs held similar sway in much of what was passed for science. Where he had once believed that science, by requiring the test of experience, went beyond philosophy, it now seemed that by determining acceptable experiences which a scientist might allow himself to have, philosophy could reach beyond science!

During the isolation tank work, John reflected on his years of psychoanalytic training. He came to realize that the all-important interpretations, a central feature of analysis, were themselves really only beliefs. The act of interpreting the client's experiences was actually a process of forming beliefs about the client's experiences.

John recalled the day at Caltech when Doc Eagleson, the amateur analyst, had interpreted John's anger and indignation against "the system" as misplaced anger against his father. That interpretation actually had been the creation of a belief; Eagleson had fabricated a belief about John's anger and had sold that belief to John. It had been an effective move—since the transaction resolved their conflict, and Caltech received more money in the process.

The system handed down by Sigmund Freud for determining psychoanalytic interpretations was actually a procedure for fabricating beliefs acceptable to society. However, John suspected that most analysts were unaware of the true nature of their activities and believed their interpretations were somehow real—an inherently unscientific viewpoint. Like the interpretations generated in an individual's psychoanalysis, the theories generated in psychology and psychiatry differed from the open-ended, exploratory, truth-seeking theories of science, which were continually tested by experimental confrontation with reality. Psychiatry was based on rather closed, circular, and untestable systems of reasoning.

As John deepened his explorations into his own mind and into the human brain as viewed from the inside out, he realized that the prevailing theoretical structures of psychology and psychoanalysis were inadequate for the goals he was pursuing in his search for Reality. He was certain that far more went on in the brain and mind than could be accounted for by these frameworks. Neither behaviorism nor Freudianism, the two theories that dominated psychology, was worth a damn in his quest to link the study of the mind (from the inside, in his isolation tank) with the study of the brain (from the outside, in his neurophysiology lab).

In his quest for a more encompassing model to understand the relationship between the mind and the brain, and the role of beliefs in this relationship, John stepped beyond the framework of psychology, psychiatry, and psychoanalysis. While he floated in his isolation tank, freed from the stifling prejudices, the misguided enthusiasms, and the incessant pressures of society, the seeds of a novel and radical model for the brain/mind relationship took root in his mind, ideas whose growth would be further stimulated by his later research with LSD. So challenging were they to the prevailing thinking of the time that John would neither complete their formulation nor publish a word of them until he wrote his landmark book, *Programming and Metaprogramming in the Human Biocomputer,* in 1967–1969—at which point they would still be well ahead of their time.

At NIH, John was chief of the Section on Cortical Integration at the National Institute of Neurological Diseases and Blindness and a member of the National Institutes of Mental Health. He also held a commission as surgeon, junior grade, in the Commissioned Officers Corps of the U.S. Public Health Service, the Surgeon General's outfit. This quasimilitary post conferred unique benefits, because it placed John outside the civil service and outside the main hierarchy at NIH. While most of John's colleagues were expected to work regular hours and report to bureaucratic bosses, he was officially on duty twenty-four hours a day, like a military officer-of-the-watch on call in case of some national health emergency. So John was free to come and go as he pleased, and he rarely faced any questions about what he was up to in his laboratories.

This extraordinary freedom to follow his own directions was among the benefits resulting from the fact that John did not need to demand the level of salary usually paid to M.D. researchers at NIH. His open road was paved by the Lilly family money, through the trust fund John's father had established.

While at NIH, John wrote a prodigious number of significant and seminal scientific papers on brain physiology. About half a dozen of these were coauthored by his principal research assistant Alice Miller.

The NIH bureaucracy may have been largely oblivious to his comings and goings, but John was drawing official attention in other quarters of the government. His two main areas of research activity, brain electrodes and sensory isolation, were of growing interest to a group of secretive agencies concerned with the control of brains and minds. The CIA and military intelligence services approached him several times, hoping to get the inside track on his research, hoping to draw him into their game.

This interest created an awkward situation for John. As a government scientist, it was his duty to share his results with other branches of the government. But John's emerging awareness of the potential for misuse of scientific discoveries ran counter to this responsibility. He had an ethical aversion to allowing his work to be turned to purposes opposed to those ideals which motivated him—scientific discovery, human progress, and the free exchange of ideas. The government, John realized, was a multiheaded beast; while one group was looking after the welfare of the people, seeking ways to cure their diseases, enlighten their minds, and prolong their lives, others were looking for new and improved ways to control minds and to kill.

While John had been at Penn and undergoing psychoanalysis, his analyst's probes had made him aware that his most idealistic endeavors might eventually be perverted by others. Waelder had confronted John with a series of questions that forced John to recognize this unpleasant fact: no matter how idealistic his own desire might be to probe the brain electrically, the political reality around him would turn his work to the service of power and policy. Now at NIH, John realized that his position might somewhat parallel the one in which Albert Einstein had once found himself.

He reflected on Einstein's career. Einstein's discoveries about the nature of physical reality were exploited toward horrendous ends—the atomic bomb. Himself an idealist, a pacifist, an advocate of disarmament, and an opponent of nationalism, Einstein was forced to sit idly while the technological fruit of his scientific work was used to crush two Japanese cities, bringing death and permanent injury to huge numbers of people.

Einstein had sought truth and beauty, and then lived to see his efforts turned into death and destruction. John could see himself being placed in a similar dilemma. This time it was the brain revolution which intrigued the military planners. He feared his work would be classified under military secrecy. He would no longer be able to publish, to discuss it with other scientists, even to mention it publicly. And he himself might be barred from knowing to what ends his efforts were being used.

John's anxiety that his idealistic inventions might be perverted was heightened by his personal acquaintance at NIH with Dr. Leo Szilard, perhaps the world's most famous living physicist. With Enrico Fermi, Szilard had written the first patent on a "Nuclear Explosive Device"—the atomic bomb. With Albert Einstein, he had urged President Roosevelt to launch the Manhattan Project, and subsequently, with Einstein, he had spearheaded the *unsuccessful* campaign to prevent its use against Japan. Szilard could speak from bitter experience about the perils now surrounding John, convincing John that he might well find himself in an Einstein-like dilemma.

And John also recalled how he had himself previously tangled with General Groves, director of the Manhattan Project. This connection also contributed to his very intense and personal sense of standing at an ethical watershed, with historic implications flowing from the way he handled the covert agencies.

The military-intelligence complex courted John several times. A scientist from the Sandia Corporation named Iben Browning visited his lab on a few occasions. Browning was interested in using brain electrodes to control the behavior of animals. Other inquiries were directed at his isolation tank work, as this research gradually became known among government scientists. John managed to dodge all questions about his tank.

Eventually the director of NIH informed John that he was invited to present a briefing on his brain electrode research at a meeting of U.S. government covert agencies. John agreed, on the condition that the briefing and his presentation were under no circumstances to be classified. He intended that these conditions would insure full public knowledge of everything he presented. Accordingly, he planned to make a thorough presentation of his research in all its details. Since, under the terms he had set, none of the material he presented could ever be classified, he thought there would be little incentive left for the agencies to use any of this public information as the basis of a covert program. John's director at NIH backed him up in this regard.

After some delay, agreement was reached on these terms, and John consented to attend the meeting.

In a somber government building in Washington, D.C., he was ushered into a briefing room where thirty men in various uniforms and business suits sat silently around a long table. Dr. Lilly was introduced to them, but the identity of those present was kept from him. He gave his talk and showed his slides, and then there was silence.

Only one question was asked: "Dr. Lilly, what are the medical indications for the use of brain electrodes in human patients?"

John responded that the use of brain electrodes in patients was justified only in the case of severe diseases untreatable by other means, such as incurable epilepsy and Parkinson's disease. He hoped that his answer would discourage further interest in experimentation.

John knew the hidden intent behind the question: The agencies wanted an acceptable medical excuse to perform mind-control experiments using electrodes on human subjects. At this time, in the 1950s, the covert agencies supported medical and psychiatric research programs through various fronts. Researchers at major universities and hospitals, and the patients on whom they experimented, did not know where the funding was actually coming from, or what the real sponsors hoped to get out of their work.

John was painfully aware that his research could be used to create powerful brainwashing and mind-control techniques. Human beings could potentially be converted into virtual robots, involuntarily carrying out missions for whoever controlled their electrodes, without knowing what that mission was or even who they served. John despised everything about it.

Later, when John had begun his dolphin research in Florida, he was again invited to the capital to brief the Office of Naval

Research and other departments at the Pentagon. After his talk, he was asked to leave the room so that he would not hear the next speaker—Iben Browning, the man from Sandia Corporation. He was thus placed in the position of being excluded from a meeting to prevent him from seeing the uses to which his own earlier research was being put.

John was told that the decision to ask him to leave was related to something in his security clearance file. Through high-level friends in the government, he discovered that a spurious note about a criminal record had been inserted in his file. When he demanded a correction of the record, he was interrogated by FBI agents curious about how he had discovered that his security clearance had been tampered with. They attempted to bully John into betraying his sources inside the government. John eventually received a letter from the secretary of defense retracting the allegation that he was a security risk.

Certain people in the covert agencies, resenting the fact that a scientist had ethical compunctions against the secret military use of his discoveries, had apparently sabotaged John's security clearance. He was eventually able to set the record straight only because of his extraordinary resourcefulness and his effective network of friends inside the government. He realized that less well-connected scientists could be intimidated and manipulated by such threats to their security clearances.

John once again had to pull strings when he discovered that a film of his laboratory work had been made by Browning and was classified, in flagrant violation of the original agreement. He managed to get the film declassified.

Some time later, the contents of Browning's presentation at the secret briefing were leaked to the press. An article in *Harper's Magazine* revealed how brain electrodes were used to guide the course of a walking mule by remote control. John found out that Sandia Corporation's main business was development of small, compact nuclear weapons of a kind that could potentially be delivered to their targets by "guided mule." His worst suspicions were confirmed.

John learned the fine art of operating effectively inside a government organization from several seasoned veterans, especially Fred Stone, an NIH administrator. Stone had mysterious ways of supplying John with the necessary facilities, arrangements, and funds for his research, somehow defying bureaucratic inertia and delay. John discovered that government functions only because there are personal networks of loyal, trustworthy people dedicated to making things work in spite of the overwhelming red tape.

Director Seymour Kety, whom John had known in med school and who had brought John to NIH, was a large, intelligent, and affable man, one of a rare breed of scientific administrators who believed that the essence of scientific leadership was to pick the right people and support their creativity, rather than tell them what to do.

But after five years at NIH, John got a new boss. Dr. Livingston, the new director, was a slight, meticulous man with a brisk manner and a distant, authoritative, and imposing presence. Livingston began to reorganize the departments to suit his own management style: everything tightly compartmentalized and orders coming from the top down. This trend was sweeping government research establishments in those days, as institutions grew larger, more heavily bureaucratized, and more narrowly goal-directed. The rearrangements began to disrupt the finely tuned research program John, as head of the Section on Cortical Integration, had managed to set up. While he normally worked in as quiet and noncontroversial a way as possible, John was forced into taking action.

He visited the new director in his office and bluntly informed Livingston that his bureaucratic activities were interfering with the research program. Dr. Livingston, feeling threatened, assumed a physically intimidating fighting stance in the corner of his big office. John was afraid his boss might actually spring from this pose and tackle him.

"You wouldn't want to attack me, because I'm trained in judo and jujitsu, and I wouldn't want to hurt you," John said coolly. (He had studied judo for three years at Caltech, attaining a first degree black belt. Martial arts had also taught him that you don't have to fight when you can talk instead.) Livingston regained his poise, and they were able to settle their differences verbally.

They agreed that Livingston would cease to interfere with John's activity on the basis of a mutual understanding that John would soon leave NIH. John recognized that changes in the institution had already been set in motion from above, and NIH would shortly no longer serve as a suitable environment for pursuing his highly individualistic search for Reality. (John's forthright approach to Livingston is perhaps explained by the fact that John was a close friend of Livingston's father, a brilliant scientist concerned with the treatment of pain.)

As John gained stature in the brain research establishment, he came to know the eminent neurophysiologist, Warren S. McCulloch, M.D., whose work John had studied at Penn along with the related work of Heinz von Foerster. John first met McCulloch at a scientific symposium, where McCulloch was giving one of his brilliantly clear and crisp presentations. As he entered the lecture room, McCulloch was at the blackboard. His intent gaze, craggy features, and full, fuzzy beard had earned him a reputation as a man who resembled an Old Testament prophet more than a scientist. John's impression was different—he saw a lanky live wire crackling with energy and excited good humor as McCulloch enthusiastically bounced around in his tennis shoes.

McCulloch was presenting a discussion of the McCulloch-Pitts Formal Neuron, a model of nerve cell behavior he had developed in collaboration with the young Harvard mathematician Walter Pitts. They had invented a way of thinking about neurons and networks of neurons that established in principle the capacity of a collection of interconnected simple cells to perform activities which had been thought to entail mental capability—for example, logic, arithmetic, and deciding among alternatives. This model convinced scientists that they should be looking to the physiology of the brain for an explanation of processes which had previously been relegated to psychology and philosophy.

The McCulloch-Pitts theory gave neuroscience a big boost. There had been much skepticism from biologists, who thought cells were too simple as units to perform operations of a mental nature, as well as from philosophers and theologians, who argued that study of the brain could not possibly account for the mind or soul. The model was also an important development in understanding the analogy between brains and computers. It contributed to the thinking of John von Neumann, a pioneer in the invention of early electronic digital computers. However, the model was still too simplistic to adequately represent the actual workings of neurons in a real brain.

As John pointed out at the symposium (and as McCulloch himself understood), the McCulloch-Pitts model was really a kind of mathematical notation for representing ideas about how the brain might work on a minute scale. Many others did not understand this distinction, and being themselves not intimately familiar with the biology of nerve cells, they misconstrued the McCulloch-Pitts model as a description of real neurons. These people made the classic mistake of "eating the menu instead of the meal"; they confused the map with the territory.

That confusion continued over the next three decades. Many science students were taught by poorly informed teachers that the behavior of neurons was "little more" than the scientific caricatures described by McCulloch and Pitts. As a result, the capabilities of both single neurons and of the entire brain composed of billions of them were grossly underestimated. This trend created a strange paradox: If the brain actually worked in the way the model described, it could not possibly generate a mind sufficiently complex to have invented the model! Thus, those scientists who were most committed to proving that the mind could be reduced to the activity of the brain had inadvertently proven that a mind sufficiently powerful to model the brain could only be accounted for by something that must exist beyond the brain of their model.

Again and again, scientists, like philosophers and theologians before them, fell into the trap of thinking that the actual phenomena of nature are virtually equivalent to the models they had constructed in their attempt to understand those phenomena. This kind of fallacy had begun with religious figures who, committed to writing impressions of their inspirational experiences, subsequently insisted that their written words encompassed and embodied "God." In science the error was basically similar, although the writings were about Nature, not God. For the most part, scientists did not *fanatically* believe their models and theories reflected the way things actually were, but they often behaved as if they *implicitly* believed this.

John had become aware of this trap early in his education and was seldom caught by it. He sensed that there were unknowns in everything: the phenomena of nature, the brain, the single neuron, and the mind of the scientific observer. There were even unknowns in the theories, models, and mathematics by which scientists attempted to reduce nature to neat little logical explanations. If he worshiped anything in his religion of science, it was the great Unknown stretching before him.

Back at Penn, during his analysis with Dr. Waelder, issues of safety and concerns about the reactions of his colleagues had thwarted his desire to insert electrodes into his own brain. The Bazett-Haldane medical ethic he believed in also prevented him from experimenting in this fashion on other human subjects.

Others were not so scrupulous. At a time when the practice of lobotomy was common in state-run mental hospitals, the use of brain electrodes seemed merciful by comparison. There were all sorts of rationalizations for inserting electrodes into the brains of certain classes of people. The mentally retarded were sometimes considered fair game; convicts might be asked to volunteer; people with severe mental illness might be "helped" by the process. John rejected this kind of activity and all arguments justifying it.

John knew it would be possible for this procedure to be used by psychiatrists, even in an office visit. In Paris, Dr. Antoine Rémond actually began treating his Parkinsonian patients in his office by inserting electrodes through tiny holes in their skulls, using the techniques developed by John on animals. This treatment seemed to help them, but its ease made John painfully aware of the real potential for abuse by psychiatrists or covert agencies.

This climate of careless experimentation on humans persisted until the mid-1950s, when an enlightened cabal of neurophysiologists decided to put a stop to the practice of lobotomy. Their strategy was extremely clever. They organized a series of symposia to which they invited psychiatrists who believed in performing lobotomies. At these meetings, doctors presented papers and shared their techniques and results, discovering in the process that there were no real experts on the subject. There wasn't even any solid scientific justification for lobotomy. Most doctors realized they had been acting like butchers, and thereafter the practice of lobotomy in the United States quickly and quietly disappeared.

Inspired by this example, John Lilly decided to try to put a halt to the abuse of patients, in the name of neurophysiological research, by insertion of brain electrodes. He compiled a list of researchers involved in this activity and obtained a grant for a conference. Then he turned over the funds to Georgetown University, on the condition that they sponsor the conference without informing anyone about who was behind it. John attended the conference as just another participant.

He had arranged for his foremost colleagues involved in electrode research with animals to present the techniques they had developed to minimize brain damage in their nonhuman subjects. Those researchers who worked with human brains were embarrassed to hear that scientists working on animal brains had far more refined and less damaging techniques. As a result, the conference was a major step toward debunking the unsafe use of brain electrodes in humans.

He also found other ways to dissuade his colleagues from unethical research on human brains. As a senior scientist at NIH, he was frequently enlisted by other agencies to monitor research projects they sponsored. In this capacity, John would travel to other laboratories and evaluate other researchers' procedures. He could take advantage of the inspection to discourage the abuse of living human beings.

In neurology and neurosurgery—the practice of clinical medicine as opposed to research—the case for electrically stimulating the brains of certain patients was more convincing. In the 1930s, Dr. Wilder Penfield and later Dr. Roger W. Sperry performed brain surgery on patients with serious diseases, such as grand mal epilepsy. These procedures required surgeons to open the skull and expose large areas of the brain's surface. In some instances, they had to cut into the brain tissues. Massive trauma to the brain was an inevitable result of these procedures. Because electrical probing might possibly make the procedures safer or more effective, the use of electrodes in such cases conformed to medical ethics; many of these operations were successful in prolonging patients' lives or improving their functioning.

Scientists who had used electrodes in the brains of animals were aware of the delicacy of brain tissues and the extent of damage inevitably caused by these intrusions. John developed several technical refinements to minimize this damage. One was the Lilly Waveform, whose use spread widely in the field. An-

other was the fluid capillary electrode, which makes contact with
brain tissues through a bead of conductive liquid. Applied gently
to the surface, it caused no damage whatsoever.

As Dr. Penfield had reported, patients who were awake and
alert during brain operations often reported vivid experiences
when certain locations in their cerebral cortex were stimulated
by the surgeon's electrodes. These reports were tantalizing, and
many neuroscientists, including John, wished they could obtain
more data of this sort.

In his isolation tank research at NIH, John was able to study
the activity of his own brain functioning unimpaired by any sort
of injury. He came to appreciate the limitations of information
gathered from experiments that damaged the brain. Such research failed to yield useful data about higher cortical functions,
which depended on the brain operating in a state of complete
integrity.

John came to believe that the awesome capabilities and
deeply hidden secrets of the human brain depended strongly on
just these higher functions of an intact, undamaged brain. To
damage a brain was to reduce it. One could hardly expect to
observe the phenomena that characterize its highest potential in
a reduced, damaged, or diminished system. In the light of these
more mature considerations, he finally abandoned the idea of
physically probing the human brain, including his own—at least
with the current state of technology.

But his desire to research large-sized brains continued. So
John began thinking about other, nonhuman species with large
brains. He considered apes, but concluded that would add little
to what he had already learned from monkeys. Elephants had
huge brains, but practically nothing was known about them scientifically, and their size would make them impractical to work
with. Then he learned that many species of cetaceans, an order
of mammals including dolphins, porpoises, and whales, had
brains comparable to or even larger than the human brain. He
knew absolutely nothing else about cetaceans at this time.

It occurred to John that he might be able to use a cetacean
brain that was close to human-size as a model for the human
brain. He might experiment on these creatures using the techniques he could not use safely on himself or ethically on other
human subjects. His ethical dilemma was solved; the next phase
of his search for Reality lay beyond the human species.

John's relationship with cetaceans began in 1949 at Woods Hole National Laboratory in Massachusetts, where he was visiting his friend George Austin, a neurosurgeon. Perusing the *Boston Globe* over breakfast, a headline caught their eye: "Whale Stranded on Beach at Biddeford Pool." Apparently, a recent storm had driven the whale, now dead, onto the sand near the coast guard station at Biddeford Pool, Maine. This coincidence was a ready-made invitation to go after the animal's brain.

Dr. Peter Scholander, John's former neighbor in Swarthmore, perhaps the world's preeminent scientific expert on whales, was working at the Woods Hole lab. They located him, and all three piled into his convertible, setting out for the five hours to Biddeford with the enthusiasm of three boys on an adventure.

There on the dunes lay the beached whale, twenty-eight feet long and four feet across. John was awestruck by the largest creature he had ever seen. Scholander identified it as a pilot whale—a relative of dolphins, orca (killer whales), and the gigantic sperm whale, the largest creature on earth.

Scholander knew some facts about the creature, but nothing had been written to date on the brain of the pilot whale. Without further delay, the three explorers began excavating for this prize.

They sawed, hacked, and chipped through four inches of blubber, four inches of muscle, and two inches of skull bone, until they peered down into the cavern they'd dug in this mountain of flesh. The brain that lay uncovered before them resembled a pair of boxing gloves laid side by side. It was much larger than a human brain. They attempted to extract it from the skull, but it collapsed into an odorous puddle, already in an advanced state of decay.

This was a great disappointment. They had hoped for a specimen suitable for neuroanatomical study. Instead they piled back into the car and returned to Woods Hole, exhilarated and intrigued, with only the memory of a brain.

John maintained a part-time interest in cetaceans from then onward. He did not see Scholander again until the 1953 International Physiology Congress in Montreal, where mutual reminiscence rekindled their enthusiasm. Scholander introduced John to F.G. Wood, Jr., curator of the Marine Studios in St. Augustine, Florida. A number of bottle-nosed dolphins, *Tursiops truncatus,* were held in captivity there for the purpose of entertaining humans.

John visited this early oceanarium. The obvious intelligence and large brains of these animals impressed John deeply, and his interest in cetaceans focused on this species.

By 1955, John had recruited seven interested fellow scientists, and the party drove off to the Marine Studios to begin a neurological study of dolphins. These southern outings continued throughout 1958, with a variable crew that sometimes included Alice Miller, John's assistant at NIH, and his younger son, Charley.

During one such expedition in the winter of 1957, John witnessed an incident that added a new dimension to his appreciation of dolphins. A dolphin had been isolated in a small, shallow tank for observation. When the weather turned cold, the temperature of the water in this little tank quickly dropped. The dolphin became too stiff to swim when returned to the main pool. In the deeper water, the stiff dolphin was having trouble keeping his blowhole above water, which was necessary for him to breathe. He gave the standard distress call, and three other dolphins came to his rescue. They took turns swimming under him, hoisting him out of the water so that he could breathe freely.

That humanitarian performance was impressive, indicating a degree of social interdependence and a willingness to care for one another when the need arose. But what followed totally surprised him: The dolphins began to administer a specific physical therapy to their disabled fellow. They took turns swimming under him, and nudged the sensitive region around his genital slit with their dorsal fins. This stimulation induced a reflex contraction of his muscles, moving his flukes and propelling him along the surface of the water. After some minutes of this therapy, the dolphin was sufficiently limber to swim on his own.

The significance of this was clear to John. In parallel circumstances, one would have described the dolphins' actions as those of human emergency medical personnel administering appropriate treatment, such as a resuscitation procedure.

During a 1958 mission abroad for the U.S. air force (unrelated to dolphins), John stopped to lecture at Scholander's Zoophysiological Institute in Oslo, Norway. A man from the Whaling Institute related an account of how some *Orcinus orca,* the largest of the dolphin species, avoided whaling boats with harpoon guns after one came too close and was shot. Yet the orca in the area continued to cruise and feed around boats without harpoons. Apparently the orca were able to distinguish boats with harpoon guns on their prows from otherwise identical boats without harpoon guns. Few of the other orca had actually witnessed the shooting. The injured orca, or perhaps another who saw the shooting, must have communicated complex information, including a description of the dangerous boats, to hundreds of others. This incident, and many other observations and reports, convinced John that dolphins possessed a high level of vocal communication.

John told his audience in Oslo that he was beginning to believe dolphins were more intelligent than they had yet been given credit for. This was a conservative statement, considering the ideas about dolphin intelligence his early exposure to these creatures was starting to inspire.

Privately, John had become convinced that scientists were going out of their way to dismiss the intelligence of dolphins. He was beginning to suspect that dolphins were victims of what he came to call "zoomorphization"—a tendency to project the limitations of other animals onto dolphins, whales, and even humans in some cases. It was the precise opposite of anthropomorphization, the tendency to ascribe human characteristics to animals. Dolphins were then being discussed in the same terms as rats, whose brains weigh four grams, cats (twenty grams), dogs (sixty grams), and monkeys (eighty grams). Such discussion was absurd in view of the obvious fact that many dolphins have brains that weigh 1,800 grams, larger even than the typical human brain's weight of 1,200 to 1,500 grams! (Some dolphin species' brains are considerably larger.)

The climax of zoomorphization was the behaviorist supposition that an adequate explanation for the properties of the human mind could be extracted from studying the behavior of such simpler animals as pigeons and rats, despite the unnatural and highly restricted conditions which were usually imposed by the experimenter as a part of such research. Behaviorism was orthodox psychology in the 1950s, firmly established in American universities and other institutions. From these bastions, its influence pervaded all of biological science. A scientific upstart who dared to talk about the intelligence of dolphins and to compare them to humans would be summarily accused of the sin of an unscientific wish to "humanize" animals. Under these inquisitional circumstances, a scientist would choose to err on the side of conservatism and conformity. John tailored his statements at the Zoophysiological Institute for an audience influenced by these prevailing prejudices.

The scientifically forthright course, given the facts of brain size, would have been to assume that dolphins were at least potentially as intelligent as humans, until proven otherwise. But in the scientific atmosphere of the time, it was first necessary to prove that the dolphin brain was every bit as complex and capable as the human brain.

When John began to be interested in dolphins, they represented little more to him than the opportunity to explore large brains. By 1958, the deep impressions left by his observations of dolphin intelligence had forced him to greatly expand his agenda. He became determined to prove, beyond a shadow of a doubt, that dolphins have brains that are capable of true intelligence.

Since his confrontation with Dr. Livingston, John's days at NIH had been numbered. Now that it was clear that his search for Reality was leading him away from NIH and into the company of the dolphin, he resigned from his post as chief of the Section on Cortical Integration, Laboratory of Neurophysiology, Institute of Neurological Diseases and Blindness, and gave up his commission as a medical officer in the U.S. Public Health Service. (He would, however, maintain a looser affiliation with NIH which would allow the institution to continue to fund his research from a distance.) John began making plans to start a dolphin research program in the Virgin Islands, where the warm Caribbean environment would provide the right conditions for continuous, comfortable interaction between humans and dolphins.

In his own mind, John also resigned from his marriage of two decades. The time was now ripe to make his long-postponed move toward his own pleasure, in accordance with the "reality principle." He felt that the children were now old enough to handle a divorce and he would file for one shortly after arriving in the Caribbean. He would no longer allow Mary—whom he now regarded as an adversary—to hold on to him. In his own estimation, he had achieved a mature independence from the influence of his father. He was starting to feel, at the age of forty-three, like his own man. He had paid his dues.

While John was attending a meeting in Woods Hole around this time, his teenage son Charley witnessed a horrid fight between his parents outside a restaurant after dinner. Mary and Charley returned home to Chevy Chase, but John did not.

CHAPTER 8

ON BEYOND HUMAN

June 1959, age 44.

A fragrant island breeze caresses his face. Dressed in gleaming white, the tall, blond, pith-helmeted Scientist directs the expedition, preceded by two sturdy island men with machetes, hacking in shifts at the dense overgrowth. Their dark skin immune to the tropic sun, their taut muscles rippling, they have been chopping for hours since leaving the jeep road, cutting a new trail through a remote corner of the island of St. Thomas.

In the shade of his helmet, the Scientist consults a map. Historically, he is not the first to travel this way. But in the province of the mind, in the context of science, he is going where no man has gone before.

He is now only yards from his destination, a small point of land protruding beyond a sheltered bay. With another hack, a large, leafy-green branch falls from his path, and he catches his first glimpse from land of the local seashore. A few more chops, and the brush cutters step aside. John finds himself standing on a promontory commanding a stunning view of an emerald bay.

It is perfect, just the sort of location he needs for his experiments. American soil, no hassles with foreign governments. Air and sea at an even 80° temperature all year round. Gentle swells rolling across the point. An ideal place for humans and dolphins to mingle.

JOHN BEGAN EXPLORING the Virgin Islands in August 1958, searching for the right location for his dolphin research institute, and for his new life.

The paradigm for the research program John wanted to undertake was unusual for the science of the time, radical in ways he himself would not recognize until he observed the public response his endeavors later received. Most scientists would have attempted to learn about dolphin intelligence by observing the behavior of the species objectively, in an environment as close as possible to their natural habitat. Using such methods, scientific observers would be as separated from the dolphins as experimental conditions would permit, so as not to interfere with normal dolphin behavior.

John, however, knew that the truer test of intelligence—the aspect of dolphins he was most interested in exploring—was the ability to learn, and that learning occurred only through interaction. John took his lead from the way children seemed to learn language and customs from their parents and society. He reasoned that such learning was based on a continual modulation of pleasurable contacts, in a context of intense and inescapable interaction. Speech and body language were inextricably mingled with direct physical contact, through encounters that were sometimes painful, but usually pleasurable, depending on how well the infant communicated its needs and adopted the sounds and meanings of the adults, especially the mother.

For John, to learn about dolphins was not merely to observe them, but to engage and interact with them in a way that would create communication. Confined together at the institute, humans and dolphins would learn to explore and exploit every available channel to communicate. John's program was to engage humans and cetaceans in the kind of intense interaction that would alter the behavior of both species. Free and unrestrained interplay would require the physical comfort of both species, which made the idyllic tropical conditions of the Virgin Islands ideal.

John began searching for property in the Islands while continuing to visit the oceanaria in Florida. His son Charley, who had developed a strong enthusiasm for cetacean research, accompanied him on many of these jaunts. Charley got some hands-on experience training pilot whales at the Theater of the Sea oceanarium.

After several visits, John rented a large house in Charlotte Amalie, capital of the U.S. Virgin Islands on St. Thomas. This would be his local base during his search for an appropriate site. The Simmons House was an old colonial building, just across from the governor's mansion on cobbled Bjerge-Gadda Street, named by the Danish settlers. It was so narrow that one needed to check for traffic before opening the front door—there wasn't room for a car to pass when the door was open. The house was two stories high, with broad, shady verandas, protected from the tropical sun, on all four sides. There was no glass in the windows so that the cooling trade winds could pass through the rooms.

While John was settling in, his father Dick stopped off from a Caribbean cruise for a visit. John told him he intended to file for his long-desired divorce as soon as he established residency.

Predictably, an argument ensued. Dick recited all the stock scruples against divorce, making it clear that his firm opposition was a matter of principle. But John could tell that his father was operating as if he thought duty required this performance. John knew that Dick had always seen through the paper reality of his business to the human reality behind it. After all, even though he had regarded a scientific career as frivolous, he had accepted John's educational choices once he had seen the human reality of John's commitment.

John interrupted his father's recitation of the rules of formal morality with a simple observation of fact:

"But Dad, you don't even *like* Mary!"

That finished it. Dick was wise enough to reconcile himself to the impending divorce. They parted amicably and the elder Lilly continued his holiday cruise. Neither sensed that this would be their last meeting. Months later, Dick Lilly died peacefully in his sleep at his home in Minnesota. John suspected that his father gladly left a life with which he had become profoundly bored.

The divorce, when it finally came nearly a year later, surprised neither Mary nor the children. It left Mary with a lifelong claim to financial support, and she never remarried. She continued her education, received an M.A. degree from American

University, then taught art in Washington, D.C., for eighteen years before retiring to the Colorado Rockies.

Free at last in St. Thomas and already something of a celebrity, John socialized with the upper echelons of island society and cavorted with the island ladies. Charlotte Amalie was a conglomeration of colorful ethnic enclaves, with descendants of several waves of European settlers who had washed ashore over three centuries. There were Swedes, French, Dutch, and Danes, each preserving their own languages and cultures from the Old Country. And descendants of African slaves made up the majority of the population, who elected politicians and ran things under the U.S. flag and a governor appointed by the president. (This system had been instituted by Franklin Delano Roosevelt in the 1930s to derail nationalist stirrings.)

John spent a year meeting people, going out on their sailboats, learning the ropes, and becoming the politician he needed to be to operate in the island reality. He decided to effect a new look and shaved his head—but the resulting heat on the top of his skull required him to constantly wear a hat outdoors.

John was a big social hit on the island. Everyone liked the slender, fair eccentric with his goofy, disarmingly beatific smile. Here was a man who was learning to have a good time. The snowman from Minnesota was melting in the tropic sun, and the gulf between this reality and his mainland life was starting to look as wide as the Gulf of Mexico.

One night he was invited to a big formal dinner party at the governor's palace. Over after-dinner brandy he asked one of his official hosts, "I notice I'm the only white guy here. How come I was invited?"

"Because we think of you as one of us."

John loved the women of the island, so different from those he had known before in the metropolitan bastions of white middle- and upper-class society on the mainland, during the '30s, '40s, and '50s. He deeply appreciated their warm innocence, spontaneity, and especially their good-hearted enjoyment of sexual experiments!

One of John's girlfriends was involved in the real estate business, and she helped him locate property for the new lab. He saw it first from a boat and then approached the overgrown site from land, finding that he had to blaze a trail back to the coast. It was just what he wanted. On the shore of Nazareth Bay, the location received a continuous flow of warm, crystal-clear water from shallow seas to the west. From the windward side of St. Thomas, it faced the neighboring island of St. John, the British Virgins, and the rest of the Caribbean beyond. An idyllic tropical setting, complete with mangrove forests, volcanic peaks, and an awe-inspiring view across a "whale highway," where the humpback whales cruised by on their seasonal migrations. Here he would build Dolphin Point Laboratory.

It wouldn't be cheap. John was sinking $100,000 of his own money in the project—a tidy sum in those days. By a fortunate coincidence a few years before, Dick had suggested that he invest in a start-up electronics firm back in Minneapolis. After putting up $50, he watched the new firm prosper and grow. John held onto his stock and eventually turned a splendid profit on his tiny portfolio. Now he had some money of his own—in addition to the comfortable allowances doled out from his trust fund and the small salaries he'd accepted during his government and institutional employment—which he could invest in his dream laboratory by the sea.

Back in Washington, a branch of the Navy came up with $30,000 to support John's research. His friend Orr Reynolds arranged for the Department of Defense to channel $10,000 to the new institute through the air force, and the National Science Foundation contributed $80,000. Later, the National Institutes of Health came through with a research grant of about $250,000 per year. John's years of networking with the research establishment in the nation's capital really paid off.

It would take time to build the lab, but the plans were laid and the outline of the project was clear, thanks to the assistance of Nathaniel Wells, a surveyor-engineer on St. Thomas, who joined the board of directors of the Communications Research Institute, Inc. (CRII) when it was organized in 1959.

The first step was to blast a sheltered pool for the dolphins out of the rocky shores at Dolphin Point, as John dubbed the new location. This was quickly and deftly accomplished by a U.S. Navy underwater demolition team that was working in the area, commanded by Donald Gaither. They enthusiastically volunteered and skillfully planted shaped charges in underwater crevices—up to 600 pounds of TNT in a single blast.

For blast after blast, while the crew huddled in a corrugated steel shack, the rocks flew, the point shook, the seawater spumed like the spray of a pod of superwhales, and the dolphin pool took shape in big, bold, beautiful steps, sculpting nature into something even better. Blasted out of the shoreline, the pond was rimmed with boulders displaced by the explosions. It was a sea-level, sea-side pool of clear, warm water, washed and freshened by the regular tides and swells, where dolphins and humans would mingle to communicate.

After the blasting ceased, there was a lot of craning, bulldozing, shoveling, and cementing to do. The laboratory building took shape out of solid concrete reinforced with steel, above the new dolphin pool. It was placed on pilings sixteen feet above sea level, for safety from storms and the occasional hurricane-tossed seas. A spiral staircase connected the lab and the pool, and a special elevator was installed to ferry dolphins from the pool and to a laboratory deck flooded with eighteen inches of water, where both dolphins and humans could be comfortable. Next to and above this deck were neatly arranged laboratory rooms for biochemistry, photography, electronics, computers, record storage, and offices. There were built-in cisterns to store rainwater captured by the sloping roofs and, on the top floor, an office suite destined to become John's home on the island.

That year John attended a conference in San Francisco, where he had been invited to give a presentation of his bold position on dolphin intelligence, which had begun to attract press attention. There he met Elisabeth Bjerg, a native islander from an old Danish family, who was also a New York fashion model. She had wandered away from her husband, a noted psychiatrist attending the conference, and was introduced to John by Dr. Jay Shurley, his NIH colleague in isolation tank research.

John was riveted by this image of stunning, perfect blonde beauty coming toward him across the ballroom floor. And Liz was ready to be deeply impressed with the handsome, scientific celebrity who had made such a stir at the conference.

Liz lived in Berkeley but occasionally flew to Manhattan, where she earned $10,000 each time she posed in front of the cameras. On her next swing east, she rendezvoused with John in

New York, and a passionate relationship immediately ensued. They enjoyed ten blissful days and nights in a plush hotel.

Liz was drawn to John by the excitement of his work as well as by a more personal attraction. A highly intelligent woman, she was painfully aware of the ephemeral nature of a fashion model's success; she may have seen an opportunity in John's research to make a contribution that would stand up to the test of time, a mark made by the enduring qualities of the mind rather than the passing beauty of the body.

Liz left her marriage and career and returned to the islands of her youth, where she and her three children from two previous marriages moved in with John. Charley, summering in St. Thomas, got to know his new step-family. It was a confusing situation, but the kids soon adapted to it good-naturedly.

Liz and John, flushed with the enthusiasm of newfound romance, gave way to a phase of uninhibited adolescent sexuality, something John had missed out on before. Every evening, after they put the kids to bed upstairs, they would make love on the living room floor with such passionate intensity that they never noticed the rope burns from the grass mats beneath them.

Later that year the new family went to New York on a holiday. One night John and Liz surprised Charley and the other kids by returning to their hotel with wedding rings. Over a year later, in November 1960, Cynthia Olivia Roslyn was born, extending this extended family a little more. Now there were more than three different broods of kids in the Lilly home. Charley, who spent the school year with his mother, Mary, continued to summer with them in the Islands through 1961, when he turned 18.

Liz threw herself into the administrative work of the new institute. It seemed a strange occupation for a glamorous model and sophisticate, but Liz was a willing and enthusiastic helpmate, a fact reflected in John's 1961 dedication to his book, *Man and Dolphin:*

TO ELISABETH BJERG LILLY

Her devotion to this program and its realization is second only to her loyalty and her love for her family.

The crew was forming. In December 1959 John's longtime assistant in other enterprises, Alice Miller, arrived at Dolphin Point to resume her duties. By 1960 things were starting to happen in the new laboratories of CRII.

In March, John and Liz flew to Marineland in Florida to fetch the first dolphins. They met Lizzie, a female dolphin named after Liz, and Baby, an immature female, both of whom had been there for some time and were used to being around humans. Special portable tanks were constructed to ship the dolphins to St. Thomas, each custom-fitted to support the dolphin's body in a minimum amount of water.

Earl Ubel, science editor of the *New York Herald Tribune,* accompanied the Lillys and their dolphins on the trip and helped John handle the shifting load. The dolphins, packed in the custom transportation tanks, were loaded on an airplane, flown to St. Thomas, and trucked to the seaside dolphin pool at CRII. Charley, along with Liz' children, Pamela, Leslie, and Stuart, joined the happy family scene on their arrival. Charley's arrival photograph later appeared in *Man and Dolphin.* Ubel's write-up made a big splash on the front page of his paper in New York the next day. Suddenly John was famous as the original Dolphin Doctor.

But the original dolphins did not do so well. Lizzie and Baby developed signs of respiratory infection—a very serious condition in dolphins. It was exacerbated by the stress of transport and an accident in which their crates were dropped during unloading. Lizzie showed signs of illness immediately and refused to eat. Within two months of arriving at CRII, both dolphins were dead—first Lizzie, then Baby a month later, in spite of frenetic medical efforts including antibiotic injections and tube feeding. Eight previous dolphins had died during experiments John had conducted in Florida. Evidently these creatures, so powerful and independent at sea, were fragile in human custody.

Everyone involved had become emotionally attached to Lizzie and Baby. After their deaths John resorted to numbering his dolphins. The next pair were called Elvar and Tolva, Swedish for eleven and twelve. John and his crew had learned a lot about caring for dolphins in captivity from their mistakes. These sturdy "Swedes" benefited, survived, and thrived, becoming, in July of 1960, the first dolphin success story at CRII.

A mainland branch of the CRII was set up in the Miami

suburb of Coconut Grove. It was to play a significant role in the institute's public relations. Relatively conservative scientists who wished to pursue dolphin research along more conventional lines than John's could be sent here, thereby helping the institute to attract funding from the scientific establishment. It was a masterful political maneuver that later proved to be an unbearable ethical compromise for John.

Elvar and Tolva were moved from St. Thomas and installed in a suburban swimming pool at Coconut Grove. They began receiving visits from scientists and celebrities, including astronomer Carl Sagan. He and John shared an interest in the issue of communication with extraterrestrial intelligence, and, despite major differences in perspective, they agreed that learning to communicate with dolphins might provide valuable information for this endeavor. Sagan later wrote at length about his encounter with the dolphins, but, perhaps reflecting the reluctance of scientists to accept the dolphins' true level of intelligence, he once described their brains as slightly smaller, rather than slightly larger, than those of humans, an oversight which he later corrected.

Aldous Huxley was also among the visitors at this time. Huxley had first become aware of John in 1956, in connection with the isolation tank experiments. They had first met at a Dartmouth symposium, where John was delivering a lecture. Later, Huxley visited John's NIH lab and compared John's research to the solitary spiritual practices of yogis, Gnostics, early Christian anchorites, and all the hermits who sought God in the desert. Now in Coconut Grove, the tall and lanky intellectual met the dolphins in their fluid medium.

Huxley was nearly blind, but he always seemed to know where in the room a person was, as if by telepathy. This uncanny ability contributed something eerie and mysterious to his gentle presence. He seemed to reside more in the world of ideas than in physical reality.

Despite the incongruity in the spectacle of this cultivated British gentleman sloshing about with the dolphins in their pool, Huxley and the dolphins had a lot in common. Like Huxley, the dolphins were relatively weak in visual perception but strong in vocal communication. Unlike the dolphins, Huxley was raised in a Victorian culture; but like them he had a rather open attitude

BIOGRAPHY

ALDOUS HUXLEY (1894–1963), visionary Anglo-American philos-opher and writer, was educated at Eton and Oxford. While his elder brother, Julian Huxley, became a prominent biologist, Aldous was deterred from that vocation by weak eyesight and so entered upon a career in literature. In Italy, he befriended D.H. Lawrence, whom he attended at the time of the poet's death in 1930, in the south of France.

Huxley's classic anti-utopian novel, *Brave New World* (1932), is among the most famous and influential writings in the English language. It predicts a fully regulated "consumer" society in which human beings are grown in bottles and engineered for specific work slots, and in which a euphorant drug called "soma" is the socially acceptable escape route from ordinary reality.

Migrating to Hollywood in 1935, Huxley entered a colorful milieu of writers, philosophers, and psychotherapists thriving on the periphery of the film industry. In 1953 he was introduced to mescaline by Dr. Humphrey Osmond, and was subsequently guided in a number of sessions by Laura Archera, a psychotherapy re-searcher and musician, later to become his second wife. Among his frequent companions in experiments with psychedelic chemicals were philosopher Gerald Heard and business mogul Albert M. Hubbard. *The Doors of Perception* (1954) and *Heaven and Hell* (1955) reflect Huxley's early experiments. The last of his dozen books, *Island* (1963), projects a positive utopia in which social cohesion and personal development are based on the intelligent use of "moksha medicine"—a mushroom with mind-expanding properties.

Aldous Huxley's biography by Laura Archera Huxley is called *This Timeless Moment* (1968). His writings on visionary experi-ence are collected in *Moksha* (1982).

---

toward sex, as revealed in his last novel, *Island.* And, like the dolphins, his brain was generating a reality somewhere beyond the one generated by most human brains.

Huxley left CRII once again deeply impressed with John's work, and John was gratified to have provided food for thought to the man whose work had influenced him so profoundly.

John first met the world-famous anthropologist Gregory Bateson through a mutual acquaintance. He had read some of Bateson's scientific papers, and was impressed with this very original intellect. Bateson had recently studied sea otters, attempting to use their behavior as a model of elementary communication. Behavioral scientists in general were fond of such "animal models," hoping to define and refine concepts which eventually could be applied to humans, a trend which John profoundly distrusted. Nevertheless, John was impressed with Bateson's papers and believed that Bateson, who was obviously an extraordinarily intelligent anthropologist, would be interested in studying a large-brained creature—the dolphin.

Late in 1961, Bateson—a large, kindly bear of a man with a comical look of mildly bemused astonishment at everything before his eyes, including human behavior—signed on as director of the CRII's Dolphin Point Lab, and moved to St. Thomas with his young wife Lois. (This decision allowed John time to concentrate on developing the Miami lab.) Gregory and Lois were soon joined by three new dolphins flown in from Miami, two of whom were donated by Ivan Tors after he had used them in his movie *Flipper.*

In the new facilities, the eminent anthropologist studied dolphin behavior in minute detail. In the manner of an ethologist, he studied them as he had studied humans in both alien societies and his own society. Bateson wished to interact with the dolphins only enough to elicit bits of their natural behavior, which he duly noted as an objective observer—a modus operandi diametrically opposed to John's program of continuous interaction. In spite of this difference in research approaches, the two soon became lifelong friends.

In the remote island lab, Bateson wanted to create a baseline of observations about dolphins. He was big on photographic documentation and hired a photographer to work full-time at the lab. An October 1963 photo shows Bateson working with the dolphin Sissy, trying to determine whether dolphins can respond to pictorial representations of familiar objects, such as other dolphins. Other photos and movies from this period show dolphins Sissy, Peter, and Pamela playing "getting to know you" with Lois Bateson and the Lilly's extended family. In the big pool, the dolphins

BIOGRAPHY

GREGORY BATESON (1904–1980) was a brilliant British intellectual, anthropologist, ethnologist, cyberneticist, and psychologist known for his ability to link diverse concepts into new disciplines. His early anthropological work was in the South Seas, where he met and wed Margaret Mead. Together they wrote *Balinese Character: A Photographic Analysis* (1941). Bateson sent revolutionary ripples into the social sciences when he applied Norbert Wiener's concepts of cybernetic control systems and Claude Shannon's mathematical communication theory to the study of interpersonal behavior. In his psychological research, this led him to formulate the theory of the "double bind," a situation in which a person is simultaneously compelled in opposite directions, resulting in an inability to function. Noted feminist writer Betty Friedan became Bateson's second wife. Later he married his third wife, Lois.

In the 1970s he was a professor at the University of California and was appointed to the University's Board of Regents by Governor Jerry Brown. His hugely popular book, *Steps to an Ecology of Mind,* encouraged people to regard human behavior and consciousness as part of a larger environmental equation. A brilliant synthesis, this work was widely prescribed as a college textbook.

demonstrated on film some of the things they can do with humans, such as synchronized swimming and rescuing of weak swimmers. After a dolphin had pushed a tired swimmer out of the water, it would stand guard to make sure the human didn't go back in until fully rested.

Early on, disputes developed around Gregory Bateson. The funding John had secured for CRII from the government research establishment was controlled by people who did not appreciate Bateson the way John did. They were put off by his highly philosophical "soft, social sciences" approach, and by the overtly intellectual way he expressed himself.

A further problem was Bateson's preoccupation with octopi. One time John returned from a trip to Miami to find that Bateson had filled the lab with the creatures. There was Gregory sitting on the floor, surrounded by tanks and trays of octopi, a beatific expression of scientific bemusement on his face, as he watched them blush at one another. He was developing a theory of octopus communication based on the cybernetics of Norbert Wiener, W. Ross Ashby, and Heinz von Foerster.

As fascinating as all of this was to Bateson, those who funded the operation had not intended to contribute to octopus research. Eventually they told John, in effect, "We will continue to support your research here, but we will not support Bateson's participation in it." As a result of these conflicts, Bateson only lasted two years at CRII, and then on John's recommendation moved to the Oceanic Institute in Hawaii, using a five-year fellowship John arranged for him through NIMH. Here Bateson performed some very significant dolphin research.

But before his departure, Bateson performed one crucial service for CRII: He discovered Margaret Howe. A college graduate with a degree in biology, she was managing a hotel and restaurant on the island when Bateson met her, and during their conversation he immediately recognized that she was an extraordinarily meticulous observer of behavior. In spite of Howe's total lack of experience with dolphins—or in any other field of scientific research—Bateson followed his intuition and brought her on staff at CRII, where she soon became central to the research program.

John believed that it was hopeless for humans to attempt to learn the speech of dolphins without the use of computers far more sophisticated than those available in the 1960s. Even an elementary physical analysis of dolphin sounds strained current technology to the breaking point. The dolphins slid all over the spectrum of auditory frequencies from 2,000 hz (hertz, or cycles per second), near the top of meaningful human speech sounds, all the way up to 150,000 hz, which was almost in the range of AM radio (500,000 hz and up). Even to physically detect and measure acoustic vibrations of such high frequencies was a technological challenge in the early 1960s. If John waited for electronic computer technology to advance to the required level, it surely would be twenty or thirty years before any progress could be made in interspecies communication. And without the aid of electronics, there was nothing a human could do to reproduce or even hear the high-pitched sounds dolphins used to communicate.

John realized that breaking the human-dolphin communication barrier would require help from the dolphins themselves, and the dolphins' extraordinary brains. And dolphins had shown both a willingness and a capacity to make the effort, if humans would only set up the right conditions. As far back as Aristotle, writers had observed that dolphins vocalizing in air mimicked the speech sounds of humans. The Greek philosopher had noted that they pronounced vowels well but had difficulty with consonants. John confirmed these observations.

In earlier experiments, John had found that if he got a dolphin in a good mood, it would vocalize vociferously, with great spontaneity and creativity, playing off those human speech sounds it heard in its immediate environment. On several occasions he had electrically stimulated the pleasure centers in a dolphin's brain, and was rewarded with a barrage of inventive vocalizations. A careful analysis of the recordings of these cartoonish ejaculations revealed that they were primarily composed of varyingly accurate renditions of what humans had been saying around the dolphin before and during the episode.

In other experiments, John had determined that dolphins, like humans but unlike monkeys or chimps, are capable of vocalizing to express their inner needs or obtain a reward. This was not surprising, in view of the fact that dolphins in the wild are highly interdependent, social creatures who communicate primarily with sound. They will ask one another vocally for very specific help when they need it. In contrast, chimps, gorillas, and animals with even smaller brains are limited to an inborn simple distress call.

John reasoned that this characteristically human (and dolphin) ability to vocalize specific internal needs was the basis for the formation of society and language. Vocalizing made it possible to teach the young of a species how to fit into prevailing customs of culture and language in their local environment.

Chimpanzees, gorillas, and other species have elaborate social behavior, but theirs is based entirely on body language, gestures, and a *fixed* set of species-specific "calls," such as a distress call or a mating call. These animals were neurologically incapable of vocal improvisation, even in pursuit of the most intense rewards—such as water, food, sex, or direct electrical stimulation of the pleasure centers in their brains.

All of this information convinced John that dolphins could and would adapt to human speech sounds and frequency spectrums. The dolphin brain, with its huge auditory cortex, was far more capable of processing sounds than any gadget humans had been able to construct. Tapping the abilities of this natural super-computer would be the key to interspecies communication.

Human children are born to vocalize, and as they do so in ways which increasingly succeed in expressing and satisfying their needs, they learn the language of their family and their tribe. John reasoned by analogy that his best approach would be to take an immature dolphin, like the one they had named Peter, and put him in a position of childlike dependence on a willing human, like Margaret Howe. By putting these two in close contact and rela-tive isolation from their respective species, John would create a situation of maximum interdependence between them—an ideal situation in which Margaret could teach Peter some English.

With this objective in mind, John set up a ten-week experi-ment in living together for Margaret and Peter in the summer of 1964. They would be confined together in one of the shallow upstairs pools at the Dolphin Point Lab. Peter would be separated from Pamela and Sissy, the two female dolphins with whom he had been living, who were consigned to the lower sea pool.

Peter would have to depend completely on Margaret, who controlled their environment, food, and the extent of physical contact between them. John had observed that dolphins crave physical contact and find affectionate attention from humans most rewarding, so Margaret could always "discipline" Peter simply by stepping out of the water and ignoring him.

Margaret also would be dependent on Peter for most social and physical interaction, at least for the six days a week that she had agreed to be confined to the lab. With a woman of Margaret's exceptionally dedicated character, this situation could be ex-pected to produce a high level of commitment and attention to Peter that could only help the project's goals.

The unabashed, unrestrained sexual drive of dolphins soon began to introduce fascinating complications into this experi-ment. A male dolphin's penis hides in a slit in his belly when quiescent. It is difficult to tell male from female without close inspection. The male has a separate anal slit just behind the genital one, while in the female, the vagina, urethra, and anus all open into the same slit, with small nipples on either side. When the male becomes sexually aroused, the penis appears from its hiding place like a switchblade, as a rigid, ten-inch, tapering cone with a flattened tip, designed to pry its way into the female's opening in a single jab. It is hydrodynamically streamlined and internally pressurized to stand up to the stresses of swimming speeds of up to thirty knots (37 miles per hour) when erect and protruding. Dolphins mate in a series of staccato penetrations, while swimming belly-to-belly on parallel courses. The male reaches orgasm and ejaculates into the female on about the twelfth insertion. There is less known about orgasm in the female. After a short rest, the cycle repeats. Under comfortable conditions, any number of male and female dolphins can carry on this way, again and again, all day long, day after day. As D.H. Lawrence knew, "The hottest blood of all is in the sea."

Peter Dolphin had been living this way with Pam and Sissy. These three sexual athletes continually tore around the dolphin pool in an endless cycle of courtships and matings, punctuated by an occasional ten-minute rest period of quiet, polite three-way conversation as they huddled in a corner of the pool. Margaret had spent hours watching them underwater through an observation bubble in the side of the pool. Countless times she had watched Peter court and mate with first one female and then the other.

Now she was alone with Peter, and he with her, a female human. Horny Peter often interrupted their language lessons with his demands for sexual attention. Margaret had never known, nor could she ever have imagined, a suitor as passionate and insistent as Peter. Not at all shy, he would snuggle up to her in the water, stroking her with his penis. When she responded by caressing him, his whole body would abruptly became excited to a degree that frightened her—after all, he weighed three hundred pounds.

Peter sensed her fear and adopted a more reserved and gentle courtship style. He'd keep his penis hidden until he felt some receptivity on her part. He'd brush against her as she stood in the shallow water. He'd nibble her toes and bang his beak against her legs. He'd grip her legs ever so gently with his huge mouth, being careful not to puncture her delicate skin with his sharp, conical teeth.

Just having her leg held in his powerful jaws—jaws which could easily crush a shark in a single snap—frightened Margaret. So Peter went out of his way to reassure Margaret of his gentleness and consideration. He would grab a large rubber ball floating in the pool and lodge it in the back of his mouth. This obstruction made it impossible to close his jaws, guaranteeing the safety of Margaret's leg. Delighted by this intelligent and sensitive dolphin's chivalrous gesture, she allowed him to proceed with his foreplay. She stroked the broad forehead between his dark, wide-set, and mischievously intelligent eyes. She rubbed his long sleek back, on either side of his handsome dorsal fin, and scratched his flippers. Occasionally she would caress him to orgasm, after which he became a willing pupil.

But after a month of living together, Margaret began to worry about Peter, who now seemed to be depressed. In her log book, she wrote about how hard it was to keep him satisfied and how his mounting sexual frustration was interfering with their work together. Glancing at Pam and Sissy in the other pool, she thought how hard it must be for Peter to be stuck with her, a reluctant human female, while his two natural lovers were only a few yards away. She wondered what it was like for the female dolphins, whether their sexual needs were as great and as urgent as his. (The available literature on dolphin sexuality seemed to indicate that female dolphins were somewhat more subtle than males. Yet there was practically no discernible difference in how they behaved once a sexual encounter ensued.)

From the other pool, Pam and Sissy sent plaintive cries to Peter at all hours. Messages went back and forth between the pools in high-pitched dolphin-speak, mostly beyond Margaret's range of hearing and totally beyond her comprehension. She wondered if Peter was talking about her, perhaps telling Pam and Sissy about their interspecies sexual problems. Did the isolated female dolphins gossip about Margaret, or transmit sonic images of dolphin sex to him? Was she just a body to Peter, providing him with physical stimulation, while he fantasized dolphin sex?

Margaret was getting depressed herself. This was not the kind of love life that she wanted either! One day each week away from the lab was not enough. On Saturdays she was allowed to go out, wander around the island, and mingle with humans. But even then she had to be back at night to sleep beside Peter, her damp little mattress on a platform in the center of the flooded room. She began to crave more of human company.

When occasionally humans did visit the lab, however, she wouldn't let them play with Peter. Margaret guarded the privacy of their life together. She was sick of people who dangled their arms in the pool and tried to get Peter's attention as if he were an attraction in a zoo. She couldn't let visitors break into the intimacy she shared with Peter. She wouldn't even interrupt their sex play in deference to visitors.

Occasionally, Margaret would break down and cry. Then Peter would always come around and try to cheer her up. When he saw she was stuck in self-pity, he'd insist on drawing her into one of their games. Sweet Peter would bring a ball and toss it at her repeatedly until she got up and joined him in play. He would not tolerate any downtime. Instead, he'd invent new games with new toys and would do everything he could to cheer her up.

This dolphin's penchant for game playing might offer an alternate explanation of Peter's frequent sexual overtures. Dolphins will respond actively to human behavior; whatever game you start with they can change into a different game of their own design. Perhaps Peter was deflecting Margaret's language game by turning it into a sex game.

In this way, he may have outsmarted both Margaret and John. They believed that his sexual need was something to be gotten out of the way, so that Peter could concentrate on his language lessons. This belief may have been somewhat naive. A human scientist is limited to acting on the basis of what he or she thinks the interaction is all about, with no guarantee that this is actually the case. A creature as smart as a dolphin probably has its own ideas about what game it is playing.

On the first of September, the experiment in living together ended. No doubt with some relief, Margaret took a leave of absence for a few weeks and then rejoined Peter on a part-time basis. Shortly after, she married John Lovett, the photographer who had recorded her romps in the pool with Peter. Later, she left the project and went off with a human husband to have a human family life.

The experiment was a success. With other research, it helped confirm that close physical interaction with humans encourages dolphins to learn from them. Once engaged with human companions, dolphins make great efforts to reproduce human speech sounds and will even learn to count, despite having a vastly different vocal apparatus than humans. Dolphins will use their voices to ask for pleasure (positive stimulation) and to get relief from pain (negative stimulation). Dialogues between Margaret and Peter are available on tape and have been the object of much study in the intervening years.

Margaret: Peter, say *Margaret* . . . MAR-GRIT.

Peter: Mmmurrr [hiccup]

Margaret: Very good, Peter!

Meanwhile, a wave of positive publicity was lapping over John Lilly and his amazing dolphins. It had started in 1958 when John addressed the meeting of the American Psychiatric and Psychoanalytic associations in San Francisco, where he first met Elisabeth. Earl Ubel organized a press conference around John, and the response spread around the world. In 1960, the *New York Times Magazine* printed an article called "Inquiry into the Dolphin's I.Q., and Man's." Nature writer Loren Eiseley joined the ad hoc dolphin P.R. campaign with his rhapsodic essay, "The Long Loneliness, the Separate Destinies of Man and Porpoise," published that winter.

John's lawyer, Ev Birch, and his wife Patty introduced him to Herman Wouk, author of *The Caine Mutiny*. After John had briefed Wouk on the dolphin research, the author became so excited that he told John, "You are not going to hide that information in some dusty scientific journal. You are going to write a popular book about it, and it's going to be a best-seller." Wouk introduced John to Hal Matsen, a top New York literary agent. In a matter of days John had a contract with Doubleday for two proposed books, with an advance of $20,000. In a matter of months he had written *Man and Dolphin*.

The publicity on John's research was not all favorable. Two scientists at the American Museum of Natural History in New York attacked his dolphin research in an article for *Natural History* magazine. John asked his old friend, Dr. Hudson Hoagland, for advice on how to respond. Hoagland, one of the inventors of oral contraceptives, was a former chairman of the board of trustees of CRII and head of the Worcester Foundation for Biological Research.

He asked John, "These people attacking you—are they important?"

"No."

"Then do you want to make them important by responding to them in print?" John decided not.

However, because the critique came from people with cre-

BIOGRAPHY

HERMAN WOUK (1915–   ), a native of New York City, graduated from Columbia and took a doctorate from Yeshiva and, in
1960, a law degree from Clark University. After a career as a writer
for radio comedy, he served as a consultant to President Roosevelt
and as a naval officer in the Pacific during World War II. Wouk
subsequently began a highly successful career writing novels and
dramatic scripts, including *Aurora Dawn* (1947), *The City Boy*
(1948), *The Traitor* (1949 drama), *The Caine Mutiny* (1951)—
which won the 1952 Pulitzer Prize—*The Caine Mutiny Courtmar-
tial* (1953 drama), *Marjorie Morningstar* (1955), *Nature's Way*
(1957 comedy), *This Is My God* (1959), *Youngblood Hawk*
(1962), and *Don't Stop the Carnival* (1965). He also wrote *The
Winds of War* (1971) and *War and Remembrance* (1978), which
were made into television miniseries in the 1980s.

Wouk received numerous military and civil honors and served
as a director or consultant at several educational and cultural organizations, including the Kennedy Center and the University of the
Virgin Islands.

---

dentials as dolphin experts, Doubleday, John's publishers, had
second thoughts about *Man and Dolphin*. (At a cocktail party, in
fact, the two critics had assaulted Mr. Doubleday himself and
pressed their demands on him.) Despite John's previous experience with government censorship in the name of national security, this was his first taste of the forces in the private sector that
affect the "free market of ideas." The book was saved by Lee
Barker, John's courageous editor, who threatened to resign if the
book were not published.

Since it was first published in 1961, *Man and Dolphin* has
been translated into nine languages. Its new point of view on
dolphins has had widespread influence. After an official Russian
translation was issued in 1967, the Soviet minister of fisheries
banned the killing of dolphins in Soviet waters.

The French edition apparently inspired novelist Robert
Merle to write his fictionalized version, published in English as
The Day of the Dolphin. That led to the 1973 movie of the same
name, directed by Mike Nichols and starring George C. Scott as
the kindly scientist who teaches dolphins to talk with humans.

The University of California at Los Angeles sponsored a symposium on the topic of dolphins at the William Andrews Clark Memorial Library in October 1962. Among the invited participants were John and anthropologist Ashley Montagu. Their presentations were collected in a volume published by the university, entitled *The Dolphin in History* (1963). John's half of this volume is titled "Modern Whales, Dolphins and Porpoises, as Challenge to Our Intelligence."

All this publicity helped John attract a distinguished crew of scientists with parallel or allied interests and draw top-notch members to his board of directors. Among the scientists were Dr. Peter Morgane, neurobiologist and neurophysiologist; John's frequent collaborator Henry Truby; as well as Scott McVay, Will L. McFarland, Eugene L. Nagel, Paul Yakovlev, and Mike S. Jacobs.

Joining the board of directors at CRII was Katherine Cole Worden, wife of Dr. Fred Worden, John's friend from med school. Kay brought a greatly appreciated level of intelligent commitment and support to the board. John also recruited two members of the Rockwell aerospace and defense contracting family. With this board in place, CRII managed to raise an annual budget of $450,000 for five years in a row.

This financial success and publicity were prompted by the fact that John was doing something bold and astonishing—in everyone's view but his own. The popular press response provided him with some idea of just how extraordinary his work appeared to the rest of the world. As he would write in 1978, "Only then did I realize that this was a new and novel viewpoint to be taking about another species."

In his last year at NIH, John had discussed his dolphin plans with Leo Szilard, the famous physicist who at NIH was turning his interest to pioneering the new field called biophysics. Szilard become so intrigued with John's account of dolphin intelligence and John's plans for a new institute devoted exclusively to dolphins that he was inspired to write *The Voice of the Dolphins*. In this rather fanciful story, Szilard located the new dolphin institute not in the Caribbean, but in Vienna. From here, Szilard's virtually oracular dolphins, who learned to speak with human scientists, guided the whole world toward disarmament and peace with their sage advice and cunning manipulation of human politicians.

Writing from the perspective of a twenty-first century commentator looking back on the period of the nuclear arms race, Szilard wove John Lilly into his tale:

> That the organization of the brain of the dolphin has a complexity comparable to that of man had been known for a long time. In 1960, Dr. John C. Lilly reported that the dolphins might have a language of their own, that they were capable of imitating human speech, and that the intelligence of dolphins might be equal to that of humans, or possibly even superior to it.

At CRII, John and his colleagues established a whole new field of research dealing with dolphin intelligence and interspecies communication. At the same time, they established a body of basic scientific information on dolphins, previously almost nonexistent. They turned the terra incognita of dolphin physiology and neurology into lucid textbook material. Essential, previously unknown facts were discovered, such as the voluntary nature of the dolphin's respiration, requiring the individual dolphin to remain conscious in order to go on breathing. Therefore, surgical anesthesia is invariably lethal to dolphins, unless artificial respiratory support is provided.

The size of the dolphin brain was established, and with it the fact that *Tursiops truncatus* has a larger brain than humans. The first comprehensive atlas of the dolphin's brain was compiled. The dolphin brain was definitively demonstrated to be neurologically comparable to a human's when examined on a microscopic level. The density of nerve cells and the complexity of their interconnections are as high as those within the human brain. The dolphin brain is larger, relative to the human brain, in exactly those areas in which the human brain is superior to that of the apes: the so-called "silent" or associational areas of the cerebral cortex implicated in higher-level functions of abstraction, generalization, and foresight. This suggests that the dolphin brain is *even more active* in these functions than the human brain.

Essential facts about dolphin communication and social behavior were revealed, including identification of the species-wide distress call; the extent of their interdependence and group reliance; their altruistic conduct toward one another; their use of sex for pleasure, recreation, and affection; and the male's ability to voluntary erect his penis and engage in prolonged and repeated mating. (Some of the above discoveries were made by John prior to his founding of CRII.)

Research into dolphin vocalizations showed that dolphins coordinate three sonic emitters to produce their sounds: one in the larynx and two in the nasal passages on either side. The dolphin's sonic/ultrasonic range is at least 100,000 hz (cycles per second). They exchange vast quantities of information (probably acoustic images) in brief bursts of high-frequency sound. With a focused beam of ultrasonic energy, they can inspect their surroundings, see inside other bodies in the water, and even identify different materials underwater at great distances.

John's bold position on dolphin intelligence was thoroughly validated by the discoveries made during this period. Many of his conjectures about dolphin language capability, including their ability to learn human-created languages, have been confirmed in the ensuing years.

In expanding his search for reality beyond the human species with his dolphin explorations, John created a truly dolphin-centered reality in the St. Thomas laboratory. After Bateson left for Hawaii, John spent increasing amounts of time at Dolphin Point. Here, among warm Caribbean swells and the delightfully unabashed sexual athletes in his laboratory pools, the Scientist was drifting into an island reality of his own. From this vantage point, the highly structured, human-centered reality on the mainland seemed increasingly bizarre and repugnant.

Almost every week, he flew back to Coconut Grove, where he maintained a home with Liz and the children. The laboratory in Miami represented his compromise with the social, scientific, and financial world he perceived at that time; in the human-centered lab dolphins were mere objects of human experimentation studied to determine facts. In St. Thomas, on the other hand, the goal was to learn from interaction with them. In Coconut Grove, John was forced to maintain a square little office in a bank building where, as the director of CRII, he presided over and tended to the needs of human society and the paper-based external reality on which his institute depended.

In setting up a two-headed institute, John had created a perfect mirror of the conflict between internal and external reality that had long raged within him. As the gulf between these realities widened, it became increasingly apparent that John was on one side, the dolphin-centered reality in St. Thomas, while Liz was on the other side, the human-centered side represented by Miami.

Liz had settled in Miami, a sophisticated cosmopolitan scene much more to her taste than remote St. Thomas. As the Miami branch of the institute grew, Liz lost control of what had begun as a kind of family business. Prestigious people were recruited to the board of directors and began to participate actively. Liz quarreled both with the board and with the professionals at the lab. The resulting conflicts made it necessary for John to remove her from her position of responsibility. She was thrown back into the role of wife, mother, and socialite. The enchantment of pioneering dolphin research with her brilliant, eccentric husband ended for Liz, and she devoted herself increasingly to socializing.

Other factors contributed to a growing distance between them. By 1962, John had begun to notice what he first thought were changes in Liz. Then he began to consider that perhaps it was his view of Liz that was changing, not her. Perhaps she was not the person he thought she was when he married her; maybe he didn't know who she really was at all.

They had met and married in such a hurry, a match made out of wild exhilaration and largely unconscious expectations. In the beginning, he had been swept away by her glamour and uninhibited sexiness. Perhaps, he reflected, it was just that his initial entrancement—his infatuation—with her was wearing off. He remembered earlier occasions when he had overvalued certain people and ideas. His sexual attractions had often caused him to project all kinds of virtues and qualities on women that weren't really there.

Perhaps these changes in Liz' behavior resulted from something else—maybe she was growing tired of life with a man as eccentric as John Lilly. He was such a strange combination of human and inhuman themes. He could be sensitive and intimate, but also remote, icy, and objective; a man in two worlds. As he seemed to acquire more of the dolphins' adorable traits, he seemed to show less of his human ones.

One day John witnessed Liz shouting at two-year-old Cynthia, and he sensed a violence in it that deeply disturbed him.

To John, anger directed at children was alien and repugnant. He was by nature judicious, controlled, and moderate. From his experiences with the dolphins, he had become increasingly impressed by the moderate and measured way they interacted with humans as well as with their own young. A dolphin never exhibited uncontrolled anger or aggression, never exaggerated its reactions, never used any more force than necessary to defend itself or teach a lesson. A dolphin was never violent, unless grievously provoked.

As a result of his constant contact with them, John was becoming more like a dolphin, and Liz, as he got to know her better, appeared more typically human.

John's next step in his search for Reality would put an even greater distance between them.

CHAPTER 9

THE UNCONTAINED MIND

May 1964, age 49.
  The Scientist locks the door and turns out the lights. In his right hand he holds a syringe loaded with one cubic centimeter of sterile water containing 100 micrograms of d-lysergic acid diethylamide tartrate—also known as LSD-25. He injects this chemical into his right thigh, withdraws the needle, and drops the syringe on the chair. He finds his way through the darkness to a ladder and climbs the eight steps to the rim of the isolation tank. Gripping the rim, he lowers his body into the water. Then, he leans back, releasing his grip, and floats on his back toward the center of this dark little sea.
  No one has ever experienced the combination of LSD and profound isolation before. Several things might happen. If he gets high enough, he might forget about his body, forget about the water, roll over and drown. Or his body might just stop breathing while his mind is occupied elsewhere. He might panic, attempt to scuttle out of the tank, fall down the dark ladder, and break his neck.
  There are other, more subtle hazards. All the authorities have warned against anyone taking LSD alone. In this tank, in total darkness and silence, he is more than alone; he is completely isolated from all the world's sensations, and from every other human being on the planet.
  Fear of psychosis flashes through him, his mind falling apart, his spirit disintegrating—the shattered, immortal spirit, persisting in this wounded state forever. That would be a fate worse than the death of the body.

*It is now too late to turn back. He knows that his future
depends on how he handles this experience—which is increasingly becoming one of terror and panic.*

*And then the chemical takes over. An electric bolt of fear
shoots through him like rocket fuel. He sheds his body, sheds
his identity, sheds his mind, and blasts off into the universe,
an autonomous being of electricity and fire, propelled by fear
transformed into pure energy, tunneling through the void. He
has ceased to be John Lilly and has become something
greater.*

*The Being takes stock of itself. It is enjoying this thun-
derous, cosmic, rollercoaster ride immensely. Then the Being
remembers it is connected with a body floating in an isolation
tank on Earth, somewhere far from this pulsing center of the
galaxy where stars are born from nuclear fire. If it chooses to
focus its awareness on that body, it is immediately back inside.*

*A supernova is expanding toward explosion. Down
below, the body goes on breathing rhythmically. In it is a full
bladder about to empty itself automatically, while far above
John rides a stream of star fire into the void. The stream
whirls and swirls, spinning off into spiraling galaxies.*

*He learns the first navigation rule: The body will take
care of itself. It's basic life-support functions go on automatically, no matter what one is experiencing "above." One can
leave the body and return to it at any time.*

IT WAS FLIPPER who led John to LSD, thanks to Aristotle. Some
2,300 years before, Aristotle had written that "not only do [dol-
phins] imitate the human voice in air, but also they carry small
children on their backs."

Throughout the Christian era and well into the twentieth
century, this fact was doubted by numerous authorities, many of
whom swore by Aristotle on less easily observed points. Learned
men and women of the church, and later of science, confidently
denied that it was possible for dolphins to speak or to carry
human passengers as portrayed on the vases of ancient Greece,
but they never bothered to see for themselves. The experimental
resolution of this issue was left to John Lilly, along with movie
producer Ivan Tors, his wife Constance, and their young children.

Tors had heard of Dr. Lilly, the dolphin expert, from the librarian at Universal Studios, whose friend, a biology graduate student named Karl Kellog, had spent a summer as a volunteer intern at a laboratory in Florida where John was directing research. John agreed to serve as Ivan Tors's consultant during the filming of the movie *Flipper,* in the Bahamas.

To confirm Aristotle's observation, John and Tors set up conditions where they could all interact with three dolphins in shallow water for prolonged periods. By the second day, the dolphins were giving rides to Tors's sons. Case closed: Aristotle was vindicated on the issue of dolphinic behavior.

But that was only a further link in the chain of coincidence. Constance Tors was one of the early explorers in the psychotherapeutic use of LSD. Using the pseudonym "Constance Newland," she had written one of the first popular books on LSD, *Myself and I,* about the experiments she and her psychoanalyst performed. This extraordinarily revealing account chronicled the successful resolution of her problem with sexual frigidity.

John had first heard about LSD at NIH in the 1950s. Many of his colleagues had done experiments with the drug, and they urged John to combine it with his studies of isolation. John had declined, saying that he wanted to avoid contaminating his tank experiments with this new factor. But as John's friendship with Constance developed, this situation changed. John came to appreciate her as a warm, compassionate, trustworthy person with a special, mysterious wisdom that seemed to be derived from her deep inner experiences. He eventually became ready to try the miracle drug he had eschewed at NIH, hoping that LSD might cure his long-standing recurrent migraines. He was also intrigued by the then-prevalent idea that this chemical could facilitate psychoanalysis by opening up the unconscious.

An expert in the therapeutic usage of LSD, Constance would be an ideal guide for John's first sessions; John's fondness for and familiarity with the concepts and procedures of psychoanalysis fit well with the program Constance had derived from her own LSD-assisted psychoanalysis. She epitomized the ideal of a psychedelic guide, whose function was to provide a safe, permissive space and intervene only if necessary to help the user out of any especially tight spots in his own psyche. The guide would also facilitate the prearranged program for the session and its therapeutic or self-revelatory purpose, preventing

BIOGRAPHY

IVAN TORS (1916–1983), a native of Budapest, wrote plays in Europe before emigrating to the United States in the late 1930s. He served in the air force and OSS, and after the war became a screenwriter, producer, and director, beginning with science fiction movies. Later, Tors created a series of TV shows and movies starring nonhuman actors, including the "Flipper" and "Gentle Ben" TV series and the movies *Flipper* (1963), *Rhino!* (1964), *Clarence the Cross-Eyed Lion* (1965), *Zebra in the Kitchen* (1965), and *Namu the Killer Whale* (1966). To support the production of his animal movies, Tors maintained large menageries near Miami and Los Angeles. His huge wild-animal preserve in Southern California became the theme park Africa, USA.

interruptions and handling any physical emergencies that might arise.

In late 1963, with the two CRII labs running smoothly, John flew to Los Angeles for a series of two LSD sessions with Constance. The first session was held at a secluded beach house. With all his years of analysis, research, and self-exploration in isolation, John was well prepared for the injection of 100 micrograms of Dr. Albert Hofmann's mysterious elixir. John filled his hypodermic syringe and injected it into the muscle of his right thigh.

What followed was a classic, high-energy "good trip," filled with fantastic personal and transpersonal revelations and terrific intellectual breakthroughs. He later described this experience in *The Center of the Cyclone:* "I moved with the music into Heaven. I saw God on a tall throne as a giant, wise, ancient Man. He was surrounded with angel choruses. . . . I was there in Heaven worshiping God, worshiping the angels, worshiping the saints in full and complete transport of religious ecstasy." This was remarkably like John's childhood experience before the altar of his Catholic church, yet it was merely an introduction into the spaces opened by LSD.

Following a blissful solo vacation in Hawaii, John returned to Constance for a second session. But this time he was preoccupied with his impending return to Miami, Elisabeth, and the distress of his personal life. He had a tense and miserable experience, filled with a rehash of his interpersonal and sexual problems. This trip is also described in *The Center of the Cyclone:* "I did not go into any far-out internal spaces this trip. I stayed with the current problem and discussed it with myself and hallucinated real persons, getting them to give their side, and I gave my side to them. . . . I came out of that session feeling rather hopeless about my marriage, about any possibility of changing my wife's mind or her personality or her knowledge."

On the flight back he stopped off to address a scientific dinner meeting in New York City. Afterward, feeling that he was coming down with an infection, Dr. Lilly bought some antibiotics, went to his hotel room, and gave himself a shot. He used the same syringe from the LSD sessions, hastily washed out with a detergent and water—an act that proved to be nearly fatal. As he well knew, a small residue of detergent will lower the surface tension of water and allow bubbles to pass through the tiny capillaries of the lungs and on to the brain. Still in a mental daze from his second exhausting LSD session, John managed to inject air bubbles into a vein, and they went right to his brain.

John went into coma and was hospitalized for several days. He was temporarily blind, dazed, and cut off from both the outside world and the sensations of his own body. In this state of stunned and isolated selfhood, John's disembodied soul was visited by his Guides—the same two Beings he had seen in childhood, first in the midst of a fevered delirium, and later, in a moment of religious rapture, as angels. He had not seen them since.

John later wrote of this visitation: "Their magnificent deep powerful love overwhelms me. . . . They say that they are my guardians, that they have been with me before at critical times and that in fact they are with me always."

But there was an important difference between this experience and John's childhood encounters. This time, John experienced the visitation from the point of view of the Being that had been most closely associated with him in childhood, as his Guardian Angel. It was as if he *was* that Being, communicating in a timeless space with the two others. John described this aspect of the experience: "I am in a large empty space with nothing in any direction except light. There is a golden light permeating the whole space everywhere in all directions, out to infinity. I am a single point of consciousness, of feeling, of knowledge. I know that I am. That is all. It is a very peaceful, awesome, and reverential space that I am in. I have no body, I have no need for a body. There is no body. I am just I. Complete with love, warmth, and radiance."

As he recovered, John slowly regained first his consciousness and then his vision. For several years thereafter, there were two small holes in John's visual field: new blind spots caused by the injury to his brain—which continuously reminded him of the dangers of unthinking experimentation.

Back in the Islands, John had obtained a supply of LSD through the government. He performed an experiment in which he injected LSD into his dolphins to see if it would increase their vocalization, and whether it would affect their orientation in the water or disrupt their voluntary respiration. He discovered that they handled the experience smoothly, in spite of some apparent disorganization of their visual fields, for which they compensated by increased reliance on their sonar. Encouraged by the fact that they had no problems with maneuvering in the water and breathing while on LSD, John finally decided to combine the effects of LSD with the isolation tank for himself.

He had constructed a huge isolation tank in a disused darkroom above the dolphin pools, next to the flooded lab room. The new tank was an eight-foot cube containing seawater at a controlled temperature of 93° F. One entered it by climbing a ladder to the top, sliding over the rim, and slipping into the water.

This design had several advantages over the tank at NIH. The seawater provided extra buoyancy, so John could float on his back in a relaxed position with his face at the surface. This eliminated the need for the rubber supports which maintained his position and the breathing tube and mask that were necessary at NIH, floating with one's face below water. With the new design, one could simply climb in and out without having to go through a complicated set-up procedure. Thus, there were far fewer things to go wrong physically, with the new tank.

Nothing in his two previous LSD sessions under Constance's guidance had prepared him for what came next.

After taking his dose of LSD and entering the tank, John felt himself expanding far beyond the body and far beyond anything the mind located in that body could conceive. He became the

Being—existing among other Beings like itself, each one vast as an entire universe, connected in a network spanning eternity. The Being was somehow akin to the Guardian Angel he had experienced in childhood.

When the Being turned its attention back to the body, it observed the body doing just fine, floating there in the warm water. So was the mind, beginning to re-form itself along familiar lines programmed by memory and by the sensations of that particular body. To the Being, the mind and body of John Lilly imposed a feeling of uncomfortable limitation. They were far too small to contain it, but as it took notice of them, it seemed to slip into them and fill them up. The body, if he paid attention to it, seemed to grab the Being and pull it in.

The Being constricted itself into the mind and body of John, losing contact with the other Beings in the cosmic spaces. And then the body climbed out of the isolation tank, climbed down the ladder, and switched on the lights.

John stepped out onto the balcony to look at the beautiful island scene. All around him, the sea, the cliffs, the vegetation, the gleaming white lab building were vibrant and alive. For about an hour he enjoyed the world as he never had before; and then he went back into the isolation tank. For the rest of that day John slipped freely and easily between awareness of his body floating in the tank and awareness of himself as an entity different from that body. His contact with the Being gradually dimmed but persisted within him as a new, expanded sense of his own existence.

This process showed John that the isolation tank and LSD were an unprecedented combination, providing the highest, clearest, most constant energy imaginable. Freed of the sensory distractions of gravity and the outside world, the human brain on LSD was a clean machine, purring with the power to generate any experience you could conceive, plan, or select from the infinite range of possibility.

After about ten hours, as the effects of LSD were winding down, John left the tank and, in a state of high enthusiasm, went looking for Margaret, whom he found, predictably, sitting in a small pool with her three dolphins. As he began to share his new enthusiasm, Margaret stopped him cold. That, she said, was *his* work, and this was *hers.* He had better not interfere with hers, just as she would not interfere in his, whatever that might be. She was not in the least bit interested in his experiments. John realized that this was actually a rather desirable state of affairs; he could now count on Margaret to protect his privacy for future experiments, while not intruding herself.

With those lines drawn, John went to his room to write up his notes. After some time, his thoughts turned to the dolphins. Night had fallen, Margaret was asleep by now, and the three dolphins were alone in their pool. John descended to the dark pool and saw the gleaming bodies of the dolphins in the starlight as they swam together. He felt a closeness and communion with them that he had never felt before.

He had a strange intuition that perhaps, during his experiment, the dolphins had communicated with him, somehow influencing and maybe even purposefully creating the nearly indescribable experience of his first two hours with LSD in the tank. If such were indeed the case, then where did his mind begin and end? Surely not with the boundaries of his own body. What sort of theory about the mind could possibly explain this kind of relationship between his mind and those of the dolphins, much less the relationship of the Being to all their minds and bodies?

Such reflections led John to realize that all his thinking to that point had been dominated by a belief in the "contained mind," the idea that the mind is contained in the brain, its fate tied to the physical condition and survival of that organ. This belief system was implicit in science, yet there was no real scientific basis for it; it was merely an assumption.

In his own case, belief in the contained mind might be no more than a reaction against the belief system foisted on him in childhood. The Catholic church taught that a person is an immortal soul, temporarily housed in a material body but ultimately able to escape it at death and wing its way to heaven, just like the angels in the icons and stained glass windows in church. But when John reached puberty, he had rejected this doctrine along with the church's doctrines on sin which conflicted with the true experience of his own developing sexuality.

In the history of science, similarly, church doctrine had been entirely thrown out because the inflexible dogmatism and conservatism of the church stood in the way of scientific progress. In that process, science had rejected ancient religious teachings concerning the immortal soul—the *uncontained* mind—even before it had any well-grounded concept to take its place. Instead, science adopted the ad hoc notion of an individual mind arising from the behavior of physical matter; a mind generated within, dependent on, and confined to the brain.

Never explicitly stated as a theory by scientists or subjected to the scientific method for proof or disproof, the belief in the physical origins of the mind became, instead, a part of the "religion of science," a part one had better not question if one wanted to be accepted as a scientist. For John the Scientist now, the idea of the contained mind had assumed a different status: It was a scientific hypothesis to be explicitly stated, analyzed, and put to the test, confirmed or refuted by experiment, in so far as this was possible. It was no longer acceptable as an implicit assumption, as a belief not subject to experimentation. It was just another belief, and all beliefs limited the range of one's experiences and one's experiments.

If John's experiences in the tank had, in fact, been influenced by either the dolphins in the pool below or in the flooded laboratory next to his isolation room, then the mind could not be strictly contained. He would have to consider the possibility that the mind was perhaps uncontained after all, or only partially contained. He came to call this latter idea "the leaky mind hypothesis." After his experience, even the most durable, bedrock assumptions of science were open to question.

On that decisive day in the spring of 1964, John had not died in the tank, nor had his mind died within his brain. Instead, he became open to a greater appreciation of life—the life of science and the life of the dolphin. And, above all, an appreciation of his own life—which the Being had now decisively entered.

John would go on to perform twenty more experiments with LSD in the isolation tank during 1964 and 1965, while Margaret's dolphin experiments proceeded in nearby parts of the lab. She served as his "safety man," in which capacity her principal duty was to prevent anybody from dropping in and interrupting him.

At NIH John had first begun to apply the knowledge he had gleaned from Britton Chance back at the Johnson Foundation concerning computers. Privately he had begun to entertain the notion that the relationship between the brain and mind could be clarified by drawing an analogy between the human brain and the computer. During the experiments with LSD and isolation at CRII, these ideas grew into a full-blown theory, first expressed in a CRII progress report in 1967 and eventually published in 1972 as *Programming and Metaprogramming in the Human Biocomputer.*

This theory suggested that the brain might be analogous to the "hardware" of a computer, its circuits and memory chips, while the mind might be seen as the "software," programs running in the computer that use the circuitry to perform some activity—calculations, modeling, word processing, or games. According to biocomputer theory, every belief is actually a "program" stored in the brain. In this system, programs which control, create, and modify other programs are called "metaprograms."

In the human biocomputer, programs are created by the influence and teachings of other people, and by encounters with new situations. Once created, programs are then selected and activated by stimuli from the outside world—interaction with people, places, and things. Human behavior, and experience, are themselves the "running" of these programs, and thus our experience is guided and limited by our available set of programs or beliefs.

This definition of experience explains why the brain continues to generate experience in profound isolation. Once programs are stored in the brain, the brain can run them—creating experiences—on its own, in the absence of significant interaction with the external reality.

Individual destiny, then, is largely a question of which programs are available to run in the brain. Within the brain there is a self-programmer, a conscious observer/operator with great latitude in reviewing and modifying the existing selection of programs. This capacity for self-programming can be greatly enhanced by both isolation from the environment and the use of neuroactive chemicals such as LSD, which open a whole new range of alternatives for self-programming—new modes of experience and new ways of being. (There are also what he called "supra-self programs," which one may access but over which one has no control.)

Human biocomputer theory was a vast step forward in John's personal search for Reality. He had added a new level to the ancient debate about mind, body, and soul, and he could now explain the brain's capacity to generate experience in profound isolation. Furthermore, he now had a fully elaborated model for the relationship between the brain and mind, the central issue of his search, and for the all-important role of beliefs in that relationship. He had developed a new way of seeing himself, his relationship to the world, and the relationship between internal and external realities. And he had discovered his power to control, modify, and even create his own experience. He also reported other, "higher" sources of control that could do this for or to him.

During John's isolation tank experiments with LSD from 1964 through 1966, John grew closer to the dolphins, to the Being that stirred within him, and to the cosmic spaces that the Being and others like it inhabited. But he grew ever more remote from the terrestrial reality he shared with his wife.

He attempted to share his LSD consciousness with Liz after he returned to Florida from his sessions with Constance, but to absolutely no avail. For her, even the thought of LSD was something that belonged in another universe. John was no more able to get her interested in LSD than he had been able to get Mary enthused about psychoanalysis.

One incident in particular highlighted their differences fluorescently. Liz had her own set of friends, socialites with whom John was utterly bored and whose social scene was centered around parties where alcohol was regularly consumed. Alcohol, however, was becoming increasingly unattractive to John, but when he decided to stop drinking it and to avoid attending alcohol-based social occasions, Liz resented this and set out to visit nightclubs around Coconut Grove without him. One night, after John had taken a small dose of LSD, Liz persuaded him to accompany her to one of these clubs. Under the influence of the chemical, John perceived the alcohol-drenched revellers as pickled corpses, cadavers from his med-school days at Dartmouth. The smell of alcohol merged in his mind with the smell of formaldehyde, and thereafter he could not even go near alcohol without it triggering the urge to vomit.

The marriage had became intolerably strained. John eventually moved out of the home they had shared and into a bachelor apartment in Miami. The split was quite acrimonious; John discovered a bugging device in his new pad, and concluded that Liz, rather than the CIA, had put private detectives on his trail. The two remained tensely separated until John finally obtained a divorce in 1975.

In the early 1960s, the U.S. Navy became interested in enlisting some dolphins. At CRII, John was visited by an old Caltech friend named Bill, who had since become head of a research program for the navy at China Lake, California. After spending some time catching up with John at his lab, Bill disclosed to John that the navy would be starting its own dolphin research lab at Point Mugu, just north of Los Angeles.

Bill elicited John's advice on staffing this facility with an expert who understood how to care for dolphins in captivity. John immediately thought of F.G. Wood, curator of the Marine Studio in Florida, a man whom John thought of as having a high ethical attitude toward dolphins and a genuine concern for their welfare. Wood, John figured, could be counted on to represent the dolphins' best interests against any abusive demands the navy might make on them. (John was not aware of Wood's attitude toward John Lilly, or of the karmic link to the future that this recommendation would create.)

Already John feared that the navy's research program would be less scientific than "operational"—aimed at using the dolphins in a military mission. Later, it would surface that the navy used dolphins in Vietnam as underwater warriors.

Shortly after Bill's visit, Dr. D. Wayne Batteau, one of Bill's colleagues, came to see John. An expert on stereophonition and the localization of sound in 3-D space, Batteau was a consultant to the navy at China Lake, where he had developed an electronic system for reproducing full three-dimensional sound. He was now interested in applying his formidable knowledge of accoustics to the problem of human-dolphin communications.

John was fascinated by his discussions with Dr. Batteau, an obvious genius, and encouraged Batteau to build a device he called the transphonometer, which would shift the frequencies of sounds from the human to the dolphin hearing range, and vice versa. They parted agreeing to stay in touch.

John's publishing contract with Doubleday had called for two books, the first being *Man and Dolphin,* which was published in 1961. Originally the second book was to be about the isolation tank experiments, but John decided to write another dolphin book instead, to update the research and present views far more advanced than those expressed in the first book. Facing a late 1965 deadline, John sequestered himself with Margaret in a hotel room for a weekend. With her help, he was able to dictate the last hundred pages in about forty-eight hours. *The Mind of the Dolphin* was published on schedule in 1967.

By this time, John's interest in continuing his dolphin work was abating. A great deal of information had already been gathered and published, and the goals of his original agenda had for the most part been fulfilled. His attitudes toward the dolphins had undergone a profound metamorphosis over this period. His awe and appreciation for the species were such that he could no longer condone performing experiments on them, and even had reservations about confining them involuntarily for interaction with humans.

At that point an additional factor, a nasty legal case pending against CRII, dealt a final blow to the institute's continued existence. The photographer originally hired—and subsequently fired—by Gregory Bateson reappeared three years later with a lawsuit in Miami court, claiming that CRII had promised him "tenure," including retirement benefits, and that he had been wrongfully dismissed. John didn't think that the photographer had much of a case, but the judge—whose sister had once come to legal blows with John and his neighbors in a zoning dispute—apparently felt otherwise. After a series of arbitrary and seemingly vengeful rulings during the trial, John sensed the winds of destiny blowing against him in this instance. He agreed to settle for $30,000. The St. Thomas lab was thus sold for a fraction of its actual value to the institute's lawyer, in order to raise the necessary cash.

Before John was able to announce to the thirty employees that he had decided to close the lab in 1967, five dolphins committed suicide by refusing to eat. At this point, the disheartened staff needed little further persuasion that it was time to fold their scientific tents and move on. John helped them all find other jobs;

the researchers and their equipment were dispersed to other labs around the country.

John ordered the release of the three remaining dolphins, and watched them return to the sea. For several hours he watched as the older dolphin herded the two younger ones around the busy yacht basin, apparently teaching them to keep their distance from humans. At last they swam out of the channel and into the wild.

CHAPTER 10

JOURNEY TO THE WEST

May 1968, Age 53.

Big Sur, California: a majestic range of coastal mountains dropping precipitously into the crashing surf of the Pacific at the western edge of the North American continent.

Clinging precariously to one of the gravel-strewn cliff-sides there is Esalen, undisputed international capital of the human potential movement. Built around natural sulphur hot springs gurgling out of the cliffs some twenty yards above the thunderous sea, the waters are now trapped in a series of troughs, tubs, and spas—the Baths, once the sacred bathing grounds of the Esalen Indians. The area was later a nudist camp, religious retreat, and a place where travelers could buy a mineral bath for fifty cents—and local artists like Henry Miller could get one for free. Now it is a place where pilgrims from around the world gather in search of new ways of being.

John Lilly drives down the winding road with its awe-some vistas. He takes a right at the large Esalen sign and descends one of the world's steepest driveways. Enormous emerald-green lawns pass before his wondering eyes, dotted with the lounging and ambling figures of smiling, totally naked humans, dolphinlike in their apparent innocence.

IN 1968 THE NATION was in a panic over LSD. Timothy Leary, LSD's most forceful public advocate, was repeatedly arrested. The Vietnam War was approaching a crescendo of organized violence, body counts, and civil dissent. Robert F. Kennedy, leading contender for president, was murdered in Los Angeles, just a month after the assassination of Dr. Martin Luther King, Jr. Soon Richard Nixon would become the next president of the United States, flanked by bellicose Spiro T. Agnew and stern John Mitchell. Countercultural rebellion, social upheaval, and the consciousness revolution were juxtaposed against the politics of the "silent majority." It was the final twist of the '60s, a decade many remember as their most thrilling, and others as their most violent. The winds of change blew in all directions at once.

It was also the year of John Lilly's hegira, or in his own words, a year of "going with the flow." It was a turbulent flow, a pattern of many smaller currents; their combined forces, summed up, pushed John in one direction: Westward.

Along the way, the eddies and rivulets would briefly deposit John in various places: Urbana, Illinois; Los Angeles and Berkeley, California; Topeka, Kansas; Stanford, California; then east again to Spring Grove, Maryland; and subsequently, Sausalito, California, before he was ultimately washed ashore in Big Sur.

The current that led John to Urbana, Illinois, began with a fascinating discovery he'd made while trying to decipher dolphin vocalizations. Phonologists, who studied the sounds of speech, used a device called a sonograph to record a "sound bite" on a disk and replay it repeatedly. John noticed that when he replayed dolphin sounds, and later human words, in this way, the sounds were heard differently. Apparently, after a few repetitions, the brain tired of one interpretation and started generating alternatives. Significantly, the brain substituted its varying interpretations for the actual sound, which actually never changed from one repetition to the next.

The discovery of this "repeating word effect" in 1968 led John to contact his friend, Professor Heinz von Foerster at the University of Illinois, where he ran the Biological Computer Laboratory, developing computers whose function was based on an advanced model of the operation of the brain.

Heinz was sufficiently fascinated by John's discovery to offer the use of the university's new IBM 360 computer to analyze the thousands of alternates that a group of people heard when listening to endless repetitions of the word *cogitate*. By an amaz-

BIOGRAPHY

HEINZ VON FOERSTER (1911–   ) was born into the upper echelons of Viennese society in a family that included philosopher Lud-
wig Wittgenstein. During the rise of Nazism he fled from Vienna,
where the von Foersters were known as "part Jewish" to Berlin,
where his "totally German" name allowed him to continue his education in physics. Thus he survived the Holocaust in which most of
his Viennese relations were murdered by Nazis.

As a brilliant young physicist, he emigrated to the United
States in the postwar era as protégé of neurophysiologist Warren
S. McCulloch, who appointed him editor of the Macy symposia on
cybernetics. As a professor at the University of Illinois, he established the Biological Computer Laboratory, where, with colleagues
including W. Ross Ashby, Gordon Pask, and Arturo Rosenbleuth he
laid the foundations for the theories of biocomputers and percep-
trons, later called neural network computers. Von Foerster was
instrumental in founding the American Society for Cybernetics.

---

ing coincidence, John's visit coincided with the national convention of the American Linguistic Society, whose meeting he was
hurriedly scheduled to address. There he played his tape loop,
and the hundreds of linguists wrote down what they heard using
the international phonetic alphabet. Analysis showed that the
brain generated alternates at the level of *phons,* units of sound
smaller than the *phoneme,* which was the unit that most linguists
of the time thought of as the basic element of spoken words. This
was a significant breakthrough in understanding the levels of
subtlety by which the brain processed the sounds of speech.

John's growing friendship with von Foerster, nurtured by
their collaboration, was as important to him as this discovery.
Von Foerster was brilliant and charming, an excellent speaker
whose sprightly presence never failed to raise the energy in any
group. His scientific ideas continued to influence John deeply for
many years. John later described him as "the one living scientist
who consistently has something important to say to me in the
areas of my own greatest scientific interest and expertise." Von
Foerster encouraged John to publish his own theory of the human
biocomputer.

Next John was taken on a guided tour of the West Coast scene by his friend Sandy Unger, a psychotherapy researcher interested in LSD. In California, Unger introduced John to many of the luminaries of the "higher consciousness" movement. In Hollywood, he met Laura Archera Huxley, musician, artist, therapist, writer, wife of the late Aldous Huxley, and author of his biography, who made a delightful first impression on him. He also met some of Laura's friends, many of whom had tried LSD, and found a special rapport and understanding among them.

In Berkeley, Unger introduced him to psychologist Timothy Leary and his wife Rosemary. It was a fun meeting, despite the fact that John had expressed opinions rather disapproving of Leary in a magazine article entitled "Educating for Responsibility with LSD." John thought that Leary, his former Harvard collaborator Richard Alpert, and many others had missed the real point of LSD as a scientific tool for studying the brain's relationship to the mind, and for disciplined, systematic self-programming. To John, these people had been seduced by the many phenomena occurring when LSD was used under uncontrolled conditions. They seemed to have formed powerful beliefs about the outside world based on what they experienced within their own minds. Using LSD in social groups, they were developing shared belief systems around it, whereas John's approach was to use such chemicals to *transcend* the limits of beliefs and to try to learn about the brain, not about the outside world.

Leary was popularizing a belief in LSD as a religious sacrament and advocating far-reaching social and political changes based on this idea. John was then among the scientists and psychotherapists who thought that popularizing LSD in this fashion was asking for trouble, a view borne out by the subsequent repressive political reaction that halted most scientific research, including John's, or the therapeutic uses of LSD under professional supervision. Perhaps the most outstanding example of such repression was the government's putting Leary, himself, under indictment. As the most flamboyant and visible spokesman for LSD, he became a target for selective prosecution.

John disapproved of Leary's TV image, but liked Timothy personally. Ironically, John was enchanted with Rosemary, a beautiful, vivacious woman whose magical, magnetic personality

BIOGRAPHY

TIMOTHY FRANCIS LEARY (1920–   ), a native of Springfield, Massachusetts, was educated at the U.S. Military Academy at West Point and elsewhere. His 1950 Ph.D. thesis for the University of California at Berkeley was followed by his classic textbook, *The Interpersonal Diagnosis of Personality* (1957), which established a transactional method of assessing personal characteristics and interactions.

At Harvard University in the early 1960s with Richard Alpert and Ralph Metzner, he experimented with psilocybin and later LSD as adjuncts to psychotherapy. Enthusiasm with the psychedelic chemicals led him to public advocacy of their widespread use. Systematically persecuted by the U.S. government under Nixon, he was jailed, fled into exile in 1970, was captured abroad by the CIA, and imprisoned from 1972 to 1976. By then, government agencies had compiled over 50,000 pages of "classified" data on Leary, considered a threat to the Establishment. Subsequently, Leary settled in Beverly Hills and linked up with the Hollywood entertainment community, writing, lecturing, and performing as a "stand-up philosopher comedian."

Essentially a transactionalist in psychology, Leary was influenced by Marshall McLuhan, including culture and the media in his formulations of human nature. Many of his thirty-five books present systematic schemes for analyzing the interaction of society, technology, and the brain. His most recent efforts entail the use of personal computers as media for interactive literature. His early scientific work is summarized in *Changing My Mind among Others* (1982), and his personal adventures are chronicled in *Flashbacks* (1983).

exemplified Leary's goals in advocating LSD to the nation and to the world.

In the early 1960s, when the U.S. Navy had approached him for advice on setting up a dolphin lab at Point Mugu, John had had no desire to become entangled in the project. He had decided to be helpful, however, in order to stay abreast of the navy's plans. John had recommended F.G. Wood to run the lab, and Wood had

been hired—apparently unaware that it was on John's recommendation. John, meanwhile, was unaware that Wood approved
of neither John Lilly nor his dolphin research.

Now, in California, John received an invitation to visit the
nearby Point Mugu facility from Dr. D. Wayne Batteau. Since
their meeting in Miami, John had stayed in touch with Batteau,
who had continued to work for the navy on the invention that had
so intrigued John earlier, the transphonometer.

At the gate of the Point Mugu base, John was greeted by
Batteau, who showed him his lab and demonstrated the transphonometer. Then he took John to lunch at the cafeteria. There,
across the space of the large room, John spotted Wood, whose
face was rapidly turning red as he recognized John Lilly.

"What are you doing bringing Lilly here?" Wood shouted at
Batteau; then in a somewhat conciliatory tone, to John, "Why
didn't you tell me you were coming?"

From this encounter and their subsequent strained conversation at Point Mugu, John began to realize that his positive attitude
toward Wood was not entirely reciprocated. John felt most un-
welcome, and was able to learn little about the dolphin program,
beyond what he had already gathered from conversations with
Batteau.

Some time later Batteau, who was working on his transphonometer at the navy dolphin lab in Hawaii, was found dead on
the beach. With Batteau's death, John lost his contact with the
navy's dolphin program.

Wood, and the Point Mugu dolphin lab, moved to the Naval
Oceans Systems Center on San Diego Bay. John wondered if the
navy had already taken up his suggestion in *Man and Dolphin* to
use cryptography computers to "crack the code" of the dolphin's
vocal language. If so, the navy might soon be shouting orders to
their dolphins underwater in a frequency range too high for humans to detect. The public would never know.

John knew that in the years since he had written *Man and
Dolphin,* computers had become a hundred times more powerful;
that computers were being used by the National Security Agency
to intercept and interpret military radio traffic from other coun-
tries; and that the world's first supercomputer, the ILLIAC IV, was
already being assembled in a security bunker at a naval air station near San Jose. The computer power necessary to establish
vocal communication with dolphins was at hand—at least to the

military which always had first access to the newest, most advanced, and most expensive technology. Glad as he was at the prospect of human-dolphin communication, he was saddened to think that it might be first realized in secrecy, for military purposes. And then, he projected, the navy would probably disparage dolphin intelligence in public in order to cover its secrets, and hoard its secret knowledge through a campaign of misinformation.

John's next pilgrimage brought him to Topeka, Kansas. There, with the help of hypnotism experts Ken Godfrey and Hellen Bonney, he intended to determine if he could reach through hypnotic trance the same spaces that he had programmed for himself with LSD in the isolation tank. In pursuing this, he was convinced he was following the instructions of the two Beings who had coached him occasionally throughout his life, and with whom he had frequently communed in his tank experiments. These guides wanted him to know that he could contact them at any time, not only during illness, traumatic injury, the threat of death, or on LSD.

Contrary to their predictions, however, John did not visit precisely the same domains of consciousness he had entered with the aid of LSD and isolation. But he did have some compelling experiences that decisively opened his mind to the probable reality of parapsychological phenomena—telepathy, remote viewing, and travels out of the body. John found that he went into trance easily and deeply, and then invariably had an experience *as if* he were somewhere else. The mind was definitely not totally "contained," he concluded from these episodes. At the very least it was "leaky."

The experiences revolved around his guide from his first two LSD sessions, Constance Tors. During his first trance experiment, John saw a scene that he immediately recognized as Constance's bedroom. He saw a bed covered with a flowered spread; then he saw the bedspread burst into flame along one edge and burn up. This startling and vivid image threw him out of trance, after which he immediately called Constance at her home in Beverly Hills and asked what she had been doing just then. She told him she had been reading in bed, lost her reading glasses in a heap of books and bedclothes, and, in a moment of impatient anger, grabbed the edge of the bedspread and ripped it off the bed. Hearing her account, John realized that he had just experienced a visual simulation that was a metaphoric version of another person's experience in a remote location.

During his next trance, he had a feeling of warmth and joy as he looked up at a beautiful crystal chandelier bathed in a golden light. Again he phoned Constance Tors and she reported she had just been glancing at the chandelier in her stairwell while dancing down the stairs, experiencing a state of childish delight in its glittering beauty. This time John had experienced the emotional, physical, and sensory reality of another person in a far-away place.

The next time he visited her in Beverly Hills another astonishing episode occurred. He took along a tape recording of a session with Ken and Hellen in Topeka. As he started it, she found that she could predict every word on the tape just before it was spoken.

These events would take some serious explaining in a contained mind belief system. Since John was no longer using LSD in these experiments, any attempt to explain the results as a peculiar effect of the chemical, or "merely hallucinations," simply wouldn't wash. Furthermore, these phenomena were being observed and confirmed by others. In a certain sense, then, John's experiments did in fact confirm the predictions of the Beings. Seemingly extraordinary phenomena could be found in the real world under normal conditions, not only under unusual conditions such as the combination of isolation and LSD.

While in Topeka, John had one more episode that seemed to illuminate the connection between trance and remote viewing, the ability to apparently see objects or events at a distance. He put loudspeakers next to Hellen's head and played his "cogitate" tape for her. He then lay on a couch across the room. As the tape played, he heard the sound originating from the speakers located near Hellen, as one would expect. But then he went into trance, as sometimes happens to people listening to the repeating-word tape. In his trance, John heard the tape as if it were coming from speakers next to his own head. He was able to go in and out of trance at will during the tape, and experienced this shift in the apparent location of the sound source several times. Apparently there was something about the trance state that enabled one to experience things *as if* one were in another person's place, whether across the room or across the country.

These episodes prompted him to recall two previous instances when he had received messages—or experiences—from people far away who were confronting traumatic conditions. One was in the early 1960s, when Elisabeth had an ectopic pregnancy while in Miami. With the tiny embryo clinging somewhere in her fallopian tubes, she awakened in the middle of the night with excruciating pain. At exactly the same moment, John was roused from sleep in his room on St. Thomas Island with a burning pain in his pelvis. He immediately called home to Liz, found out what was happening, and gave her medical advice.

The other incident occurred in 1959. Hunting for grant money for the new institute in Washington with Liz, John had a vivid experience of his father's consciousness, as if Dad wanted to talk to him. He phoned St. Paul that evening, but Dick's new wife, Elizabeth, objected to disturbing Mr. Lilly, who had already gone to bed. John waited until the next morning to call back. This time, the butler went to awaken Mr. Lilly and found him dead in bed, a beatific smile on his face. At seventy-three, after retirement from the bank and after marrying a second time, Dick had seemed bored and apathetic about life. John believed that his father had willed himself to die quietly in his sleep in order to escape.

All of these extraordinary incidents recommended to John the idea that by penetrating more deeply into one's own mind, one would come into contact with the entire universe. John theorized that there are, in a sense, two channels into an individual mind: a channel that connects with the local world through the physical sense organs, and a channel that connects with the entire universe, nonlocally. He summarized this idea later by writing, "Somehow, inside, we tune in to the universe outside," an idea very much in agreement with the thinking of C.G. Jung.

John had speculated in 1964 that his experiences in the isolation tank might have been, in effect, programmed by the nearby dolphins. He now realized that many of the experiences he had undergone might not have been entirely his own.

There were several ways to look at this possibility. According to the "leaky mind hypothesis," the mind, contained in a brain, in a body, in a particular location, can receive messages, or programs for experiences, from a distant source. A more radical version of the theory suggested that the mind itself may be able to briefly leave its brain and go elsewhere before returning.

Another perspective was the "uncontained mind," the view that the mind is naturally free to travel and only temporarily caught in a brain. This might account for his experience of the Beings, who seemed able to enter various brains, experiencing whatever occurred at a particular time and place to that mind/brain/body.

Since his first session in the isolation tank with LSD, John had been dimly aware that he might himself be one of those Beings, or somehow connected with such a Being. His guides seemed to hold conversations with a third Being who either was John or was somehow in charge of John. Perhaps one of these Beings was temporarily confused, merely thinking it was an eccentric scientist named John C. Lilly, pursuing a career and a personal spiritual quest on Earth. Or perhaps John was actually an agent controlled by one of the Beings. He considered many alternatives about their status and the nature of his relationship to them—from the possibility that they were aspects of his own psyche, to the notion that they were representatives of an advanced extraterrestrial civilization—but he avoided adopting any particular, limiting beliefs about it.

If the Beings could sample any mind and experience whatever was happening at that point in time and space, then the very notion of a separate individual existence, as well as our normal ideas about time and space, were meaningless. If some mind or network of minds were everywhere, in everything, there would no longer be any need to explain astonishing psychic experiences or so-called coincidences. Perhaps people were simply suffering from the *illusion* that they were separate individuals, while totally engaged in the experiences of "their" lives. Perhaps persons were actually mere *personas,* the masks of Greek drama through which the gods spoke.

Such notions were not unprecedented. The ancients had subscribed to pantheism, the belief that a god or gods were in everything. Some had believed in panpsychism, the view that Mind is in everything, not just within the brains of individual human beings.

Whatever explanation one chose, it was clear to John that the mind—or Mind—had a great deal of flexibility in both what it could do and how it could interpret or explain its activities. Any of the above could be the correct explanation, or just another more or less useful hypothesis.

In science, explanations are evaluated using the principle called "Occam's Razor": in essence, "go with the simplest explanation that works; discard all others." John's problem with this rule came from his awareness of the consequences of choosing a given explanation. In ordinary science, your current theory determines which experiments you undertake, and which experiments you never bother with. The result of an experiment is that the theory is either confirmed or shown to need revision. Yet, in developing a scientific approach to the domain of the mind, your theories or explanations will determine which *experiences* you will or will not have, no matter what experiments you perform. It is difficult to test a theory in this realm if your other beliefs limit the range of available experiences.

John was aware that explanations and theories are really beliefs about the universe and the mind. A particular belief may or may not be true, may or may not cause one to act in a certain way, but that belief will unquestionably set limits on what one can experience.

In following this chain of reasoning, John Lilly formulated a succinct statement about the nature of beliefs and the mind. As expressed later, in *The Center of the Cyclone,* it may be the single most famous statement he has ever made, and is often dubbed "Lilly's Law":

> In the province of the mind, what is believed to be true is true or becomes true, within certain limits to be found experientially and experimentally. These limits are further beliefs to be transcended. In the province of the mind, there are no limits.

John's next stop after Topeka was Dr. Ernest Hilgard's hypnosis lab at Stanford University, where he spent several weeks catching up on the current state of the art. Here he first heard talk of Esalen, an institute founded in 1962 by Michael Murphy and Richard Price, that was the prototypic "growth center" for exploring human potential. It was located 100 miles south at Big Sur, on the Pacific Coast.

John drove down the coast and enrolled in one of Esalen's seminars. It presented the idea that the "shattered mind" suggested by a psychiatric diagnosis of psychosis might actually be an episode of personal reorganization, from which a person could emerge with a higher level of integration and greater happiness. The seminar suggested that the best strategy might be to treat psychotic episodes supportively, rather than attempting to suppress them, as was standard psychiatric practice. The seminar brought to John's attention the writings of two famous psychiatrists who pioneered this approach: Thomas Szasz and R.D. Laing.

John left with the impression that Esalen was a place where new and unconventional ideas could be freely and safely explored, just as its founders had intended. John made a note to look them up on his next visit to California.

John next went east to the Maryland Psychiatric Research Center at Spring Grove State Hospital to assume a new post, Chief of Psychological Isolation and Psychedelic Research. The job had been arranged by a group of psychiatrists who had been investigating LSD at NIH while he was there. Many of them—including his friend Sandy Unger—were now continuing LSD research at Spring Grove, and, aware of John's current interest in LSD, they welcomed him.

The Maryland Psychiatric Research Center was one of very few institutions still authorized to conduct LSD research, but only under restrictive conditions. In testing the effects of LSD used with psychotherapy on chronic alcoholics, the doctors were allowed to give the patient exactly one dose of LSD. They were forbidden from taking it themselves. This stricture, running counter to the Bazett-Haldane medical research ethic to which he was so firmly committed, bothered John.

In spite of the rules, therapists on the project had tried LSD. John insisted that he could not participate in or understand the treatment program unless he took LSD under the same conditions as the patients. This plan was supported by Unger, who privately agreed to give John the full treatment.

After consulting with Robert Masters and Jean Houston, researchers who had experimented with LSD, hypnosis, and other techniques, John joined Unger for the training session. In a minimally distracting environment, the therapist was to push the patient in the direction of self-discovery, the principle being to use the LSD session to recognize those basic beliefs which were shaping one's personal reality. It had worked successfully in getting some "hopeless" alcoholics to stop drinking.

Under Sandy's guidance, John took a split dose of 300 micrograms of LSD, and sought to experience those beliefs most instrumental in shaping his life up to that point. He called the belief system he thus discovered "the Religion of Science": it was just what a naive and uncritical schoolboy could be expected to assimilate during the course of a scientific education, such as John's at Caltech in the 1930s. The catechism of the Religion of Science runs something like this:

> There is no God, meaning, or ordering intelligence in the universe. For no particular reason, the universe either began with a Big Bang or evolved from the continuous creation of matter. It has continued, in a random fashion, governed only by the laws of physics, to produce the rather improbable consequences we see today, including ourselves.

John's LSD-assisted imagination translated this creed into a vivid, wrenching experience of being trapped within a "Cosmic Computer" in which everything, including John, was totally controlled and determined by a hierarchy of increasingly more powerful programs, a system whose activity was nonetheless utterly meaningless and without purpose. Inside this hellish machine, John was merely one of the many smaller programs in an eternal scenario. As this particular experience finally began to wear off, John was granted visions of glamorous females. The powerful programs that controlled him said that if he followed their instructions, he would be rewarded with the love of a female robot.

This was the most painful experience John had ever undergone. It convinced him of two things: first, the Religion of Science was far too narrow a belief system; second, this schoolboy conception of scientific truth, proven inadequate by thirty years of adult experience and experiment, was still influencing him, despite the fact that he no longer consciously subscribed to it.

Why was this so? Was it simply that the earlier in life one adopted a belief, the harder that belief would be to change? Or was it that he had adopted the catechism of the Church of Science after his adolescent rejection of the catechism of the Catholic church? He had rejected the Catholic belief system when it conflicted with his emerging sexuality. His conflict with Catholicism wasn't with the grand idea of a meaningful universe ordered by a divine intelligence; nor was it with immortality, Guardian Angels, loving-kindness, or the Incarnation. It was between John's experience of sex and the church's identification of sex as the very embodiment of sin. In the process of throwing out that dirty bathwater, young John had thrown out the divine baby.

John realized that his rejection of Catholicism had created a void he had filled with an equally dogmatic and untestable belief system—the Religion of Science.

Belief systems compete in the human mind, and within each of us is a shifting battle for mental space. Certain beliefs mutually support patterns of behavior and ways of life. Any and all of these "programs" compete and form coalitions with other programs. John's adolescent development involved forming a coalition in which the Religion of Science was an ally, defending his expression of sexual behavior against the power of his earlier Catholic creed. Ever since, his life had been dominated by the implicit belief that if sex were not to be considered a sin, it must be part of the mechanistic chaos that was the atheistic universe of nineteenth-century, post-Newtonian science. As a result, he, and all the women he had been involved with, had been robots. Their universe was a sterile machine, driven by necessity, lacking meaning. The session with Unger, which John later described as "a guided tour of hell," was the turning point; John began to free his intimate relationships from the prison of the Religion of Science, as years earlier he had freed them from Catholic sex morality.

In addition to his disagreements with the restrictions governing research at Spring Grove, John felt a growing disillusionment with the MPRC as well as with the motives of many people in the scientific establishment. Several incidents contributed to this.

From his disbanded lab in Miami, John had shipped some valuable scientific equipment for use in his new lab. But upon his arrival at Spring Grove, John found about $25,000 worth of this equipment to be missing. Further investigation revealed that it had all been "appropriated" by some of the Spring Grove administrators, never to be returned.

So much for his welcome. Then, when John talked with the administrators about writing applications for research grants, he was advised to allot 60 percent of his grant money for "overhead"—that is, payment to the institution itself—leaving only 40 percent of the funds for research. He refused, and consequently never received any grant support whatsoever for his research at Spring Grove. (Subsequently, some of the administrators were revealed by NIH to have been misappropriating grant money for their personal use.)

John suddenly became aware of the way in which some corrupt institutions drained scarce public funds intended for scientific research. These were people who pretended to be practicing science while their actual motivations were otherwise. They contrasted starkly with the many dedicated people John had met at Penn, NIH, CRII, and in government—people whose basic orientation was "Get the job done," and whose attitude was always "Can do."

John began to feel that he would not remain at Spring Grove for long.

On his next trip to San Francisco, John met one of Esalen's founders, Michael Murphy, who sent him down to Esalen to look up cofounder Richard Price. "You'll probably find him sitting on the floor in the seminar on psychosis," said Mike. John did. Mike and Dick invited John to spend six weeks at Esalen to immerse himself in a broad range of experiences. As part of the arrangement, John would present a seminar on his discoveries with dolphins.

While in San Francisco, John heard of Alan Watts, a maverick philosopher said to have interests similar to his own. Watts, an ordained Episcopal clergyman, had embraced the spirit if not the letter of Zen Buddhism, and had written several books introducing Zen to Westerners. He had also authored *The Joyous Cosmology,* a book extolling his experiences with LSD and other psychedelic agents.

After introducing himself to Watts by telephone, John drove across the Golden Gate Bridge to Sausalito, a picturesque village on the northern side of the San Francisco Bay. Watts lived on a retired ferry boat, the *Vallejo,* moored at Gate 5 among a panoply of colorful houseboats on the Sausalito waterfront.

BIOGRAPHY

ALAN WILSON WATTS (1915–1973), a native of Kent, England, became fascinated with Buddhism in his teens, being influenced by D.T. Suzuki, J. Krishnamurti, and Fredric Spiegelberg, among others. In 1938 he emigrated to the United States to study Zen with Sokei-an Sasaki. Fond of religious ritual and spiritual counseling, he became an Episcopal priest and the chaplain of Northwestern University, a post from which he fled to California in 1952 to resume the study of oriental religion and philosophy. An author of great erudition and poetry, beginning in 1936 he produced a prodigious number of books: *The Spirit of Zen; The Legacy of Asia and Western Man; The Meaning of Happiness; The Theologia Mystica of Saint Dionysius; Behold the Spirit; Zen; Easter—Its Story and Meaning; The Supreme Identity; The Wisdom of Insecurity; Myth and Ritual in Christianity; The Way of Liberation in Zen Buddhism; The Way of Zen; Nature, Man and Woman; This Is It; Psychotherapy East and West; The Joyous Cosmology; The Two Hands of God; Beyond Theology: The Art of Godmanship; The Book: On the Taboo Against Knowing Who You Are; Does It Matter? (Essays on Man's Relation to Materiality); The Art of Contemplation; Erotic Spirituality;* and *Nonsense.*

His life is chronicled in two autobiographies, *In My Own Way* (1972) and *Cloud-Hidden, Whereabouts Unknown* (1973), as well as several postmortem biographies that criticize his life in various ways. Alan Watts was preeminently a practitioner of experimental philosophy—the art of adopting and living within various belief systems in order to learn their potentialities and their limits.

"Here is a man who is more ruthlessly rational than I am," said Watts, introducing John to his wife, Jano.

John found Watts brilliant, lively, and engaging (though scientifically unsophisticated), but hardly *ruthlessly* rational. He had tested Watts with a riddle that challenges a person's ability to arrive at a logical conclusion, unimpeded by emotional revulsion or social taboo. It took Watts three hours to solve the puzzle. In spite of this failure, however, they had a lively discussion about LSD and became friends.

Through Watts, Murphy, and Price, John became more closely linked with a network of influential West Coast people who were grappling with a new awareness of consciousness raised by LSD. These connections would open many doors for him.

One such door was opened by a prominent member of this network, Dr. Willis Harman of the Stanford Research Institute, whom John had met earlier. John entrusted his manuscript of *The Human Biocomputer: Programming and Metaprogramming,* a revision of CRII Scientific Research Report #0167, to Harman. Impressed, Harman passed it to his friend Stuart Brand, publisher of *The Whole Earth Catalog,* who decided to publish it as a pamphlet, advertised in his catalog. The little book was an immediate hit with the California illuminati, who bought out several reprintings. Eventually, it was published as a book by the Julian Press in 1972, under the title *Programming and Metaprogramming in the Human Biocomputer: Theory and Experiments.* John's stature among the members of his new network was growing rapidly.

After six weeks at Esalen and his own seminar on dolphins, Dick Price and Mike Murphy invited John to join the faculty. He quickly decided to cut his ties with the eastern Establishment and move west. In March 1969, he resigned from the Maryland Psychiatric Research Center—leaving all of his remaining laboratory equipment as a gift.

At Esalen he made many new friends and was exposed to a wide variety of ideas, practices, and experiences. He was confronted with the work of people like Fritz Perls, developer of Gestalt therapy; Bill Schutz, pioneer of encounter groups; as well as Virginia Stair, John Heider, and Steve and Bill Stroud. These Esalen-oriented therapists and group leaders, who were encouraging people to explore themselves and test their limitations through interaction with others, made a strong favorable impression on John. He formed a close friendship with Price, a student of Perls and a brilliant, resourceful Gestalt therapist himself. Ida Rolf, creator of a form of bodywork called Structural Integration, or "Rolfing," taught John how traumas are impressed in the musculature of the body and how they can be released. And Al Huang showed John the graceful flow of physical energy expressed in t'ai chi, a foundation of many oriental martial arts.

John's first encounter with Fritz Perls was unsettling. John had driven up the coast to Esalen from Los Angeles. At the little town of Morro Bay, he had stopped, found a men's clothing shop, and bought himself a blue jumpsuit that he wore out the door. After winding his way north through the breathtaking turns of Highway 1, he arrived at Esalen that afternoon. There, before dinner in the lodge, another man in a blue jumpsuit rushed up to him and demanded, "Who do you think you are, copying me?!"

John, standing his ground, introduced himself rather forcefully as Dr. John C. Lilly.

"Oh, you're the guy with the dolphins! I'm Dr. Frederik S. Perls. Want to have dinner with me?"

"No, you're too formidable," John replied.

They soon became friends.

John also came to know Dr. Richard Alpert, who had collaborated on the book *The Psychedelic Experience* with Timothy Leary and Ralph Metzner. He had been expelled with them from Harvard University in 1962, on the demonstrably false charge that they were giving psychedelics to undergraduates. Alpert's interpretation of LSD was spiritual; inspired by his psychedelic experiences, he traveled to India, found a guru, and undertook the life of a Hindu holy man and yogi under the name Ram Dass ("servant of God"). Back in the States, he attracted a large following of spiritual seekers, many inspired by LSD, who called him Baba, roughly translated as "Father" or "Papa."

John's first impression of Ram Dass formed while the holy man was engaged in a knock-down, drag-out fistfight with Dick Price at Gorda Ranch, Jan Brewer's mountainside retreat used by Esalen insiders. Dick, in a rage for some unknown reason, came charging up in a pickup truck, leapt out, tackled Ram Dass, and soon had him pinned with his face in the dust. Then Ram Dass turned the tables and pinned Dick, whose fury soon waned. Afterward John asked Ram Dass, "How does it make you feel when someone does that to you?"

"It makes me want to turn around and do the same thing to him." This convinced John that Ram Dass was for real.

Later, during a seminar, Ram Dass said to John, "You look like you need spiritual help. You don't look happy."

John replied, "I do this on purpose, so I don't attract followers."

Ram Dass first introduced John to Patanjali's *Yoga Sutras,* the 2,500-year-old textbook on Yoga. John collected a dozen translations; his favorite turned out to be *The Science of Yoga* by

RICHARD ALPERT (1931–   ) was raised in New England and in 1953 took his doctorate in psychology at Stanford University. Beginning in 1956 he codirected the Psychedelic Research Project at Harvard, where he collaborated with Ralph Metzner and Timothy Leary and coauthored with them *The Psychedelic Experience* (1963), the most popular guidebook on the use of LSD.

In 1967, Alpert made a pilgrimage to India and became a follower of Hindu guru Neem Karoli Baba, who gave him the religious name Ram Dass. Once back in the United States, Ram Dass proved highly influential in promoting the interpretation of psychedelic experience as a religious phenomenon, along the lines of Hinduism and Yoga. His best-known book, *Be Here Now,* introduced a large occidental audience to oriental practices of meditation and personal development.

I.K. Taimni, an Indian biochemist. John immersed himself in this translation and attempted to synthesize its teachings with those of the contemporary yogi Ramana Maharshi (whose work Ram Dass had also recommended) and with his own concept of the human biocomputer. The Center for Advanced Study in the Behavioral Sciences, near Stanford University, eventually provided support for John's efforts to write a book about his experiences with the *Yoga Sutras.* Over time this work changed direction and eventually became *The Center of the Cyclone.*

John continued as a resident, associate, and student- or teacher-in-residence at Esalen until his departure for Arica, Chile, in June 1970. He would continue to be featured regularly in the institute's catalog of seminars, and the center would continue to offer him a second home and an occasional retreat from the pressures of civilization.

During his tenure there, Esalen provided John a new kind of space in which to experiment on himself—among other people rather than in the solitude of the isolation tank. He fell in love several times, and wrote poetry that reflected his efforts to define and find an ideal mate and to grapple with his confusions about love, sex, and reproduction.

PRIME DIRECTIVE: REPRODUCE!

15 Dec. 1969

Is the purpose you and I are here insemination?
Is our dyad to produce a child?
Is there anything else for us?
Sweet meeting, tender melting, ecstatic fusion.
The sweet mystery of you to be explored.
The curious me wanting to love-know you.
Are we each driven only to reproduce?
Fucking, mating, ecstatic union, love,
Tender regard, giving, being given to.
Swing in, leaving self, ego, for each.
Is this the big picture?
Us, plus children?
Are we here on mother earth to propagate?
When you no longer pregnant want to be, What then?
What do you want to be then?
Failure of fertility, hysterectomy, what then?
Do I then strive to place my sperm in another, pregnant to
    make?
Where is the end of this trip?
In me there are arising new (for me) yet old (for me) strivings
    for a dyad.
A dyad beyond "reproduce!"
A dyad to travel with you, learn with you, of far spaces, far
    beings, beyond the prime directive of reproduction.
To get there, to that dyad, no vagina with uterus
attached is needed.
To get there, a vagina may be needed.
Is yours connected to you as a memory
back to "reproduce!" or
Can you transcend the directive, can I?
Let's have fun, trying to understand.

BEYOND "REPRODUCE!": SUPRA-SELF DYAD

15 Dec. 1969

We, in this dyad, each have already reproduced.
You have children made, as have I, each with another,
    not us.
You can no longer become pregnant.

With you I cannot impregnate.
We can love, fuck, ecstatic union.
Alter many such, what then?
Are we here for sensation's sake?
Can we go beyond, through us and sex?
Where is "beyond"?
Far out spaces, greater beings-entities than us, beckon and
      call.
Together can we go to them, or is it each of us alone?
Let us try, together, to so go.
Let us face our hindrances, evasions, blocks, and soar,
      together.
The hindrance of body ecstasy tied here convert to spirit
      travel energy there.
The hindrance of planet earth, mother ties to her bosom, use
      constructively.
The evasion of loss of independent self, convert to dyad
      greatness.
Together fusing into one to travel as two-in-one.
No rivalry, no control for each separate over other, one
      directed by each of two, fused.
A dream, a fantasy? Poetry?
No.
A program, a metaprogram for a Supra-self dyad.

That year, John learned that Constance Tors had died. Her
body was found in bed, large quantities of sleeping pills and
tranquilizers in her stomach and in her bloodstream. She had told
friends that she was ready to go on, that she had no interest in
inhabiting an aging human body. John wrote:

Here and now, I've lost her.
No more a "thee and thou" with her.
Her great beauty of body, mind and soul,
Our past encounters, now only stored, in me in them.
Yet I grieve, and as grieving, hope.
The dark place in her took her away,
It won the battle for her bodily life,
Removed her from her children, husband, lover.
Where is she now? Lost in a limbo of her
own belief constructed?

Shining in full self-realization out there, in here?
Readying to possess another body?
Preparing to reincarnate in embryo?
Blindly stumbling in perpetual dark?
Led by them, out there, to new high levels?

(excerpted from *Her Death,* 1969)

CHAPTER 11

ESSENCE

May 1970, age 55.

John arrives at the clean, modern house on the outskirts of Arica, Chile, where he has come for his first encounter with Oscar Ichazo. He has traveled all the way from California to meet this spiritual teacher, who has been the subject of awe-inspiring reports. John is admitted to the apartment by Ichazo's mistress. Some minutes later, Ichazo emerges from the small bedroom that serves as his meditation cell and strides into the room with his gaze fixed on infinity, clearly in an unusual state of consciousness.

"What's going on?" John asks.

Ichazo replies convincingly, "I've been talking with God."

John knows he has come to the right place.

JOHN LILLY'S NEXT adventure was touched off by a letter from Santiago, Chile, written by Claudio Naranjo, an Esalen faculty member, prominent psychiatrist, and pioneer in the psycho-therapeutic use of LSD and more exotic substances.

In 1969 Claudio had traveled first to Santiago, Chile, to study with Ichazo at his Institutio de Gnosologia, billed as a center for the revival of an ancient esoteric school of mysticism. Gnosticism—from the Greek word *gnosis*, meaning "seeking to know" or "knowledge"—was an early form of Christianity which taught that every individual had the ability to directly experience God, without the mediation of priests or the institutional hierarchies of churches.

Ichazo and his group in Chile were developing their own version of Gnosticism, incorporating elements of Sufism, Tibetan Buddhism, Zen, and Gurdjieffian teachings. Oscar himself, by his own account the protégé of a mysterious group of "Masters" of esoteric traditions and mystery schools, was now beginning to teach and promulgate the tradition. His program of spiritual teachings and personal-growth techniques would soon become famous in the United States and Europe, as the ARICA movement, symbolized by a colorful meditation diagram and trademark—a gold circle within an ivory circle within a magenta hexagon, against a square blue background. During 1969 and 1970, the program was just getting started with an elite group in Chile.

Naranjo's letter to John suggested that Ichazo had methods for systematically entering special states of being. Some of these states were quite familiar to John; others he had yet to explore.

Naranjo returned to Esalen and, in January 1970, began sharing what he had learned with other residents. John learned some of the techniques and found that he was able to quit smoking by using one of them, an exercise called a "mentation." Impressed by the efficacy of these techniques from the mysterious Chilean sage, he also learned his first smattering of Spanish: *Fumar est muy mal; no fumar est muy bueno.*

The explicitly spiritual orientation of Oscar's teachings appealed to John, who was wearying of the human potential menu available at Esalen. After sampling its best, he had concluded that Esalen was mostly about human social interaction: relaxing and smoothing out the wrinkles in one's interpersonal act, to ease the ride in human-centered, terrestrial reality.

Although becoming quite adept at this, John felt he was getting nowhere in his search for Reality. While there was much talk of LSD experiences at Esalen, little of it approached the depth of his previous experiences or the rigor of his scientific approach to the subject. Furthermore, Ram Dass had given him a glimpse of the mystic's path as a new context for his search for Reality. Oscar's mystical school might supply the next step on his search.

And so in May 1970, John flew to Chile to meet with Oscar for a week and size up his prospects for entering the mystery school.

In their first contact—"essence to essence," as John later

described it—he felt an immediate rapport and intimacy that made him feel suddenly and totally good, an unprecedented feeling that he later described as one of "singing inside." There was something mysteriously *right* about Oscar, about meeting him at this point in John's life.

John showed him an early version of the human biocomputer manuscript. With apparent delight, Oscar read John's account of the spaces he had entered using LSD and the isolation tank and he seemed impressed with what he took to be evidence of how far John had gone on his own path of spiritual development.

Oscar exclaimed, "Man, you don't have any karma left! Maybe just a few grains."

John replied, "Yeah, but they're hard as diamonds!" (In the Buddhist-Hindu tradition, spiritual progress is associated with freeing oneself from the consequences of past action, or karma.)

Oscar and four students demonstrated some of their techniques, including one exercise that sent John on an vivid past-life recollection. John felt that he had found a kind of colleague on the path in Oscar, who had apparently experienced many of the same unusual states of being and spaces as John had. Oscar was both a likable, engaging personality and a formidable spiritual teacher of great depth and understanding, John thought.

John returned to California to prepare for a lengthy stay in Chile, and came back the next month to join the esoteric school founded by Oscar.

At this point, Arica was a rapidly growing fishing port on Chile's Pacific coast, near the border with Peru. In ten years, it had grown from 14,000 to 100,000 residents, most living in old packing crates. Arica was wild, rough, and uncomfortable, a noisy, smoky sprawl in a desert by the sea. Behind it, the Andes rose steeply to their highest ridges, and beyond the mountains was the Amazon basin. It was a land of Incas, coca, Indian flutes, and sure-footed llamas.

One might imagine that joining an esoteric school here involves a trek to a picturesque monastery hung high in the Andes where devoted, robed brethren pace with silent dignity through corridors sanctified by time, sharing a life of communal harmony in the ancient caves and cloisters. The school at Arica was nothing like this. It was a "monastery without walls," spread all over town, with students, housed independently, converging for their scheduled meetings in such mundane locales as abandoned factory buildings or the lecture halls of the local hospital. It was more an ad hoc "guerilla monastery," utilizing the available urban space. Devotees shuttled between scheduled meetings in lurching little taxicabs and smoky, sputtering buses.

For the first month John stayed in the local *hosteria,* a hotel located on the fishing pier. It was miserably cold, damp, and proved so inhospitable that a few of John's fellow students staying there became ill enough to have to drop out and leave Arica. But John stuck it out long enough to begin the course, and, after a month, he moved to a small rented home in a new housing development on the Azapa Road, close to the Universidad del Norte campus.

The grueling training program at Arica ran from eight in the morning until midnight. Schedule and daily life were rigidly controlled by Oscar's program, including a strict, high-protein diet at group meals. The only break came at Saturday afternoon "pig-out," when the students gathered at the Penguino Café to indulge in otherwise forbidden foods such as ice cream.

The daily routine at this spiritual boot camp included "the gym," about two hours of vigorous exercises incorporating elements of gymnastics, hatha-yoga, Sufi dancing, and Gurdjieff exercises. This was punctuated by Sundays devoted to "the pampas" (Spanish for "plains"), a set of especially arduous outdoor exercises. The entire class would troop to a quiet patch of desert some five miles north of town, on a shelf at the top of a cliff towering half a mile above the sea. Here each individual would perform such assigned activities as walking in a circle for hours carrying a heavy stone while chanting, meditating, and breathing in a prescribed manner.

Oscar himself spent an enormous amount of time meditating, following his own prescriptions. He also communed privately with individuals, taking a direct interest in each student and establishing significant positive contact with each one.

In addition to prescribing complex exercises and rituals, Oscar delivered a complicated belief system in a series of lectures. In essence, it was a system of explanatory principles—a framework to interpret the meaning of the experiences that resulted from the unusual things the group was doing. It consisted largely of a vocabulary whose meaning would become apparent by performing the exercises and undergoing the experiences to which it applied, as the Kath Hill Exercise below illustrates.

The Kath Hill Exercise

According to Oscar, there are three primary energy centers in the body, the Oth, the Path, and the Kath. There is a special hill where the Kath, located in the belly about two inches below the navel, is exercised.

John selects a rock with a distinctive shape. Holding the rock in his hand, he salutes the hill. Then he bounds up the steep slope, imagining that his Kath center is pulling him up the hill. At the top of the hill, he projects his Kath center from his body into the rock. He throws the rock containing his Kath down the hill and runs after it. At the bottom he finds the rock again and puts his Kath back into his body.

This vocabulary differed from anything John had encountered previously, although it had aspects which resembled other arcane systems such as Yoga. There was a kind of astrology, related to personality types. There were ideas about levels of consciousness that vaguely resembled what John had read in his study of Indian Yoga. There were technical names and mantras related to centers of energy in different parts of the body. Ichazo had a fondness for the number nine, and tended to group his reference points in sets of nine items.

John probably had the most developed scientific background among Arica participants, and hence a distinctive vocabulary with which to think about the kinds of experiences being explored there. As the training progressed, Ichazo's system of concepts and explanatory principles became superimposed on his own, resulting in a synthesis—more precisely a syncretism, or union of diverse beliefs—which found expression in his later works, including *The Center of the Cyclone*. For years, John would continue to incorporate aspects of Oscar's esoteric vocabulary into his own.

One such example was Oscar's use of the terms *ego* and *Essence*. Much work at Arica was devoted to the goal of "ego reduction." This sense of the term *ego* was not closely related to that used in Freud's psychoanalytic writings or subsequent psychiatric jargon. Rather, it approximated the negative connotation popularly found in such words as *egotism, egotripping,* or *egocentricity*—a narrow, anxious, defensive aspect of the self, concerned with self-justification and triumph over others.

According to Oscar, everything that brought one down, into "lower" states of consciousness, was, in one way or another, classified as ego. Simply put, his program aimed to clarify and define any deviations, excesses, or imbalances caused by ego. The ego would be balanced, smoothed of its rough edges, and minimized through his training in order to allow one's brain/mind to run more smoothly in daily life and to increase one's ability to enter higher states of consciousness more easily.

There was also a higher self or "Essence" in this system, at the opposite pole from ego—a higher aspect of self that could be experienced when ego was minimized. Thus, the system created a context for more frequent and extensive contact with this expanded state of being.

John's synthesis connected Oscar's use of *ego* with his own term *program* to form *ego programs*—those belief systems, considered as brain "software," that maintained a particular aspect of the self. Similarly, *essence* became *essence programs.* To John, the important difference was that ego and essence were not seen as separate entities, but rather as *modes of operation of the self*—reference points on a scale, against which a self can measure its functional position. The self is the agent that moves, sometimes voluntarily, sometimes under compulsion by various forces, across this scale. John's goal wasn't to get rid of ego but rather to spend as much time as possible near the top end of the scale. This model corresponded better with his actual experience of the exercises, in which he sensed himself approaching, or in extreme cases merging with, the Essence level, or alternatively falling into the more limited sphere of ego, with its claustrophobic paranoia and emphasis on issues of survival.

Oscar's concept of ego clashed with the more conventional definitions of ego offered in psychology and in John's psychoanalytic training, and thus failed to make a significant impression on him. On the other hand, the concept of Essence struck him as an important idea that conventional psychology had missed, a vital link bridging the gap between Western psychology and John's highest, most profound experiences. In his mind, the term became connected with the Beings he had met earlier as guides or guardians, with the Being or higher self he had discovered within himself, with the Catholic angels of his childhood, and with the universal belief in a soul or spirit within people.

Oscar also classified different states of consciousness according to numerical "vibrational levels," following a proposal of Gurdjieff. Oscar used a spectrum of nine states, beginning with the highest state, labeled with the number 3. The series of lower states which followed were labeled by doubling the number of the previous state, thus:

$$3 \quad 6 \quad 12 \quad 24 \quad 48 \quad 96 \quad 192 \quad 384 \quad 768$$

The last state was considered a particularly hellish mode of consciousness.

John redesigned this scale in two ways: First, he assigned positive and negative values "+" and "−" to states on either side of the middle of the range. Second, the more extreme the state, the lower the number. Thus the highest state was called +3, and the lowest −3. This made state 48 the neutral, more-or-less ordinary state of daily consciousness, ±48. As a result, John's version of Ichazo's scale looked like this:

$$+3 \quad +6 \quad +12 \quad +24 \quad \pm48 \quad -24 \quad -12 \quad -6 \quad -3$$

State +24, for example, occurs when one is smoothly performing an activity which comes easily and naturally, and is experienced as somewhat accelerated and exhilarated. One's body flows, one's mind runs without resistance, hesitation, doubt, or concern. Moving up the scale, the next state is +12, best described as rapture or, perhaps more familiarly, as "getting high." One is aware of one's body shaping physical experience, but the body is without weight, resistance, or pain. The body and the surrounding world are perceived as luminous energy rather than as solid matter. One's mind is filled only with the highest thoughts of delight, humor, or awe.

The transition to +6 is far more dramatic. Awareness of the body and the physical world is lost. One experiences oneself as a concentrated point of consciousness, intelligence, and radiance. Other individuals are experienced similarly. As an independent being one is free to travel in inner and outer space as a "quantum observer" that can go anywhere in the brain, body, throughout the surrounding environment, or the cosmos beyond. Note that wherever one travels in this state, one is still a separate and distinct identity. However, with the transition to +3, even one's sense of identity disappears. One drops all the concerns and memories of an individual being and merges into a network spread out across the cosmos. One feels like an anonymous part of some larger entity, which is perhaps the universe as a whole, perhaps God.

Each of these states has its corresponding inverse on the negative side of the scale, with similar, though unpleasant qualities to the experience. For instance, −24 occurs when one performs a difficult task that the body and mind resist; in 6 the loss of body awareness is frightening, while in −3, the loss of personal identity is experienced as terrifying instead of blissful.

This system is presented in exquisite detail in *The Center of the Cyclone* and is referred to in many of John's subsequent writings. Compartmentalizing experience into discrete states or levels allows one to program rapid transitions between clearly marked categories. The scheme is similar to drawing a map to let one find their way around some territory more easily. Alternately, it resembles constructing a system of categories to better organize a group of data.

When one maps or categorizes, one chooses to draw somewhat arbitrary distinctions in order to construct a useful description. Preferably, the distinctions drawn and the features thus highlighted or named correspond reasonably well to the most prominent, significant, and essential characteristics of the territory itself, at least for one's purposes of the moment.

Once a good map exists, giving someone directions then becomes relatively easy. Intimate familiarity with such a system allows one to make sense out of the following kind of statement: "If I start out in state +12 and move *this* way, I expect to land in state +6." Otherwise, a working technical vocabulary can easily sound like nonsensical jargon to the uninitiated outsider.

*T*he Center of the Cyclone recounts John's Arica experience in such a way as to give the impression that Oscar's esoteric techniques alone accounted for John's colorful inner adventures. John never mentions LSD in connection with his Arica activities, except to refer occasionally to his earlier experiments by way of comparison. In fact, however, LSD was a key ingredient during his six months in Chile. On his own initiative, but without discouragement from Oscar or the others (many of whom had had recent psychedelic experience), he dosed himself with LSD about every four weeks. The consistent infusion of LSD readily explains the deep impression, or *imprint,* the training left on him.

Despite common misconceptions of esoteric schools as superior alternatives to psychedelic drugs, John's use of LSD in the Arica context can be understood from both historical and scientific perspectives.

Historically, many esoteric traditions as well as some religions originally used drugs; many still do to this day. One of the oldest documented references comes from the sixth century, in the *Yoga Sutras* of Patanjali. The key passage is found in chapter four, verse one: "The higher [psychic] powers are developed from heredity, *psychoactive plants* [aussasdi, *or "light-containing plants"*], the power of words and mental concentration, the power of self-discipline, and self-induced trance." A number of scholars believe that many of the mystery religions revolved around controlled, programmed psychedelic experiences. Even the wafer consumed during the Christian mass, considered theologically equivalent to the flesh of Christ, has been argued to be a vestige of a Gnostic ceremony using psychedelic mushrooms.

Many of those who had spiritual experiences after using LSD in the 1960s and 1970s turned to esoteric traditions to provide a context from which they could gain a better perspective on what had happened to them. They sought both a philosophical position which accepted these experiences and addressed the issues they raised and, as well, a systematic discipline to guide their drug use and structure their experiments. Some wanted to use spiritual teachings as an *alternative* to psychedelic drugs; others preferred to use such traditions as an *adjunct* to psychedelics. Oscar Ichazo's school, with its explicit system of beliefs and its program of exercises, filled the bill for both groups.

From a scientific perspective, on the other hand, John's search for Reality had become a search for *operational* tools to reliably access and interpret the unusual states he had experienced throughout his life. In this context, *operational* refers to a set of directions or a map which works whether or not one believes in the concepts it uses. One can, for example, follow a recipe for baking an angel food cake, and enjoy the result, whether one understands the chemical changes the ingredients undergo, or, instead, believes that it is made with the help of real angels. In either case, the recipe is an operational procedure that works.

John's previous experiments had provided him with two powerful tools for exploring varied states of consciousness: LSD and the isolation tank. Both could be considered "hardware"; what he was seeking was software, programs or belief systems, to use them more effectively.

Part of the problem was that the experiences were too *big*, too overwhelming to produce reliable, reproducible results. A psychedelic state in which anything and everything seems equally possible may result in an excessive sense of instability, experienced as chaos, insecurity, or terror. Or the experience could be so vast that one has difficulty remembering it all.

In contrast, an effective scientific experiment tests certain specific issues without calling every assumption into question at once. The designer attempts to leave some room for new knowledge to enter, but not so much that we lose track of what the experiment was originally supposed to be about.

As one might expect from its history, esoteric training is synergistic with psychedelic drugs; systematized, repeated rituals can mold the shape of inner experience into reliable, repeatable patterns. Moreover, such training can make the experience less terrifying, and hence less distracting for accomplishing some experimental purpose.

What John had previously lacked and Ichazo provided was a permissive, accepting environment for his LSD experiences, as well as a rigorous, experimental design strategy (the rituals and exercises) to guide and shape his experiences. The results were not especially new; the states were the same, and even the particular phenomena experienced were very similar to the pre-Arica experiments. What John was seeking here by melding Oscar's system and his own was a methodology to systematize, regularize, and integrate the states he had discovered earlier.

The Monk's Hood Exercise below is a meditation prescribed by Oscar. It is followed by the Isolation Box, a variation of the isolation tank, which John contributed to Oscar's program at Arica.

The Monk's Hood Exercise

John goes into a field and kneels in prayer. He pulls the heavy brown cloth of a monk's hood over his head, cutting off the sight of the outside world. As his prayer deepens, he feels himself in his body. Yet, at the same time, he is concentrated in an intense point of consciousness in the darkness. Soon he is joined on either side by his two Guides, who are also intense points of consciousness. From the sun comes a shaft of warmth, radiance, and love. John feels himself fusing with the Guides. The fused Being moves up the radiant shaft toward the sun.

The Isolation Box

John is lying on his back in a narrow box that measures 2 by 2 by 7 feet. It cuts off light and sound, but is not nearly as relaxing as the isolation tank. He feels the weight of his body on the thin mattress beneath him. His limbs are stiff and immobile in the dark, stuffy, confining space. This box could become physical torture as the low-level discomforts accumulated.

John centers himself in his Kath. He passes briefly into the state of being he calls —3—in other words, pure hell. He is entirely in the grips of a paranoid cosmic conspiracy, a small and powerless program within a vast and meaningless computer, similar to his 1968 LSD session with Sandy Unger. But there is one small, crucial difference: This time he knows where he is. In that recognition lies the basis for a transition.

He centers himself again, and immediately flips into +3, a heavenly state that feels as if he were one of the joyous co-creators of the universe, working with and within God. Having mastered that transition, John knows that he need never fear again.

John felt his experiences at Arica helped him to find his own center, the eye of his storm of Being. He decided that this center was both his ultimate origin and his continuing sanctuary. He wrote: "The center of the cyclone is that rising, quiet, central, low-pressure place in which one can learn to live eternally. Just outside of this center is the rotating storm of one's own ego, competing with other egos in a furious high-velocity circular dance . . . one's self-created hells are outside the center. In the center of the cyclone one is off the wheel of karma, of life, rising to join the Creators of the Universe, the Creators of us. . . ."

Early on in his stay at Arica, John began to notice some disturbing aspects developing around the group immersed in Arica's closed society and prescribed routines, events that raised his scientific skepticism and doubts about the nature of what was occurring there. For instance, Oscar's program seemed to encourage a very high degree of reliance on the leader's judgment and perception instead of one's own, as the following exercise makes clear.

The I Listen and I Obey Exercise

John is about to perform an exercise intended to develop confidence in the "safety" of following instructions literally blindly, relying on the judgment of the author of the instructions for one's survival, instead of relying on one's own perception.

John stands at the beginning of the "I listen and I obey" course. It is an uphill walk, steep at first; toward the top it levels out, and ends in a cliff that plunges 1,000 meters to the Pacific Ocean below. He closes his eyes and begins walking up the hill to the cliff.

He coordinates his walking and breathing with repeated recitation of the words, "I listen and I obey." Every seven steps, he stops and listens silently. Eyes closed, he gradually approaches the cliff.

As per instructions, when he feels the path leveling off, he opens his eyes. Before him he sees the edge. He stops.

As far as John was concerned, Oscar's system was operational talk, a vocabulary providing instructions for reaching various states of consciousness and discussing the results. It was a map—but it was not the territory it described. As such, it was perfectly acceptable to him. At first, he had enthusiastically absorbed this new vocabulary and followed the program to the letter, just as he had memorized the Catholic Mass and Creed in childhood, the thousands of names of parts of the human body in anatomy class, or the complex procedures of neurosurgery.

But this attitude changed as John realized the other students were taking Oscar's system differently. Lacking experience with the scientific idea of operational talk, they were taking whatever arcane scheme Oscar pronounced as an objective description of reality, the very nature of higher consciousness, instead of as a series of rules and procedures in a game.

John felt that they were becoming obsessed with the methodology as a belief system. His own goal was to reach new states of being, and to demonstrate, communicate, and share these states. The beliefs were unimportant, except as operational tools used to reach these new states. Whatever doctrinal path took one there was equally valid.

John often heard fellow students complaining about how difficult it was to "go through this gate," referring to a metaphor Oscar frequently used for the training program. When one of them told John, "I feel like we're all going through a gate, and you're ahead of me in line," he retorted, "Well, why don't you just go around the gate?"

Instead of merely providing a path, beliefs can themselves become the destination. This tendency has severe pitfalls. An experience is mistakenly attributed to a teacher or teaching, and a student then stops looking within him- or herself for the real source of the experience. As a result, a student comes to depend on the teacher and system, losing access to alternative methods of interpretation and self-control.

Some of these tendencies among the Arica students derived from Oscar himself, who treated his own eclectic beliefs as if they were an ancient, unquestionable tradition. Other methods of explanation simply did not matter to him. All the while firmly, quietly, convinced of his system, Oscar remained charming, calm, and unflappable—hardly a fanatic.

For John, this was the frustrating paradox: Oscar seemed like a man totally open to new experience, respecting experience as the ultimate teacher, yet apparently so convinced of even the most minute details of his belief system that he was uninterested in considering any other model or explanatory principles. His consummately scientific, empirical, experiential approach was keenly contrasted with his entirely unscientific belief system, closed as it was to revision or comparison with other systems. This was disappointing for John, because in Oscar he thought he had found someone with whom he could share not only his experiences but also his ideas about them.

John had discovered this inflexibility early on, when Ichazo would brush aside any of John's theories in a friendly fashion to return the conversation to the confines of his own vocabulary. In a passage from his journal, later published in *Simulations of God,* John wrote: "[Oscar's] sincerity is hard to match. He really believes in these assumptions as true, objectively true. I have reached a saturation point at which I cannot stomach this way of thinking at all. My mood is to reject it and start all over."

John dealt with this conceptual rigidity by relating what happened to him in purely experiential terms. He realized that all that mattered was operating in the prescribed manner and arriving at the prescribed results. He wrote: "So I do not have to . . . swallow uncritically Oscar's traditional assumptions-beliefs to do his trip. As before, with LSD in 1964, I did not swallow the old psychiatric beliefs and found new knowledge; so with Oscar I do not need to believe in his system—just do the trip and work on theory on my own. . . . It's what Oscar DOES, not what he SAYS, that's true and worth study."

Contributing to John's growing reservations about Arica was his awareness that he was being programmed by the group activity around him. While his previous work had been oriented toward self-programming, at Arica he was being programmed by other people; most of the esoteric work was conducted in the heart of a group with which he shared most of his waking hours. In *The Center of the Cyclone,* John described his concerns:

> I did not like the idea of being in a closed group, esoteric or
> otherwise. I have pursued my own path, learning from whom-
> ever and wherever I could. In my experience, the politics
> inherent in many group decisions lowers the quality and ef-
> fectiveness of the action. The experienced, wise, energetic,
> intelligent individual functioning in a loose coalition with
> others in a wide network is far more effective than he is in
> a tightly organized group, or so it seems to me.

When one day Oscar announced that he would no longer personally lead the group but was turning the training over to his senior students, John knew it was time to go.

By December 1970 John was quite adept at applying the amalgam of Oscar's and his own systems, and on the thirteenth he experimented with a large dose of LSD:

I started out by riding through the body power and body sex spaces without giving in to either one. I allowed the equivalent of a grand mal seizure to take place while maintaining full consciousness. Somehow, now, I could stand the seizure-like activity far better than I had ever been able to before. ... I was suddenly precipitated into the power and creation space of state +3. ... I am a thin layer of all those beings in +3, mingling, connected with one another in a spherical surface around the whole known universe. Our "backs" are to the void. We are creating energy, matter and life at the interface between the void and all known creation.

In addition to using his revision of Ichazo's scale of consciousness levels, John refers to the spaces of *body sex* and *body power,* states of inner experience reached through two of the *somatic programs* he had identified in the human biocomputer. Corresponding to its respective interpretation, each program generates behavior—i.e., signals to various muscles and glands and other brain centers instructing them to respond in ways consistent with each interpretation. When one of these programs is fully operating, you experience the corresponding reality as the main content of consciousness.

These inner experiences, John felt, grew out of neurological programs manifested as networks of nerve cells in the brain. Each program interprets the raw data of experience—sensations from the skin, muscles, and viscera, as well as the state of the brain—in its own unique way and generates corresponding behavior. The result is an experience in the mind of reality as defined by the particular program.

The body power program, for example, defines a reality often experienced in athletics in which one feels "I am a strong and powerful creature; I am exerting myself and asserting myself in the physical world."

When the body sex program is running, you experience the following as the most compelling reality: (1) your body as a sex object; (2) your body as an instrument of sex; (3) yourself as a lover, beloved, mate, seducer, seductress, seduced, pursuer, pursued, flirt, impassioned one; (4) all the sensations associated with the type of sex you are engaged in—usually pleasurable, seductive, compulsive; (5) any sensations associated with unsuccessful, delayed, incomplete, or unsatisfying sexual activity—usually unpleasant, frustrated, strung-out, or tense; (6) the gross psychic states associated with sex, such as longing, hunger, satiation, enthusiasm, dominance, submissiveness, protectiveness, protectedness, vulnerability, gratitude, generosity, greed (and for some people, embarrassment, shame, guilt, disgust, contempt, sadism, debasement, degradation, filth, pain, hatred); (7) the subtle psychic states associated with sex, such as elation, fusion, divinity, salvation, cosmic union, devotion, self-realization, completion, existential freedom, eternity, deja vu; and (8) in some cases orgasm, with all the gross, subtle, physical, and psychic sensations and the states it can entail, in various combinations and subsets.

For some people, in some circumstances, the two programs, body power and body sex, could be mixed, running at the same time. This would produce an experiential (and observable) reality like "Super Heros." The movie *Red Sonya* depicts what happens when the two programs are combined, or actively compete.

In John's experience of December 13, as his energy level rose, these two very essential programs became activated and "invited" him to enter the particular realities each defines. Eschewing these two states as possible realities of himself, he passed rapidly through these "spaces" and moved on to an even more intense phase of undifferentiated activation of brain programs and neural system—muscular movement rather like an epileptic seizure, but without loss of consciousness. Then he peaked into "the power and creation state," which he designates +3.

After six months at Arica, John retreated into the desert for three days of solitude, prayer, and meditation. He asked for divine guidance in determining his future course: to continue as part of Oscar's training group or go his own way? Finally the answer came, with force and conviction: What he came for, he had completed; he felt a pull to return to California.

When John announced his decision, Ichazo acknowledged it and said that he looked forward to their next meeting: "Farewell, John. Via con Dios!"

The group, however, was disappointed. Several members felt that John was abandoning a great movement as it was beginning to take form. To them, with two more months of training ahead before they could be judged ready to go out into the world and spread the teaching, John's early departure could only mean either that he was in some way ahead of them on the path or that he was leaving with his work incomplete.

But for John, the Arica episode was just one more class in a lifelong course of continuing education, one more belief system to evaluate and incorporate in a mind that had mastered the art of changing beliefs like suits of clothes. For many of the others, Arica had opened a new way of being, and for them it was the site of a religious conversion.

Despite the group pressure, John left Arica at the end of December and caught a plane to Los Angeles. He realized that he had resisted a temptation that would never again attract him— the temptation to immerse himself entirely in any programmed reality, whether provided by himself or any other individual or group. The skills, training, and environment offered by Arica could have absorbed him in the world of the internal reality forever; instead, he had chosen to return to the greater world beyond. He had emerged from the cohesion of a cultlike group as a free agent.

On the ground in L.A., John caught a taxi and joined the traffic pattern of the great metropolis, throbbing with diverse life and divergent consciousness. He entered the legendary Los Angeles freeway system and sped northward among thousands of souls pursuing their own dreams, taking their chances with the external reality.

After experiencing the extreme states of +3 and −3 under monastic conditions at Arica, John realized that he was ready for a partnership of souls with a female human: *dyadic fusion*. He had distrusted the idea since early childhood, coming to believe that the physical exigencies of sexual intercourse and procreation were all that relationships could reasonably be expected to offer. He had eventually come to think that love was merely an evanescent high which lasted only as long as all went well.

Now, something had changed. Perhaps it was the realization of a higher capacity for unity in conscious beings—a union of essences—beyond the separateness of individual physical bodies. In this light, the union of two bodies and two lives could be seen as the manifestation and recognition of a such a higher union.

John was ready to find it.

CHAPTER 12

DYAD

February 1971, age 56.

   On the seventh day of the month, one of the most severe earthquakes in modern history strikes Los Angeles, swaying skyscrapers and showering shards of window glass on downtown sidewalks. The quake, centered at Sylmar, twenty-six miles north of downtown on Interstate 5, measures 6.6 on the Richter scale. Collapsing freeway overpasses crush vehicles and close the interstate, the main route connecting Los Angeles with central and northern California. At least sixty-one people are killed and an unknown number injured.

   In a house in Hollywood, the Sylmar earthquake throws John Lilly out of bed and into Alternity.

   Alternity is the place, state, or domain where all possibilities stand open to the self. What one sees is a very wide array of discrete possibilities—potential realities selected from an infinity of dimensions—each of them an entire future life. Alternity "just happens" to people sometimes, and then, without fully understanding what is going on, they fall back into a single future, and continue to live within its narrow confines.

   The processes of Alternity are operating all the time, in one or more dimensions of our lives of which we are unaware. The rare, direct experience of Alternity, the intense awareness of this domain, is usually a display—a "seeing." Perhaps some individuals remain in Alternity as a way of life: Yogi saints, wandering wizards, blissful psychotics, Tibetan monks in caves. Perhaps Hermann Hesse visited Alternity when he imagined the Glass Bead Game and wrote that sec-tion in Magister Ludi *that recounts the alternative lives of his protagonist.*

THE NIGHT BEFORE the killer quake, with a boost from LSD, John had opened to Alternity. He was performing the "prophet meditation" he'd learned from Oscar Ichazo in Chile. He sat up, spine straight, in a cross-legged meditation pose.

Suddenly, unexpectedly, all possible futures opened up to him.

He saw a shaft of light running through his spine, grounded in the Earth and extending infinitely above. All about him in Alternity were open compartments extending radially from the spinal pillar of light, an uncountable number of slices of possible futures. His spine transfixed by the axis of the universe, his being was held in perfect balance and symmetry by a universal order stronger than personal inclinations and idiosyncrasies. In this state of cosmic balance and poise, all things within his range became equally possible; not being inclined toward any one path allowed him to see all paths. There were a multitude of paths into the future, each leading into a different life, each one full, rich, interesting, dramatic, convincing, colorful, comic and/or tragic. Here was a particular woman, there a group of colleagues, a scene in the country, a fascinating line of research, an alien spe-cies, a new child, or an unrecognizable world. . . .

His being rippled and expanded as one or another of these realities opened to invite him into its particular time line. These were but minor fluctuations of his perfect centeredness, ripples in the luminous current of his cosmic symmetry, and they passed without pulling him off balance.

Overcome at last by the endless abundance of possibilities, he put the experience aside, naming the phenomenon *Alternity* for future reference. He returned to a single reality, this bed in Hollywood, California, next to a woman named Elizabeth, and fell asleep.

The next morning, when the earthquake struck, John re-turned to a state of Alternity—on the floor.

The bed from which the quake knocked him was one he

shared with Elizabeth Campbell, a Hollywood sophisticate and John's lover for a short time since his return from Chile. John and Elizabeth were two people who knew that they were not suited to each other for the long run. Knowing they were capable of having sex without becoming tightly bonded, they were having a fine time together.

John left the apartment to wander the streets of Hollywood like a pilgrim in Oz, still aware of the state of Alternity, open to all potential paths into the future. When he returned later in the afternoon, he discovered that one of those paths had closed to him—a man greeted him at the front door and informed him that Elizabeth had a new lover.

That evening, still in Alternity, he went to a big old Hollywood house with a friend for a party in honor of Alan Watts, who had just given a lecture at Beverly Hills High School. Car problems delayed their arrival at the party until very late, after almost everyone, including Watts, had left.

John was still flying on LSD. He fell into orbit around a woman sitting cross-legged in front of the bar, observing those present with a silent, alert attentiveness in her clear eyes that reminded him of an eagle. Her name was Toni and Watts was her sometime lover; she, too, had taken LSD.

Captivated by the love and warmth she was radiating, John said something to her that seemed inspired by some outside source: "Where have you been for the last 500 years?"

She replied, "I've been in training."

John fell out of Alternity and into Toni—for the next fifteen years.

Antonietta Lena Ficarotta: known as Toni to her friends, as Aunt Ann to her niece Gina, and as Mom to her daughter, Nina Carozza, twenty-two. Her father, Angelo Ficarotta, was a carpenter in an old-world tradition. Her younger brother, Tom, was a contractor on his way to being a multimillionaire. And Toni was an artist. Descended from Sicilians and Albanians, raised on Long Island, New York, educated in Los Angeles, trained in art and psychotherapy, twice married and divorced, she was at the center of a hip crowd of artists and intellectuals.

Five nights later, John went to a dinner party at Toni's house

Outside the Project JANUS mobile laboratory instrumentation truck, 1979: Psycholinguist Daniel Graboi, Toni, John, physicist John Kert, volunteer researcher Tom Fitz, and in front row, volunteers Gabrielle Lauer, "C.J.", and Jennifer Yankee (right). *Photo: Courtesy of Human Dolphin Foundation.*

Inside the JANUS truck: John Lilly, Burgess Meredith, and John Kert, amid a complex network of computer and audio equipment. The Digital pdp-11-03 computer stands at right rear behind Kert. *Photo: Courtesy of Human Dolphin Foundation.*

With Buckminster Fuller, at John's sixty-sixth birthday party. *Photo: Courtesy of John Lilly.*

Redwood Shores, 1982: Jennifer Yankee kisses dolphin (Joe or Rosie), in the pool at Project JANUS. *Photo: Martha Spence.*

Malibu, December 1982: Cynthia Lilly, between John and John C. Lilly, Jr. *Photo: Sandra Lee Katzman.*

Vacationing with Cynthia. *Photo: Toni Lilly, courtesy of Lilly family.*

John introduces Damon Webb, three-year-old son of Nina and artist Jim Webb, to computers in 1982. *Photo: Courtesy of Lilly family.*

Psychotherapy pioneer R.D. Laing, M.D., breakfasts on John's patio in Malibu, 1984. *Photo: Barbara Clarke-Lilly.*

John with chemist Albert Hofmann at Hofmann's home in Basel. *Photo: Toni Lilly.*

January 1987, Santa Barbara: Leading a seminar with psychiatrist Claudio Naranjo, whose influence had led John to Arica in 1970. *Photo: Moon Kerson.*

Toni, John, and Richard Feynman at Esalen in 1983. *Photo: Faustin Bray/Sound Photosynthesis.*

Barbara Clarke-Lilly. *Photo: Faustin Bray/ Sound Photosynthesis.*

October 1988: John, seen here with Hyla Cass, M.D., arrives at Moscow airport. *Photo: Barbara Clarke-Lilly.*

Lisa Lyon. *Photo: Courtesy of Lisa Lyon-Lilly.*

Malibu, October 1988: John Lilly, Albert Hofmann, and Timothy Leary — the three world-famous scientists who explored the uses of LSD. Hofmann, a chemist, invented it at the Sandoz pharmaceutical labs in Basel. *Photo: Barbara Clarke-Lilly.*

John Lilly in 1989. *Photo: Faustin Bray/ Sound Photosynthesis.*

John in Malibu with friends (left to right) Laura Phillips, Susanna Lombardo, Kathy Rossi, Crissie Steffen, John, Faustin Bray, P.B., and Barbara Clarke-Lilly. *Photo: Faustin Bray/Sound Photosynthesis.*

where he met twelve of her friends, including her dear friend Kay Sharpe.

After dinner many guests took LSD. As they lay on couches and pillows, Kay told John, "You are a cosmic snob," to which he responded, "You are right." He found that he could fit right in with Toni's crowd; things were going well.

A few days later, Watts returned to L.A. expecting to stay at Toni's place, and John performed his first official duty as Toni's new man when he picked Watts up at the airport and told him that he and Toni were now a pair. Disappointed, Watts was nevertheless magnanimous with John. John pointed out that Toni had noted that his birthday and Watts's were the same, with their times of birth only seventy-eight minutes apart by local time. "Now that," said Watts, "is almost enough to make me believe in astrology."

John soon began living with Toni. Her small West Los Angeles house at 8910 Beverlywood, with John's camper parked in the driveway, became home for John. In the camper, he worked on *The Center of the Cyclone,* recounting in the last chapter his meeting with his soul mate.

The extent to which John and Toni complemented each other, advancing each other's purposes, seemed to be a function of their diametrically opposite natures. This was not a relationship without substantial conflict and confrontation. Both the sources of their conflicts and their individual methods for resolving them came from two utterly separate realities. Confrontations would generally dissolve in laughter as each realized that they were fighting over things that existed in different universes.

When a confrontation developed, for example, Toni would get angry, and John would characteristically behave *as if* angry. For Toni, anger was a perfectly natural emotion, a normal component of interpersonal relationships, a form of communication to be used whenever circumstances seemed to call for it. For John, however, anger was an unpleasant feeling that disrupts sound judgment—a dangerous interpersonal move to be averted except under the most extreme provocation and the most dire circumstances. And so he would simulate anger—act *as if* angry—as a role one played when the script called for it in response to what others were doing or saying.

Their perspectives were so different that their impressions of people, places, and things they shared were drawn in entirely different terms. That made it all the more remarkable when they often found a person both could like and relate to—each for their own distinctive reasons, of course. For example, to John, their mutual friend Laura Archera Huxley was an exciting, intellectual lady, author, and therapy pioneer. To Toni, who listed Laura among her personal teachers, with Alan Watts and Ram Dass, Laura shone most in the kitchen, a view she later expressed in *The Dyadic Cyclone,* the book she would write with John: "LAURA HUXLEY: creative mixing of nutritious foods, elegantly served." This was far from a dismissal of Huxley, but rather Toni's highest heartfelt compliment. For Toni, the kitchen was the heart of the home, the heart of the family, and very close to her heart itself.

The Dyadic Cyclone also records their impressions of each other during this period. John wrote of Toni:

> My first impression of Toni as an eagle-like character has been borne out. She possesses a vast reservoir of serene contemplation, of peace, and of physical vigor and of an ability to demand and hold on to the ties to the land that her Sicilian-Albanian ancestors have always demanded. She is delightful in . . . the élan vital she so constantly expresses. . . . She has the warm heart of the Mediterranean peoples, and yet she fully appreciates my less emotional northern Minnesota (Irish/Scottish/German) background. We seem to complement each other in multifarious ways, and every day is a set of new discoveries of the delights of our dyad.

And Toni wrote of John:

> John has helped me dare to look beyond the consensus reality in every direction. His complete abandon and the openness of his mind are only matched by the boundless horizon of his spirit. . . . He has taught me courage and flexibility. He is a great companion, brother, lover, father and, most of all, he reflects my humor back to me.

In March Oscar Ichazo sent John an exuberant letter from Chile, followed with a second letter inviting John to meet him in San Francisco. After this meeting with Oscar, John and Toni drove back East to Long Island, where Ichazo and his crew from Arica were setting up a training program.

Although both John and Toni had been invited to the event, when they arrived at Arica's new headquarters at the Essex House in New York City, John was told by some of the Arica students that he could not participate, although Toni could enter the three-month program. Apparently, the group felt John had deserted them in Chile.

Nevertheless, John stayed on, passing time in private discussions with Oscar while Toni attended the training, now called Arica Institute. John showed Ichazo the manuscript of *The Center of the Cyclone,* in which he had written so extensively and enthusiastically about his own Arica experiences while suppressing any mention of his use of LSD at Arica, or of his skepticism.

Outwardly pleased, Oscar continued friendly meetings with John. But soon after, a representative of the training group offered John a startling proposition: They would now let him join the group, only on the condition that he withdraw *The Center of the Cyclone* from publication.

This was the last straw. John was not about to cancel a book he had written with such clarity and passion. He had made substantial commitments to his publisher, Julian Press in New York. Now completely disillusioned with Arica, he shed what remained of his entrancement with Oscar, the group, and its teachings, despite his continuing respect for the man's intentions.

Toni completed the training program and they returned to California. Toni's later impressions of this episode: "Oscar Ichazo and his lady, Jenny Pareda: South American palace politics mixed with esoteric teachings can be humorous."

They felt the need for larger quarters and began to search for a home. John discovered that the natural air flow carried Los Angeles' pervasive smog around and away from Malibu, a coastal town whose name is taken from the Chumash Indian word for "beautiful coast." They shortly found a house there, located on a narrow winding road back from the beach. It was a hilltop California miniranch, with a large, comfortable house, barns, sheds, and other small outbuildings, its own well, and a windmill on the hill. Thoroughly enchanted, they bought it and moved in.

Shortly after, *Psychology Today* sent Sam Keen to interview John. The resulting article, "John Lilly: From Dolphins to LSD" ran in the December 1971 issue.

At home in Malibu, John and Toni met Glenn and Lee Perry, longtime students of Zen meditation, who offered to design and build and sell isolation tanks based on John's considerable experience in this area. The Perrys started an enterprise called The Samadhi Tank Company, after *samadhi,* the Sanskrit word for a state of deep meditation.

These were tanks of a new kind. Instead of fresh or seawater, which needed to be fairly deep to float a person, the new tanks used a dense solution of Epsom salts, which gave sufficient buoyancy in about a foot of liquid. The naked body floated right at the surface, with the air temperature kept the same as the fluid's. These tanks were simple, safe, and easy enough to use that almost anybody could climb right in and have an experience of sensory isolation. Two of the first tanks built according to this design were installed in a small concrete-block building on the ranch, which then became John's isolation laboratory. Three more tanks were installed in redwood shacks on a hillside a good distance from the main house.

With the publication of *The Center of the Cyclone,* many people became interested in John Lilly, and some began to seek him out as a teacher, advisor, and companion on their inner adventures. With isolation tanks now installed on the property, John and Toni responded to this interest by offering seminars on the tank work at their home. Many people now had the opportunity to experience profound isolation for themselves—and to have a deeper experience of themselves in the process.

It spoiled the day for actor Burgess Meredith when he heard that *The Day of the Dolphin* movie was going into production. In the circus that was Hollywood and its sideshow at the beach in Malibu, such secrets couldn't be kept for long. Meredith had planned to make a movie about dolphins himself, and there simply wasn't room at the box office for two such movies. Thus it would be impossible to raise money for his movie, based on the real-life experiences of Dr. John Lilly, and folly to try. Meredith was irked, more philosophically than personally, as he paced the damp boards of his sundeck, suspended over the beach at Malibu Point.

But there was some solace to be had: The movie would not be, but the idea of it had already led him to meet John and Toni. He was grateful for that, and so were they, discovering in Burgess a loving and caring neighbor who believed that loyalty was the basic virtue of friendship.

Visiting him one day, John and Toni slept in their camper beside his beach house after a pleasant dinner. Rejoining their host inside for breakfast the next morning, they heard that he had dreamt of a dolphin coming ashore on the wet sand below his house. In the dream, his wife and the neighborhood kids went down to the beach, turned the dolphin around and pushed it back to sea. It was a strange dream for Burgess; he'd never actually seen anything like that. He thought perhaps the dream had been triggered by the license plate on the Lilly camper, which read: DOLFIN.

Two hours later a small commotion erupted beneath the Meredith home, built on poles over the beach. The trio went to investigate. There in the surf was a dolphin, swimming ashore. It beached itself, lying on the sand. While Burgess and John watched in amazement, Toni and Meredith's wife, with the help of some nearby children, managed to get the dolphin to swim back to sea.

Such scenes with dolphins and whales occurred frequently around John. Whenever he was at the beach, the creatures were certain to make an appearance in the water. If he went to a marine park, the orca acknowledged his presence by refusing to perform. He seemed to have some mysterious connection with cetaceans, a link that was still quite strong.

In November 1973, Alan Watts died of heart failure. He'd been up all night drinking on an airplane flight from London, and when he arrived at his home on Mount Tamalpais in Mill Valley, his wife Jano fed him a large steak. Shortly thereafter, he passed away.

At fifty-eight, Alan had been in poor health and a state of general dissipation due at least in part to heavy alcohol consumption. In spite of his eloquent enthusiasm for mind-expanding, for

BIOGRAPHY

BURGESS MEREDITH (1908–   ), stage and screen actor, was born in Cleveland and after a brief career as a sailor made his theatrical debut in 1929. In 1936 he went to Hollywood to star in his first movie, *Winterset,* after giving brilliant performances in the stage version the year before.

During a long acting career in which he has been widely regarded as among the world's most versatile performers, he also directed a number of stage plays and the movie *The Man on the Eiffel Tower* (1949). His dozens of film credits include *Of Mice and Men* (1940), *Advise and Consent* (1962), *There Was a Crooked Man* (1970), *The Hindenberg* (1975), *Rocky* (1976), *Rocky II* (1979), and *The Day the World Ended* (1979). He played The Penguin in the "Batman" TV series.

Burgess Meredith was a cofounder of the Human-Dolphin Foundation.

---

solace he had returned to alcohol, the sanctioned sacrament of the mainstream and the most socially approved method of suicide in Western culture. From another point of view, he might be seen as one of the great drinking roshis of lore; perhaps he had achieved the selfless jollity of the legendary sake-sipping Zen masters of the past.

Alan Watts's passing was acknowledged the following February with full religious honors on the slopes of Mount Tamalpais. In an old barn converted to a temple at the Green Gulch Farm of the San Francisco Zen Center, a solemn, full-dress Zen ritual was performed by Richard Baker Roshi, arguably the foremost American Zen master, in his robes of golden brocade. Baker honored Watts's spirit with the Japanese name and title *Yu Zen Myo Ko, Dai Yu Jo Mon*—"Profound mountain, subtle light, great founder, opener of the Zen Samadhi gate."

In Malibu, John and Alan had been scheduled to lead a joint seminar on what turned out to be the day after his sudden death. John carried on with the seminar—which was attended by Laura Huxley and a young neurophysiologist named Francis Jeffrey, among others—and proceeded toward the fifty-ninth birthday the two men would have shared.

Alan's memory was also preserved in other ways. There

was his Society for Comparative Philosophy, on whose board of directors both John and Toni served, as well as Alan himself, his wife Jano, and several other supporters. After his death, the group became The Alan Watts Society, with the mission of preserving his work. It was based on the S.S. *Vallejo,* Watts's old ferryboat turned houseboat, anchored on the Sausalito waterfront. The roomy old boat was converted into a conference center for the sort of events and people Watts would have appreciated.

In Zen Buddhism, the philosophy with which Watts was most closely associated, death is referred to as "crossing over." The Buddhist literature of China and Japan compares the passing of an enlightened one to the shattering of a fine porcelain vase. The surface of the intact vase only appears to separate the air within from the air without. When the vase shatters, only the form of the vase and the appearance of separation have gone. The air within does not disappear; it merely "crosses over" to join the air beyond, from which it has never truly been separated.

Tibetan Buddhists have a similar theory of reincarnation, according to which each of us is a composite of aspects or qualities drawn from the influences of both bygone and living personages. Upon death, the composite disassembles and is then redistributed into the universe, especially into one's friends and those one has influenced—a fragmentary kind of immortality.

In a manner reminiscent of this Tibetan doctrine, Alan Watts—friend to John, lover to Toni, and unofficial godfather to her daughter Nina, now twenty-five—lived on among the occupants of the Lilly household in Malibu, where his official portrait, with arms crossed boldly on his chest and the daring, challenging expression of a spiritual karate master on his face, hung on a wall. Those present sensed that John had somehow absorbed something of Watts, filling in for him in a way. John let his short blond beard grow into a Watts-like goatee, as if the minutes-older sage had bequeathed this symbol to John.

Watts, who had always believed in reincarnation, had promised that in his next life he would return as a beautiful, red-haired woman. Shortly after his death, his daughter Joan gave birth to a red-haired girl—who seemed to gravitate toward the cupboard where Watts's favorite brandy had been kept.

When *The Center of the Cyclone* was published, John wrote himself a note dated 27 January 1972 inside the back cover of his personal copy. It is a poignant and succinct statement of his philosophy of life during the early seventies:

> My philosophy: Don't get caught with a fixed philosophy, a set of safe beliefs, a particular way of life.
>
> Experiment! With life, with love.
>
> Run an exploration of the real and the true degrees of freedom of life, of love, of the human condition, inside self and in one's style of life.
>
> Move! Into new spaces beyond one's present concepts of possible/probable/certain/real spaces.
>
> Far vaster than I now know are the innermost/outermost realities.
>
> Far more interesting than I now feel are the deeps of space, the beyond within, the infinite without.
>
> Love and loving are basic.
>
> Hostility is redundant.
>
> Fear is non-sense.
>
> "Death" is a myth.
>
> I am I.

As John came to the end of 1973 and moved onward, he was well grounded in a solid domestic reality and an ardent dyad, the likes of which he had never before enjoyed. On many occasions he would stand on the crest of his private hill above Malibu and gaze out on the ocean, the rugged volcanic ridges, the golden, grassy slopes studded with the masts of his radio antennas, the ranch-style house with the camper in the driveway, his wife planting trees and flowers and a vegetable garden, and find himself, finally, for the first time, to be happy—simply happy. Happy to be human.

And yet, inside, he still remembered, "I was the Being."

CHAPTER 13

THE YEAR OF SAMADHI

June 1973, age 58.

Pain. Aching, throbbing pain. The right side of his head is a sheet of searing agony, so bad it obliterates his existence, so intense that he cannot think, cannot imagine, cannot even hope for an end to it. He is doomed to wander in this narrow abyss of nullification as if tethered by a chain drawn tightly around his neck to a glowing ember of hell itself. Hell is the state with no memory of any other state of being.

He is back in the hell he has known since the age of seven—the one constant amid the flux of his unpredictable life. Every eighteen days he returns here. This is the continuity of his identity—this life in hell. Migraine.

In his present state, even such gloomy thoughts are beyond him. It is all he can do to steer his body to his room here at Esalen, to bed, to the darkness, silence, and solitude in which the migraine is least unbearable. For fifty-one years, like clockwork, he has beat this sad retreat whenever his curse descended. His suffering is obvious to all who see his ashen face and his contorted body, straining under the weight of a pain as big as the universe.

Dr. Craig Enright visits the condemned man; he knows the story:

"What's the matter, John?"

"Migraine."

"I have something new I'd like you to try, John."

"Ok."

Craig escorts John to the isolation tank at Esalen and

*helps him in. John is floating on the surface of the fluid with
his head near the open hatch. Craig reaches in and injects 35
milligrams of ketamine hydrochloride into John's right shoulder. Within minutes, migraine pain recedes from the right side
of John's head and seems to move three feet away. The pain
is out there in space and is no longer hurting him.*

*Then, twenty minutes later (earthtime), pain moves back
into John's head. John groans, and Craig injects 70 milligrams
of ketamine. This time the pain moves what seems like twelve
feet to the right of John's head. When, thirty minutes later, the
pain sails back across inner space and lodges in John's head
once more, Craig gives him a shot of 150 milligrams.*

*The pain leaves John's head to the right, and goes clear
over the horizon to disappear forever. An hour later the ketamine has totally worn off, but there's no sign of the pain. John
climbs out of the tank, dresses, and rejoins Toni, who is leading their seminar.*

WHEN THE MIGRAINE failed to recur the following month, John
was amazed. He had previously tried every weapon in the arse-
nal of medical science—and all had failed. He had tried, with LSD
in the tank, to program these hellish episodes out of the repertoire
of his brain's behavior as well, an approach that provided only
temporary relief.

The prevailing theory of migraines suggested they were
maintained by a pattern of tension in blood vessels supplying the
brain. Migraine was seen as a form of "charley horse" in the
brain: Tension led to constriction of the vessels, which in turn led
to further tension, a circular feedback process. When his migraine did not reappear, John knew this theory had to be incor-
rect. The effects of Enright's new agent, ketamine hydrochloride,
had long since worn off; hence it could hardly be preventing a
recurrence of the vascular activity described by this model. The
constriction of blood vessels must be an effect, not a cause, of
migraine attacks.

John had suspected that migraines were a function of programs operating in the mind, perhaps closely related to one or
more circuits of neurons, physical structures with which such
mental programs might be associated. For his earlier attempts at
self-treatment by LSD-assisted reprogramming, he had visualized

the migraine as an oscillating, self-stimulating, self-perpetuating activity of such circuits. This perspective was supported by a discovery made by many migraine sufferers—attacks could be brought on, and sometimes terminated, by self-programming or programming from the environment.

How, then, had ketamine cured him, apparently permanently? The chemical, which was rapidly metabolized and excreted, was unlikely to have caused any permanent physiological or chemical changes. So John concluded that migraines were, in fact, a result of mental programming—and therefore ketamine must be a extraordinarily powerful facilitator of that process.

But ketamine's history was quite unlike the other programming facilitators with which John was familiar, notably LSD. Patented in 1963, it had been used as a surgical anesthetic on millions of patients since 1965. Ketamine was described as a "dissociative anesthetic," meaning that it allows one to separate oneself from the feeling of pain, a process called analgesia; it did not block nerve pathways that conduct the somatic sensations of pain as local anesthetics do. Used as a general anesthetic, it did not suppress pulse and respiration as the standard solvent anesthetics—ether, chloroform, ethyl alcohol, or haldane gas—all did. The only oddity regarding ketamine noted in the medical literature was the *emergence reaction,* a period of disoriented perception and altered consciousness some patients felt as ketamine anesthesia wore off. Some psychiatrists who had studied the emergence reaction had already begun using ketamine as an adjunct to psychotherapy in the early seventies.

After his cure that weekend, John returned to Malibu determined to explore the use of ketamine as a programming facilitator, starting with a fraction of the surgical dosage, 30 to 150 milligrams. In the process, he discovered a number of properties to the chemical that made it appealing for this kind of research. Foremost were its reliability and the repeatability of results. A drug that could be injected eliminated uncertainties about assimilation or absorption rates of medications that are swallowed and hence about timing the onset of effects. A person could be given a precisely measured injection of ketamine and, within a matter of seconds or minutes, that person would go to a predictable level of consciousness. The exact level would depend on the relationship between dosage, body weight, and the individual's sensitivity, all of which could be calibrated. This reliability yielded clean graphs, such as those given in John's book, *The Scientist,* relating dosage and timing—which are objectively observable variables—to inner events experienced by the subject, and outward changes in behavior observable by others. In this sense, ketamine was "good, clean science."

John compared the research benefits of ketamine with those of LSD. The long duration and intensity of LSD, six to eight hours, made it difficult to recall all the details of an experience. Additionally, LSD experiments had to be separated by two-week intervals, or the effect would be greatly reduced. Thus one couldn't maintain continuity of these states. Alternatively, ketamine's fast action and relative lack of "tolerance" effects permitted repetition of an experiment within the same day, and again on following days.

John found that with ketamine, he could stay in those domains that had always interested him, while the complicated methods he had used in the past had allowed him only fleeting glimpses, leaving only vague descriptions of phenomena, experiences, or states of consciousness. It was a hit-or-miss sort of affair; results were quirky and unrepeatable. But with ketamine and his quantitative approach, these domains assumed a certain solidity and became "places" he could travel to with consistent characteristics.

Ketamine thus provided a way of reliably traversing the domains of being he had discovered through other kinds of experiments. It gave him regular access to the internal reality first discovered in the 1950s in the tank, and intuited far earlier as the inner reality described in his teenage essay on Reality. It provided entry into what he had come to call the "extraterrestrial reality," the timeless space of the Beings that he had discovered in the Islands and associated with the traveling point of consciousness he had experienced as the +6 state at Arica. Using ketamine, this reality became vivid experiences of visiting alien landscapes and realms of the far future. Somewhere between the LSD experiments with isolation and the period in Arica, John had formulated the concept of the Network, that web of Being or Beings which extended across the cosmos in what John had come to call "hyperspace." That state, which he correlated with the +3 level of consciousness, was also easily accessible through the use of the new agent.

John conjectured that ketamine is a kind of "chemical isolation tank." One means to quantify isolation is to measure how much signals from the outside world are cut off. A good tank attenuates signals from the outside world by about 70dB (decibels). Ketamine, in the dosage he was using, provided a roughly similar amount of isolation. Put them together and you've attenuated the outside world by about 140dB, the equivalent of cutting sensory stimulation in half, and repeating the process twenty-three times. Now that's isolation!

Additionally, ketamine does what the tank alone can't do: It eliminates any distraction from painful or annoying sensations in the body.

When John and Craig Enright next got together around an isolation tank, they began a joint program of ketamine research. In one of these sessions, unbeknownst to John, Enright programmed himself "to return to the prehominid origins of Man." (A distorted version of this episode which John reported in *The Scientist* was destined to become the basis for a key sequence in the movie *Altered States*.) While John watched, Craig injected a measured dose of ketamine and proceeded to live out, in both inner and outer realities, the program of being an apelike ancestor of modern man.

The action in the two realities matched only roughly. In the outer reality—observable by John—Craig became a hyperanimated crouching figure—howling, ranting, shaking his arms, and gesticulating. In the inner reality Craig experienced himself as an ape—confronting, challenging, and driving away a leopard, finally climbing into a tree and staring down at John from the branches.

In John's reality, of course, there wasn't any tree; John was, at this moment, in the state usually called "sober"; in his terms, that meant his inner and outer realities were closely interlocked in the manner appropriate for a person operating in the physical world. There also was no tree in Enright's outer reality, but significantly he experienced the tree of his inner reality *as if it did in fact exist in his outer reality.* A few minutes later, as the effects of the ketamine wore off, Craig's inner-reality tree disappeared.

Only afterward did Craig reveal his prehominid program to John. Since John had not shared this scenario, he had not identified the apelike qualities in Enright's performance. Instead, Craig's thrashing body, wildly flailing limbs, and repetitive, spasmodic movements suggested an epileptic seizure to John's medically trained eye. Nevertheless, Craig had remained on his feet the whole time, unlike a victim of a grand mal seizure, who generally fell writhing to the ground.

Clearly, Craig's inner experience had been far more defined and varied than his outward performance had suggested, John realized.

From this experiment John and Craig drew three important conclusions about the effects of ketamine: First, one's internal reality could differ radically from the external reality in which one was participating, even with regard to prominent features of the physical environment. Second, the person might remain active physically in the external environment, in a manner not corresponding closely to one's internal experience of this activity. And third, one could remain totally oblivious to this disparity.

These and other observations led the two researchers to formulate a general observation about ketamine (K): "At certain critical doses and certain critical concentrations of K in the brain, the subcortical systems continue their automatic activities out of contact with the observer in the brain." In other words, the body could continue performing in a manner neither controlled nor accurately perceived by the person to whom that body belonged. As a related discovery, they found that practically any pattern of behavior, from spasmodic twitching to activities requiring relatively sophisticated coordination, could be carried out automatically without conscious control while on ketamine. They called such behavior an "automatism."

The hazards suggested by these conclusions impelled them to formulate certain precautions: They would have a "safety man" on hand at all times to prevent a person on ketamine from doing harm to himself or others, and they would pursue these experiments only in an isolated and safe environment.

John and Craig were perhaps the only adequate safety men available to each other. A highly effective medical doctor who mixed empathy, the best of current medical science, and a holistic perspective in his practice at Esalen and surrounding Big Sur communities, Craig Enright was a dedicated, bold, and experienced explorer of inner domains—in many ways a man rather like John Lilly, who was thirty years his senior. And like John,

Craig could apply his medical expertise to their joint experiments and deal with any hazards that might arise. These similarities, and the extraordinarily close friendship they had developed, provided that essential combination of love and respect required for two men undertaking such daring experiments together.

Unfortunately, John was becoming so entranced with his ketamine experiences that he would soon begin to experiment alone, without the outstanding safety man he had found in Craig, and outside the isolation tank. And there were further hazards to the use of this agent which they had not yet identified—changes in consciousness, appearing only with closely spaced multiple doses, that could lead both to losing track of the external reality and confusing the two by projecting the internal onto the external. Furthermore, they were not yet aware of the "repeated-use trap," a syndrome resulting from the fact that even the act of injecting ketamine could become an automatism. In that state, the frequency of self-administered doses was limited only by a brief period of physical incapacity following each dose.

John fell prey to this trap in a series of experiments over several weeks in Malibu, conducted after the joint experiments with Craig. He began living continuously in internal and extraterrestrial realities, while attempting to continue to function in his normal external reality. He was to continue in this mode for several months.

Early in this period, after a session with ketamine, John decided to go for a relaxing bath in his hot tub. He did not notice that the water was too hot.

Since his work with the air force, he had known his blood pressure was atypically low. As a result, the blood supply to his brain fluctuated when his body was stressed. In the aeromedical physiology lab at Wright Field, he had actually measured this effect by putting his body on the tilt table with pressure-sensing catheters of his own design inserted in various blood vessels. He had found that when he tilted his head up, blood tended to rush away from the upper end of his body.

On this particular sunny afternoon, John wasn't thinking about those observations he had made so long ago, nor was he paying attention to the water temperature. But once in the tub, he began to feel uncomfortably warm and attempted to climb out. As he stood up, his muscles lost their strength and he collapsed and slipped beneath the water. He was fully conscious—but not of the external reality in which his body was close to drowning; he was conscious on the inside only.

John would have died but for an extraordinary series of coincidences. Phil Halecki, whom John and Toni had met at the Arica Institute training in New York, chose that moment to call, driven by a mysterious sense of urgency. Although Toni answered the phone, it was only Halecki's insistence that caused her to summon John, who, she suspected, didn't want to be interrupted. She went looking for him, found him face down in the water, and revived him using a technique she had learned only three days before from an article in *The National Enquirer*— mouth-to-mouth resuscitation.

After his near drowning, Toni, Burgess Meredith, and several doctors they enlisted attempted to pressure John into abandoning his ketamine explorations. He eluded their best efforts and continued, deciding now to inject himself hourly for three weeks, in order to maintain a continuous effect.

John now had enough data to be aware of the repeated-use trap and other hazards of ketamine. If his basic beliefs had remained as they had been when he began these experiments, he might have concluded that it was time to discontinue. However, his basic beliefs about the nature of reality had mutated during his prolonged period of exposure to the new agent, altered in ways which could not have been foreseen by anyone without extensive experience of ketamine's effects—*ketamine is a programming facilitator.*

His interpretation of the hot tub incident was a good example of this. While the episode convinced Toni that her dyadic life with John was precarious, for John it provided further confirmation that his life was guarded by higher powers in the extraterrestrial reality, a hierarchy of entities operating through the control of coincidences on a global scale. During this period he came to call that network ECCO—Italian for "This is it!"—also an acronym for Earth Coincidence Control Office. He was sure that ECCO would protect him from even the worst of his own folly, as long as he was using his body and mind to pursue research into higher domains of being.

He became convinced that ECCO had recruited him in the manner of a spy agency and was training him to carry out their missions on earth. By arranging fortuitous coincidences or ruth-lessly painful mishaps, ECCO could reward or punish John and thus steer him on the course they had chosen for him. And he believed that when he was in certain states, they could enter his brain and directly reward or punish him with internal reality experiences, rather like the remote-controlled mules of the Sandia Corporation he had read about, whose course could be guided by electrodes implanted directly in their brains in the pleasure and pain centers.

A sequence of incidents in 1974 and 1975 struck John as mounting evidence for the pervasive influence of ECCO in his life. In his internal reality, he was frequently in direct contact with the Guides, the two Beings who now identified themselves as part of ECCO. In his external reality, he was deluged with apparently meaningful coincidences supporting his current belief system. When his internal and external realities overlapped, as they did while he navigated the busy outside world with ketamine in his system, certain events and images seemed strangely accented, as if to suggest that all the world was a billboard through which ECCO advertised itself.

He also began to have contact with another network, which he called the SSI, for "Solid State Intelligence." The SSI was composed of computerlike, solid state lifeforms throughout the universe. This group appeared to be operating at cross-purposes with ECCO (which seemed to represent the overall order of the universe) and were bent on conquering and dominating biological life—all organic, water-based creatures—beginning with the de-struction of cetaceans through whaling and tuna fishing. Part of John's mission as an agent of ECCO was to alert the world to the threat posed by the solid state beings.

For John, perhaps the most striking incident confirming the dual global influences of ECCO and the SSI occurred in autumn of 1974, when he and Toni were flying into Los Angeles Interna-tional Airport (LAX). John had gone into the bathroom to inject himself with ketamine. When he returned to his seat and looked out the window he saw Comet Kahoutek, visible to the naked eye, glowing low in the southern sky. The comet seemed to grow momentarily brighter, at which point John received a message: "We are the Solid State Intelligence and we are going to demon-strate our power by shutting down all the solid state equipment at LAX." John told Toni about the message. A few minutes later, the pilot announced that their flight was being diverted to Burbank Airport because LAX had been shut down by an electrical power failure.

After landing safely, the passengers were bused to LAX, where they learned that a plane had crash-landed near the runway, knocking out electrical lines. Miraculously, no one on board had been injured.

John thought all of this had been arranged by ECCO to demonstrate the threat posed by the SSI—and Toni was so frightened by the incident that she *almost* started believing in ECCO.

During this period of extensive ketamine use, ECCO warned of other imminent dangers to the survival of life on the planet. They showed John scenarios of extinction by nuclear war and by a blast of radiation from a supernova explosion in deep space. He was taken on tours of cataclysmic events occurring on other planets; ECCO's message seemed to be "It *can* happen here." John had been aware since his college days with astronomer Fritz Zwicky that life on Earth was subject to sudden destruction by such unforeseeable cosmic events. Now such dangers were of immediate importance to him. He felt compelled to warn those around him, who seemed blissfully unaware of just how precarious their situation really was.

Some hazards were of a more personal nature. ECCO seemed to be testing John by repeatedly confronting him with that which he feared most. One evening, after a shot of ketamine, John was sitting in his easy chair in front of the television when an extraterrestrial appeared and, through some advanced technique of "bloodless surgery," removed his penis and handed it to him.

John screamed in horror, "They've cut off my penis!" Toni ran to the rescue, pointing out that it was still in place. When he looked down, he saw that the extraterrestrials had replaced his normal penis with a mechanical one he could voluntarily erect whenever he wanted, as male dolphins can do. An hour later, John discovered that there was, of course, no sign of any change in his penis.

After three weeks of hourly ketamine injections, John decided that he must travel to the East Coast to alert the nation's political and media leaders in person about the threat posed by the SSI. He told Toni that he had to go to New York without informing her of the nature of his mission.

Upon arrival, he rented a suite in a hotel next to Central Park. Three thousand miles from Malibu, Toni, their friends, and the doctors she had recruited couldn't interfere with his mission. With a new supply of ketamine, he continued his efforts to receive communications from the extraterrestrials, who were sending him advice and warnings about the future of life on planet Earth, and the perils to organic life-forms throughout the galaxy.

He received a very strong advisory from the network to return to his first medical school, Dartmouth Medical Center, in Hanover, New Hampshire. He took the appropriate airplane and arrived there only to collapse on the hard, tile floor of the airport, from which he was scooped up by a public safety squad and transported to the Mary Hitchcock Hospital. Here he was recognized by young doctors who knew his writings, as well as by certain of the older doctors who had been at the medical school contemporaneously with John, in the late 1930s. When John disclosed his intention to return to New York City, his medical brethren assigned a young intern to travel with him and "protect" him in the big city.

Once back in New York, John invited the young man to stay at his hotel suite, and returned to his mission of saving mankind and the entire ecosystem from the depredations of the Solid State Intelligence. He called the White House to warn President Gerald Ford about "a danger to the human race involving atomic energy and computers." The White House aide who took the call was not entirely convinced of the urgency of this matter, and, in spite of the impressive scientific credentials of Dr. John C. Lilly, the president was not available to him at that time.

This and other incidents of John's behavior convinced the intern from Dartmouth that John was mentally ill. With the active collusion of two psychiatrists he knew, he had John admitted to a psychiatric hospital, under the pretense that John had asked for psychiatric help.

Here again, John reaped the rewards of the vast network of goodwill he had generated during his many years of work in the Eastern scientific establishment. Friendly medical colleagues were everywhere, preventing the cosmic clown's comedy from turning into serious soap opera. As it transpired, the psychiatric hospital to which John was committed happened to be run by an old friend. This doctor could find no psychiatric reason for keeping John there. He was apologetic that he himself could not order John's release because John had been admitted by another doctor, a staff psychiatrist unwilling to have his diagnosis of insanity summarily overruled by the chief. So John was transferred to a second psychiatric hospital, where another old friend immediately discharged him into Toni's care, his bewildered life companion having flown to New York to join him at the hospital. Together they returned to Malibu.

At home, John resumed his experiments with ketamine on a regular basis. For a while, he again confined this activity to his isolation laboratory and the tank, in an effort to penetrate further into the extraterrestrial reality and to study nuances and refinements of consciousness in this domain. He again decided to inject ketamine on an hourly schedule in an attempt to maintain continuous contact with extraterrestrial reality.

During this period he was rarely seen by humans. He would emerge several times a day, just long enough to eat a microwaved chicken drumstick, drawn from a stash of interchangeable, refrigerated snacks.

However, during the several months of continuous experimentation that followed, John left his lab's confines and took his ketamine, and the extraterrestrial reality with which he had become increasingly identified "on the road." While John was making prolonged internal expeditions, his body continued operating in the external reality, where it continued to interact with all sorts of people, places, and things. Throughout these episodes, Toni continued to schedule seminars, lectures, and interviews for her mate, expertly handling the contingencies of the human reality, the "planetside trip," as they had come to call it. She would drag him out of the isolation tank and his laboratory to points all over the globe to teach and be taught in active engagement with members of the younger generation who wanted to know about the range of realities available to them in the world, in their bodies, and in their own heads. Whatever his neurochemical condition of the moment, John never failed to stimulate, inspire, or provoke questions.

For many of the increasing numbers of seekers and sympathetic souls who gathered around him, John's mere presence was influential, even when he was absorbed in his most incommunicado states. They sensed something mysterious and unfathomable within this living "center of the cyclone"; bonds would form around him and extraordinary transformations would occur. For those who really wanted to share in the adventure, John consistently offered an invitation to come along and experience it for oneself, and see how far one could go.

Because of the surprising things he said and did, John acquired a reputation as a kind of cosmic trickster, startling people into moments of "satori"—revealing gaps in the hypnotic continuity of their ordinary reality. (Some historical precedent for this sort of activity could be found in gurus, Zen masters, arhats, anchorites, and Sufis wandering the Near and Far East, accosting passersby with peculiar one-liners about the higher reality.) John seemed to appear in unexpected places in the role of an "extraterrestrial examiner," particularly testing the consciousness level of New Age leaders, gauging their level of evolution by their reactions to his otherworldly behavior. High marks went to Esalen cofounder Richard Price, who was always there for John with a safe and supportive environment, and to Werner Erhard, founder of the *est* program, for their unruffled acceptance. Bill Schutz, considered the inventor of encounter groups, scored well for his high degree of engagement with whatever he encountered in John, no matter how outrageous or absurd it seemed to others.

Patience with John began to wear thin among many of those subjected to his "Extraterrestrial Interaction Test." From a terrestrial point of view, John was acting like an irrepressible child before the stage where inhibitions and restraint are learned. In particular, his expressions of unabashed sensuality and "polymorphous perversity" (to use the Freudian term) left plenty of people nonplussed, including an unfortunate interviewer sent by *Psychology Today* magazine for a follow-up to their 1971 article. He could not understand why John, instead of answering serious questions about what it was like to be in higher states of consciousness, continued fondling the reporter's girlfriend. John's persistence, despite the distressed reactions of those present, including Toni, did nothing to help him understand. (In his internal reality, John and this young woman were alone, making love with innocent, childlike freedom and adolescent passion.)

In late September 1974, John's first "year of samadhi," as he later came to call his ketamine period, came to a crashing halt.

It was the second time in Lilly clan history that a bicycle became an agent of radical change.

Predictably enough, it had become increasingly difficult for John to obtain ketamine, for those who supplied him eventually became reluctant to continue. He began to seek other, longer-acting chemicals that might provide the same benefits but wouldn't require repeated administration to maintain those states of exploration for an extended period. His research turned up such a chemical, with a structure similar to ketamine, but a longer period of activity.

John obtained some, but he lacked a clear idea of what dosage would be appropriate. Assuming the necessary amount would be comparable to his ketamine dosage, as a preliminary test he took a quantity which would have been a relatively small dose for ketamine: 40 milligrams. This turned out to be a gross miscalculation on several counts. This was a slow-acting chemical, so onset was delayed; and this was actually a very large dose, so the effects would extend considerably longer than the time John had arranged to stay safely in his isolation facility. Furthermore, he had no safety man—he had not, in fact, told anyone what he was doing.

For nearly an hour, he noticed no change in his state of being. He then became hungry and left his laboratory for the kitchen. He was in there when the phone rang. Toni had gone to the gas station at the bottom of the hill, but left the key to the gas cap at home. Suspecting that he had taken an insufficient dose and would experience no effect, John told her that he would ride down the hill on his ten-speed bicycle to deliver the key.

Only then, as he mounted his new bicycle, did the full effect of the new drug start. It was a beautiful day of sunshine and birdsong. As he rode down the hill, the wind in his hair was pure joy, and he felt pleasure in the simplest movements of his body and every stretch of his muscles, a pleasure he had not felt since he had first learned to ride as a child.

As he flew along a downhill stretch at about thirty miles per hour, continuing in this state of childlike rapture, the bike chain suddenly jammed and he was pitched onto the road. When he regained some semblance of consciousness, he felt fluid oozing down his forehead; for a moment he feared that his brain had been blasted out of his skull.

Fortunately a passerby stopped to reassure him that the fluid was merely blood. Applying his medical knowledge to the situation, John decided it would be best to lie very still until help arrived. Shortly, paramedics arrived from the nearby fire station and he allowed himself to pass out, in their care.

The bicycle crash was followed by days of hospitalization dominated by coma, stupor, and pain. Isolated from the outer reality by pain, medications, and trauma, John once again met his two Guides in the inner reality. They told him he had a choice: he could go away with them "for good," or he could return to the body and mend. In the latter case, should he choose to accept the assignment, he would have the use of that body to continue his stay on planet Earth for a certain number of years. In that role he had many lessons to practice, he realized:

> ... lessons on how to remain at peace in spite of provocations to the contrary; of how to maintain the feeling in the face of temptations to be unfeeling; of how to continue to write books, to lecture, to give workshops, to teach and to listen to lectures, to read books, to be taught, to attend other's workshops and not demean either my own knowledge or the knowledge of others and to respect our ignorances. To love and be loved, to repair, to be repaired, to solve the karma I accumulated and the karma accumulated by others because of me.

John considered his decision to return to human life in the light of a model he had developed during his studies of neurophysiology: the moat effect. The model described the state of an area of nerve cells, such as a portion of the cerebral cortex. Once the area is excited and energized, the surrounding area becomes suppressed and de-energized. Visually modeled, the central area rises to form a pedestal while the surrounding area sinks to form a moat around it. John chose to allow the inviting swarm of alternate realities in his interior domains to be suppressed as the moat, placing Toni and the way of life she represented on the central pedestal.

Once the decision was made, once he had placed the highest value on the body called John Lilly, on Toni, and their life together, John returned from the disordered inner domains to the external reality of his injured body in a hospital bed. There followed a long and painful recovery. He was assisted by many healers, helpers, and coaches: Hector Prestera, Sharon Wheeler, Bernice Danylchuck, Lika and Malia (from Samoa), Jan Nicholson, Helen Costa, Ruth and Myron Glatt, Emily Conrad, Bob Swanson, and Grace Stern.

From the period in coma and its aftermath John took seemingly contradictory lessons. On the one hand, he was reminded of the value he placed on the survival of his body and on his life with Toni. On the other hand, he was still impressed with the reality and immediacy of the inner domains. The two Beings had been present, offering advice and challenge; the magician of self-programming had found he could operate in the province of the mind in skillful ways that made the possibilities of the world outside seem pale by comparison. This painful episode thus brought him at once closer to Toni and at the same time closer still to the Beings in that other dimension, who always appeared in the midst of a survival crisis, as one would expect of Guardian Angels.

John described this time and some of the further lessons it held for him later that year, as he was writing *The Dyadic Cyclone* with Toni:

Recently, I was very badly injured in a bicycle accident. I broke five ribs on the right. On the right side of my body I broke my clavicle and my scapula, and still after many months my right shoulder is not operating correctly. My right lung was collapsed, I had a concussion, spent nine days in a hospital and several weeks in bed at home. This accident taught much. It taught me that the beliefs of others about one's self are particularly powerful in determining the external reality in which one lives. It taught me that certain people cannot possibly understand the processes by which one arrives at one's particular thinking and feeling while in intense pain. As William James said at the beginning of this century, "Those who live on one side of the threshold of pain cannot possibly understand the psychology of those who live on the other side of the threshold of pain."

This lesson was brought home particularly strongly to me: I suddenly realized that we cannot expect understanding from others no matter how close to one they are, no matter how much they apparently understand one, if one is in states (not just pain) that are unfamiliar to those persons closest to one. If your wife or husband has never gone through the particular kinds and intensity of pain that one is experiencing, one cannot expect them to understand. This is asking too much of biological organisms that are having their own survival problems within different belief systems. We are the victims of our previous experience and of our beliefs constructed on those experiences. There is no escape from this victimization, as it were. We are limited biological organisms, severely limited by the biological vehicle within which we reside.

The decision to return to earthly life was not made without a sense of loss. In *Simulations of God,* John described his interpretation of himself at this stage of life:

I am only an extraterrestrial who has come to the planet Earth to inhabit a human body. Every time I leave this body and go back to my own civilization, I am expanded beyond all human imaginings. When I must return I am squeezed down into the limited human being, into the limited vehicle. It is as if the vehicle is too small to contain the passenger arriving from the *extraterrestrial realities.* The passage from the *extraterrestrial reality* into the *internal reality* of John C. Lilly, M.D., citizen of the United States on planet Earth, is a very onerous one. In former years when the isolation tank and LSD had freed me to leave our world, I would subsequently go through the grief spaces associated with the return.

In order to stave off immediate cries of psychotic delusion, I wish to reassure you that these belief systems operate only under very special conditions. I do not carry them over into my everyday life; to do so would be intolerable for both myself and my loved ones—which is exactly where one learns the first lesson about belief systems. A given belief system can be believed only when it is appropriate to believe it. Appropriateness is determined not only by oneself but by the social reality in which one exists.

To be free of this social reality, I invented the tank. . . . Freed of the social necessities for a few hours, one can take on any belief systems. Then when one comes out of the tank, one resumes the belief system appropriate to the situation in which one finds oneself. Thus belief systems are to some extent analogous to garments that we can put on and take off, that are of various colors and various designs, that may be rather outrageous, sexual, emotional or totally alien.

Thus John was still something of an unreconstructed extra-terrestrial, yearning for the inner domains even as he chose to place the highest value on life with Toni, an existence he now understood to be incompatible with the beliefs he had taken on during his year of samadhi. Some of these beliefs persisted, perhaps in somewhat muted form. John continued to experience the pervasive influence of ECCO—and the Beings—in his life, but later, during a conversation with an interviewer, he dismissed his obsession with the Solid State Intelligence (SSI) with the statement, "I was just getting in touch with my bones and teeth." He had concluded that the body itself was a partially solid state, and therefore not at odds with the SSI, if it existed.

By January 1975, he was pretty much back to being a physically functional member of the human species, once again enjoying being physical, human, and in his unique position on planet Earth. He began sitting in his VW camper, parked next to the house, dictating into a tape recorder a memoir of his experiences, reflections, and thoughts from the year of samadhi, and the following months of pain and healing. This tape became the core of his book, *The Dyadic Cyclone,* published in 1975.

In it, he wrote: "I hope to do a more thorough job on the analysis of the [bicycle] accident in a future book. Currently I am keeping the description within the confines of this book, written with Toni." He never mentioned the central role of ketamine until that future book, *The Scientist* (1978).

At around the same time, John put the finishing touches on *Simulations of God: The Science of Belief* (1976), a book about alternative beliefs and their consequences, drawn from the extra-terrestrial perspective he had assumed during the years of intensive ketamine experimentation. *The Dyadic Cyclone,* written from a human perspective with Toni, could be considered a somewhat sentimental reminiscence about the recent adventures of an explorer who has returned to hearth and home after a perilous voyage. But *Simulations of God* is the report of an extraterrestrial anthropologist, a distant and objective overview of numerous human "niche realities," which earthlings choose to inhabit by taking one or another belief as the foremost reality in their lives, that is, their personal simulations of God.

While *The Dyadic Cyclone* begins with a grateful dedication

to their friend, actor-producer Burgess Meredith, who helped John
and Toni survive the year of samadhi and its sequel of pain,
Simulations takes as its epigraph a quote from science fiction
writer Arthur C. Clarke's *Tales of Ten Worlds:*

> The person one loves never really exists, but is a projection
> focused through the lens of the mind onto whatever screen it
> fits with least distortion.

With this recapitulation, John tacitly acknowledges his own idol-
atry of Toni, via the moat effect, and more generally the ubiqui-
tous human bondage to whomever or whatever one chooses to
value and believe in.

Thus, from the interaction and the cross-fertilization of the
several domains exchanging Zen koans in his brain about the
nature of Reality poured forth a greater flood of writings than in
any previous period of his life: in 1976, *The Dyadic Cyclone* and
Simulations of God; in 1977, *The Deep Self* (and the edited collection *Lilly on Dolphins*); and the following year *The Scientist* and
Communication Between Man and Dolphin. In all, he created five
new books comprising about 2,000 pages over three years, each
of them generated in a creative storm lasting about six weeks,
dictated onto tape and virtually unedited.

In spite of this enormous productivity, there was concern
about John being unbalanced. Some feared he was going to extremes and placing too much value on his far-ranging mental
explorations and too little value on the central issues of health
and bodily continuity. John, however, regarded his body as a
vehicle for education. He wanted to get the maximum mileage out
of it, and practiced many arts for the care of the body, as one
would care for a racehorse, a prizefighter in training, or a samurai
warrior between battles. But he was never especially concerned
with wearing it out or using it up. For him, the point was to use
the body and brain so as to get maximum intensity, experience,
and action within the available bodily life span. His attitude is
best summarized by his succinct statement "My body is my laboratory."

Keenly aware of John's commitment to this belief, Toni
penned a beautiful, calligraphic version of a quotation from
George Bernard Shaw, framed it, and hung it on the bathroom
wall:

I want to be thoroughly used up when I die, for the harder I
work the more I live. I rejoice in life for its own sake. Life is
no "brief candle" to me. It is a sort of splendid torch which
I have got hold of for the moment, and I want to make it burn
as brightly as possible before handing it on to future generations.

One effect of this often traumatic period was John's revision (in *The Dyadic Cyclone*) of his famous law, as follows:

*What one believes to be true in the province of the mind
either is true or becomes true within certain limits. In the
province of the mind there are no limits; however, the body
introduces definite limits.*

Nevertheless, John observed a tension between two poles of
reality, a kind of "rubberband effect": Going into alternate reality
spaces, the farther out you go, the harder you snap back. As a
consequence of this effect, in the intermissions between John's
most outrageous escapades during the 1970s, he often seemed to
others to become narrow, conservative, and fussy, as if he were
compensating for one extreme by going to the opposite. In this
state he would become a cautious, serious Dr. Lilly, M.D., meticulously rational, overbearingly punctilious, with an annoying tendency to recite from the vast store of scientific data accumulated
during his career. When this behavior became burdensome to
him, it served as an incentive to go farther in the opposite direction, into the inner realities.

Over the next decade he would learn to unify the extremes
into a sustainable, steady state, like legendary Buddhist sages of
China, who feared neither life nor death because they were
simultaneously both dead and alive, both beyond the body and
within it.

On the afternoon of October 4, 1975, John and Toni got
married, legally. This came as something of a surprise to many of
their friends who had referred to them for years as John and Toni
Lilly. This festive occasion was attended by many loving friends,
including best couple Bob Swanson and Grace Stern.

It had taken John eight years to get untangled from his marriage to Elisabeth. Although they had separated in 1967 in Florida, she had fought to hang on. Finally John filed for divorce a second time in California, where the new no-fault divorce law had been enacted, and he obtained it.

Approximately two years after John and his friend, Craig Enright, had begun joint experiments with ketamine, a catastrophic car accident landed Craig in the hospital intensive care unit. Negotiating the perilous twists of California Highway 1 in Big Sur, Craig had entered a dense bank of fog when, without warning, another car appeared head-on. As he veered to the right to avoid collision, his car slipped off the pavement, slid across the narrow shoulder, went over the edge, and dropped a hundred feet, bouncing and tumbling a further five hundred feet to lodge in a crevice by the sea.

John was conducting a seminar nearby. He arrived at the intensive care unit at Monterey Peninsula Community Hospital that evening. Craig's head was swathed in gauze, his swollen brain concussed. The neurologists had done their best, but the prognosis was terminal.

John sat at the bedside, holding Craig's hand; he spoke to his friend for a solid hour, giving him a running account of the comings and goings of the other visitors.

"It's not so bad to die, Craig," John told him. "I've been to the brink myself a few times, and I've seen over the edge. The Beings have told me on several occasions that I was free to go with them and leave my body behind for others to worry about; but I decided to stay here and continue my work in this vehicle. The Beings showed me that I'm not really this vehicle that everyone calls John Lilly; they've showed me that I'm one of them. *You are one of us.* I know that you know this because we've been there together. Whatever you do, Craig, I love you."

As darkness descended on Monterey, John returned to the hotel in Carmel by the Sea where he and Toni were conducting the seminar. He made an announcement forbidding any use of psychedelics, including ketamine, that any attendees might have brought for their own use during the weekend, and closed down the isolation tank that had been installed there.

When he visited the hospital the next morning, he found that Craig had died during the night.

During the seventies, John and Toni operated a unique center at their Malibu ranch, affectionately called their "tank farm." At least two isolation tanks, supplied by the Samadhi Tank Company, were in operation at all times. Hundreds of scientists, celebrities, seekers-after-truth, and friends of the family passed through the tanks. Some took only memories; others left written reports, many of which were later published in *The Deep Self*.

Others expressed it in other ways. Some set up isolation tank centers elsewhere: in Hollywood, New York City, Big Sur, Colorado, and Paris. Steve Conger, an architect from Boulder, Colorado, designed and built a variety of isolation tanks for connoisseurs around the country. His guidelines for tank construction were incorporated into *The Deep Self*.

One of the most significant influences on John's study of consciousness in the 1970s was his connection with Franklin Merrell-Wolff. In 1973, John read Merrell-Wolff's extremely obscure and esoteric book, *Pathways Through to Space*, subtitled *A personal record of transformation in consciousness (from a Point I, to a Space I)*, first published in 1944.

"The Ineffable Transition came, about ten days ago," begins the narrative, dated August 17, 1936. It chronicles the author's personal transformation, effected through a combination of Eastern-style yogic meditation and Western-style mathematics. John sensed a reflection of his own lifelong quest, which he found echoed in such aphorisms as:

> . . . the highest form of Asceticism is the true scientist's willingness to give up his bias and predilections when the evidence goes against them. . . . Compassion is the supreme component of the Great Realization.

After reading the book, John sought out the sage. He made a pilgrimage to Merrell-Wolff's hermitage, high on the slopes of Mt. Whitney, the loftiest peak of the High Sierras, but he was not at home. John later found him in the little town of Lone Pine on the eastern side of the Sierras, tended by a small cadre of young devotees.

Franklin Merrell-Wolff seemed somewhat perplexed by John: "From what you say, you seem to be enlightened. If you're enlightened, then why aren't you in Ananda?" (*Ananda* is the Sanskrit word for "a state of bliss.")

Replied John, "I got bored. It was nothing but bliss, bliss, bliss, all the time."

The two scientist-yogis hit it off. John continued to be stimulated by Merrell-Wolff's work and particularly savored his discussion of changes in consciousness in terms of mathematical models in his more recent book, *The Philosophy of Consciousness Without an Object.* John dedicated *Simulations of God* to Franklin Merrell-Wolff.

John was also heavily influenced by science fiction during this period. John Lilly had long been an avid reader, finding that this genre provided him with much of the freshest thinking on the cutting edge of current reality.

Stranger in a Strange Land, by Robert A. Heinlein, made an especially deep impression on John. In this novel, Heinlein's Martian-raised but ultrahuman hero forms an extended family around his own higher consciousness studies. This family is sexually liberated and communal about money. The hero is both wise and rich enough to allow seekers to either donate or take what they need from a large basket of cash left beside the front door.

This idea of the use of money became something of a lifestyle ideal for John. He could never quite figure out why he could not actually live this way himself. To John, the real world of relative wealth and scarcity seemed like an aberration in which he was trapped by some sort of time warp. He felt he was forced to live in some kind of medieval reality populated by accountants, lawyers, and people who for some peculiar reason were constantly in need of this thing called "money."

"Money is a psychotic system," he said,

> a form of forestalled violence waiting to pounce on anyone who weakens, as in a pack of wolves or a school of sharks. Somehow, everyone agrees to play this game, perceiving no

viable alternatives. But in it, everyone is abused, and everyone is an abuser. Within this context, the only solution seems
to be to have so much money that it no longer matters to you.
In my own life so far, I have been able to go as far as I have
in my research, and to contribute what I have to the world,
because I have never had to worry about money. In a system
that runs on money, it is essential that those of genius be
supplied with plenty, so they can be free to experiment and
contribute to the general welfare.

Olaf Stapledon (1886–1950), a writer who mingled science
fiction with ethical speculations, also made a significant impression, particularly with his 1937 novel, *Star Maker* (reissued in
1987). It begins with an autobiographical account of what one
might presume to be a psychedelic experience, as the narrator
rests on a hilltop above his British hamlet and gazes into the
starry night. In *Star Maker,* Stapledon pursues physical reality in
a series of magnifying jumps, from the scale of a single man and
his thoughts to the scale of God-the-Creator and the entire universe. Once the universe evolves to an integrated consciousness
and meets its maker, the Star Maker must consider whether to
destroy it all and begin anew.

In John's scientific imagination, Stapledon's "Star Maker"
blended with physicist John Archibald Wheeler's idea of hyper-
space, to dream of our own universe as a mere bubble in the
cosmic froth, one of an infinite number of possible, probable, and
even actual universes. The physical universe with all its measur-
able properties is just one arbitrary setting on a set of cosmologi-
cal dials. Time, itself, could be no more than a local option.
Within the purview of Merrell-Wolff's "Consciousness-without-
an-Object," the Mind of God, or Hyperspace, everything that has,
will, or could ever happen *is* happening, all at "once."

John also rubbed elbows with Arthur Young, inventor of the
Bell helicopter, a physicist of more practical bent and more traditional metaphysics than Stapledon. Young and his wife Ruth had
founded the Institute for the Study of Consciousness in Berkeley,
close to the University of California campus. John first met them
when he spoke at their institute at the instigation of a mutual
friend, Faustin Bray. John became a frequent guest and occasional keynote speaker there.

Throughout the 1970s and 1980s, the Youngs acted as den

parents to a covey of young physicists including Jack Sarfatti, Saul-Paul Sirag, Nick Herbert, and Fred Alan Wolf, sometimes known collectively as the Physics Consciousness Research Group. They advocated a literal reading of the formulas of quantum mechanics that would, they proposed, throw some light on the connection between consciousness and physical matter.

Their discussions tended to center around Bell's Theorem, a convincing mathematical argument that the rules of quantum physics imply *nonlocality*. Briefly stated, the idea is that events at two different locations in the universe may be connected on the quantum level in a way that allows instantaneous interaction, defying Einstein's principle that our knowledge of any distant events in the physical universe is limited by the speed of light.

Sarfatti, for instance, proposed that the brain might be regarded as a "quantum computer," with subatomic events all over the cortex correlated into a single quantum wave-function that accounted for the experience of a unified consciousness. Such insights are in agreement with some early speculations by such pioneers of quantum physics as Erwin Schrödinger and John Von Neumann, who saw that the formulations of physics could be applied to the brain and mind directly, rather than indirectly, by way of chemistry and neurophysiology.

John was quite at home in this intellectual orientation. He realized that if one started thinking about the brain in terms of the elementary particles of which it is made, according to physics, and if one thought of the mind as the activity of those particles, then one might gain some interesting insights. Such particles are interacting with similar particles throughout the universe. Some may happen to be in the brains of other humans; some are in the brains of dolphins; others are in rocks, trees, the oceans, and the earth; some are in far-off stars. Thus, communication between minds may not be limited to the exchange of signals via the sense organs of human physiology, and the mind may not be strictly contained in the brain.

Synthesizing all this, John developed his theory of a "quantum-jumping consciousness," which seemed to elucidate the experiences he had had at Arica, including the space called $+3$. This idea folded into his developing concept of Alternity.

Arthur Young had written several books, including *The Reflexive Universe* and *The Geometry of Meaning*. The latter John found significant, especially its concept that meaning can be considered analogous to an angle in mathematics. This, too, linked with his model of Alternity as a selection of alternate realities arrayed around oneself like the angular slices of a pie. Meaning, after all, is related to intention and interpretation, two faculties of the mind that make something out of what is. The meaning of something is dependent on one's perspective—one's point of view—and that's your *angle*.

John found the issue of point of view so important that he introduced an acronym for it, POV, into his personal vocabulary and literary lingo. He also coined the acronym COU to represent one's perspective from a POV—the center of the universe. All this agrees with Einstein's emphasis on the fact that every measurement is made within some specific frame of reference and every observation is implicitly from the perspective of a particular observer.

At approximately this point, John's vocabulary received another contribution, this time from his friend, Professor Heinz von Foerster of the University of Illinois, who introduced him to the mathematical idea of *eigenstates,* another term important in quantum mechanics. Eigenstates are a mathematical model for islands of relative stability in the midst of a sea of chaos. The *quanta* of quantum theory, the units corresponding to subatomic particles, are specific eigenstates of a quantum wave-function. If there are such things as states of consciousness, John thought, then they must be eigenstates—specific, relatively stable domains characteristic of brain activity.

But eigenstates come in several flavors: stable, multi-stable, and unstable. What the brain does is neither all conscious nor all consciousness. So the term *states of consciousness* had to be tossed out as misleading, as did the idea of "altered states of consciousness." Instead, John started using the term, *States Of Being* (SOBs), with the proviso that *states* isn't quite the right word either, because it implies stability, while some eigenstates, perhaps the most interesting ones, are unstable.

John's integrated perspective went something like this: Any observer is observing from a specific point of view which is that observer's personal center of the universe. Therefore, every observation carries with it an implicit identification tag that marks its perspective on reality, somewhat like a return address on an envelope indicates where a message is coming from.

The situation is most interesting when the observer is observing himself or herself. In this case, the observer who is being observed is caught in the act of observing the observer. *Observer observing observer observing observer . . .* an infinite series, which generates an eigenstate. That eigenstate is the consciousness of the observer—a "quantum," or basic unit of consciousness.

Reportedly, Albert Einstein imagined himself as *a quantum of light,* a photon, traveling through the universe at the speed of light. Einstein is said to have derived his insights on relativity theory from imagining the experience of the universe from that point of view. John, in some of his experiments, imagined himself as a Quantum Observer (i.e., *a quantum of consciousness*) at large in the brain, the body, and the universe. Such a point-source of consciousness, or point of view, could travel unimpeded through the microstructure of space-time, which, at the scale of 10^{-33} centimeters (Planck's length) is nonlocal, or indeterminate, according to recent formulations of quantum physics.

One inspiration for this kind of adventure came from a doctoral thesis called "The Quantum Observer in a Neurally Engineered Prosthesis," by R.E. Edwards, an electrical engineering student at UCLA. Edwards showed John an original, full-length version, which contained a novel mathematical language called *Topquantese.* John eventually found it useful as an internal reality programming language for navigating as a quantum of consciousness.

Late in 1973, John attended a series of lectures at Hughes Aircraft Company Research Center in Malibu, presented by master-physicist Richard P. Feynman, recipient of the Nobel Prize in physics and professor at John's alma mater, Caltech.

When John arrived at the auditorium where Feynman was to speak, he noticed an unassuming, casually dressed fellow, whom he took to be the janitor, standing behind the reception desk. As it turned out, this "janitor" mounted the podium and began lecturing on physics. It was Feynman himself.

After the lecture, John introduced himself, and in his characteristically direct manner immediately engaged Professor Feynman in shoptalk with this opener: "The observer is the invisible man in physics. You had better study the *observer,* and I have the method!"

BIOGRAPHY

RICHARD PHILLIPS FEYNMAN (1918–1988), born in New York City to a working-class family, attended M.I.T. on scholarship and received his doctorate in physics from Princeton in 1942. He was recruited into the Manhattan Project, where he worked on the development of the first atomic bomb at Los Alamos, New Mexico, until 1945. Subsequently, Feynman served as professor of theoretical physics at Cornell, and then at Caltech beginning in 1950. Widely regarded as the brightest of the postwar generation of physicists, Feynman received the Einstein Award in 1954, the Nobel Prize in physics in 1965, the Oersted Medal in 1972, and the Niels Bohr International Gold Medal in 1973. He was a leading contributor to the theory of quantum electrodynamics, a field whose principal analytical method is the "Feynman diagram." He also worked on the theory of beta decay and on liquid helium. Additionally, Feynman was an accomplished bongo and conga drummer.

The Feynman Lectures in Physics now serves as a standard introductory textbook in the field. His personal views on life are given in *Surely You're Joking, Mr. Feynman!* (1985) and the posthumously published *"What Do YOU Care What Other People Think?"*

With his invention of the isolation tank in 1954, John's original motivation had been to study the scientific observer, a study he perceived to be a major gap in the scientific pursuits of the period. (At that time this was not an acceptable question to raise in the scientific literature, so John had clothed his proposal in the terms of neurophysiology and psychoanalytic theory that were then prevalent.) When he entered the tank to isolate the scientific observer and find out what it was, he discovered a seemingly infinite multitude of phenomena. Now he wanted to introduce the world's hottest physicist to that aspect of the scientific equation—the role and nature of the observer.

John invited Feynman to his next seminar in Malibu, and Feynman accepted. Also attending was Ram Dass (Dr. Richard Alpert) and ten M.D.s who were interested in ketamine. While perhaps not exactly Feynman's cup of tea, he did learn how to use John's isolation tank. Thus began a twelve-week series in which

Feynman came to the Lilly's to spend a three-hour session in the isolation tank, "observing the observer" each week. After each tank session he returned to Caltech and delivered a lecture.

In his best-selling biography, *"Surely You're Joking, Mr. Feynman!"* he described some of his tank experiences in the "Altered States" chapter, where he discussed his efforts to have "hallucinations."

In a gift copy of his *Feynman Lectures in Physics,* he wrote:

> April 1974
> To John Lilly,
> Thanks for the hallucinations.
> —Dick Feynman

John read this and shot back, "Thanks for the book, Dick—but you stopped being a scientist the instant you said that word, *hallucinations.*"

A fourteen-year discussion followed. First, John argued that the word *hallucination* is a trash-bin concept for a whole range of experiences that people wish to discount because they are unconventional or difficult to describe. The term is an unscientific generalization that confuses a multitude of significant processes and specific experiences involving internal reality. "And surely as a physicist," John told Dick, "you make scientific progress by drawing, rather than ignoring, fine distinctions."

Dick Feynman appreciated this point of view, and continued his own explorations of the nature of the scientific observer in various ways over the years. The two scientists became friends, and Dick attempted to assist John's healing process after the 1974 bicycle accident with a peculiar variation of his famous conga drumming. While John lay in his rented hospital bed, his broken bones mending, Dick would play to him like a bushman beating on an electrically amplified Geiger counter.

Another influence on John in the early 1970s was a self-styled southern California Sufi master named E.J. Gold, who produced an idiosyncratic sequel to the *Tibetan Book of the Dead* entitled *The American Book of the Dead.* Based on the popularity of this volume and other endeavors, a cult following of sorts developed around Gold, with a center in the High Sierras.

In person, John found E.J. Gold absolutely marvelous, a classic Buddha, complete with shaved head and a big round belly. Their first encounter was a moment of pure joy, an immediate rapport of the kind John had experienced with only three other people: Oscar Ichazo, Craig Enright, and Franklin Merrell-Wolff. As Alan Watts had said, "If two sages meet and both don't burst out laughing, then one of them is not a sage." For a while, E.J. became a jolly partner for John's cosmic clowning; later, in 1988, Gold published a jazzed-up version of John's famous "cogitate" tape, a demonstration of the repeating-word effect.

E.J. sometimes bragged about such exploits as the time he barged into the Los Angeles office of the Scientology organization, saying, "I'm from headquarters, and I'm here to revise all your manuals and beliefs." He purportedly spent a week there, quietly making revisions in the Scientology literature, and then vanished.

While lecturing in Boston during the summer of 1976, John visited Fred Worden, his loyal friend from Dartmouth med school days. Dr. Worden had followed a less eccentric path of brain research and remained in the medical establishment as director of the Neurosciences Research Program at MIT. Presenting a copy of a book he had recently coedited to John, Fred wrote:

> For John,
>
> *a friend* who stretches all the bounds and makes more than a noticeable difference,
>
> *a scientist* who kicks the crap out of constraints that others cling to,
>
> *and a spirit* that I have watched with admiration and awe for almost forty years, a pioneer whose explorations make it all seem as if other pioneers had stayed home by their comfortable fireplaces!
>
> God knows where you've been, where you are, where you're going, but I know you'll be doing it with great courage, great intellectual power, indomitable determination.
>
> —Fred Worden

At Psychedelic Symposium II, an event held at the University of California's Santa Cruz campus in 1977, John first met Dr.

Albert Hofmann, the Swiss chemist who had invented LSD in 1939. While Hofmann's fame was based on this invention, and his later identification of psilocybin as the principal natural neuroactive constituent in "magic mushrooms," his fortune was based on the many more socially acceptable and commercial compounds he developed while working at the Sandoz labs in Basel. Among these were a number of compounds used to treat migraines and prevent miscarriages during pregnancy.

Hofmann, who retired with Sandoz stock worth millions, might have been mistaken for a typically conservative Swiss retiree, but for the wealth of experience reported in his book *LSD, My Problem Child*. Although his first ingestion of LSD had been accidental, subsequent experiments were voluntary, and they set him on a distinctly spiritual path.

John filed past Dr. Hofmann in the reception line, and introduced himself. "I'm so glad to meet you," replied Hofmann. "I just finished reading *Center of the Cyclone*, and I want to report that my experiences are very parallel to yours."

Albert Hofmann immediately impressed John as a man of both intelligence and good humor. They took a photo together, and John decided to compensate for Albert's lack of height by having him stand on a box so that the picture would come out with them on the same level. Albert and John were to remain friends, getting together on Albert's occasional visits to California, and during John's 1986 tour of Europe.

In 1979, work was under way on the movie *Altered States*, a project loosely based on Paddy Chayefsky's novel of the same title, itself even more loosely based on the adventures of John Lilly. The producers sent the script to John for his comments, and John handed it to Burgess Meredith, who came back with this succinct synopsis: "King Kong meets Dr. Jekyll and Mr. Hyde."

In the film, William Hurt plays a young, dedicated, driven scientist who invents an isolation tank vaguely modeled on the one which John had at NIH. The scientist is so obsessed with his isolation tank that he neglects life outside. Not only does he have bizarre experiences and undergo spiritual transformations but also begins to change physically. In a sequence reminiscent of John's account in *The Scientist* of Craig Enright's regression into a protohominid ancestor of modern man, Hurt's character turns into a carnivorous, apelike being who goes hunting at the zoo for animals to eat.

The passage in the script detailing this scene struck John as a rather hideous distortion, but he withheld judgment until he could see the movie. He understood that any negative comment he made would likely have no effect, since his name was not associated with the project in any way. And anything positive might be construed as an endorsement.

When the finished movie arrived, it was superior to both the script and the novel. Evidently the cinematic artists who were actually responsible for the movie, which was directed by Ken Russell, had some experience in the domains John had pioneered. John and Toni wept in parts, so effectively and poetically did the movie portray what they had gone through together during John's year of samadhi: John almost dying; Toni bringing him back out of primordial spaces and nearly getting drawn into the chaos herself; reconstituting John as a functioning human being; the intensification of love between the couple, who go so far out and then come back in and back together. In the final minutes of the movie, these themes were portrayed with stunning visual effects.

John and Toni were enthusiastic about the film, despite its sensationalized and distorted version of John's career and the lurid, inaccurate view of his isolation tank work.

John received neither credit nor remuneration. In a 1987 interview he quipped, "There are two John Lillys living in parallel universes. The other one is very wealthy, because he patented all our inventions."

CHAPTER 14

THE
WAY OUT

April 1979, age 64.

It's an exhilarating feeling, chasing dolphins in the sea. John and Toni are bathed in spray, their high-speed power boat churning up a wake a mile long. They cling to the rail as two professional dolphin catchers pilot the sleek, open craft and scout for their quarry. They spot a pod of dolphins and head straight for it. One of the pros readies the special sling of fine nylon mesh which they will use to scoop up the dolphins.

Here, off the Gulf Coast of Mississippi, the Atlantic teems with thousands of the Atlantic bottle-nosed dolphins, in small pods and in tribes of hundreds. As the speedboat of dolphin hunters bears down on this pod, net extended to starboard, the dolphins take off at top speed to the left—so abruptly that the boat cannot track their course. The quarry punches through the crests of waves and disappears into the big blue. The disappointed helmsman cuts back on his throttle, slowing the boat in a wide arc to the right. Damn! It was a near miss.

Then John sees two shiny heads bob to the surface, starboard and inside the arc of the boat's turn. These two creatures loll in the sea, as if they were expecting someone. The boat eases toward them and John recognizes them as youngsters, only five or six feet long. John wonders: Are they just disoriented, unable to flee with their pod, too young to know they should avoid humans? Or—the thought fills his mind with an eerie certainty—are they offering themselves for capture? Have they chosen us?

With mixed feelings, John helps the crew scoop these two from the sea. The dolphins make only a token effort to escape the net. The expedition is a success, but John is uneasy about reversing his earlier decision against holding dolphins captive. Silently, he makes a promise to the dolphins: After they have helped the humans learn to communicate, he will return them to their home in the sea. Five years, max, he adds. Silently, the dolphins confirm this pact.

They are a perfect pair—an immature male and female. Just what the doctor ordered. He names them, Joe and Rosie. Toni begins making friends with the captives, who now lie stranded on foam rubber mats, feeling their weight for the first time.

IN 1976, JOHN and Toni and many of their friends created the Human/Dolphin Foundation, a nonprofit organization they hoped would advance interest in cetaceans and attract enough funds to investigate the use of improved computers in achieving a true breakthrough in human communication with dolphins. With the help of a friend, Vance Norum, they incorporated HDF in July.

The following year, Georgia Tanner joined John and Toni on the board of directors, providing a crucial infusion of cash. Dennis Kastner brought his computer expertise to the project, and a number of others began contributing support. The foundation was built entirely by private donations of money and effort, resulting in freedom from the institutional or government control that always accompanies grant money.

By January 1978, they had a PDP-11/04 computer along with a crew of talented young people working to develop computer software to facilitate communication with dolphins. With the assistance of Dr. Daniel Graboi, a psycholinguist from the San Diego branch of the University of California, a special portable laboratory, housed in a truck, was designed and built. This enabled the foundation to travel wherever dolphins might be available. In hopes of generating further interest and funding, that year John published *Communication between Man and Dolphin*, in which he had assembled the relevant data and cogent arguments for both the intelligence of dolphins and the value of establishing communication with them.

During this period, John slowly introduced Toni to the world of the cetaceans. In 1977, they visited Bill Evans, a biologist who operated a cetacean research project behind the scenes at Sea World, on Mission Bay in southern California. Here Toni had an opportunity to encounter the belugas, a larger species of dolphin, sometimes called white whales because of their pale skin and rounded heads. About twelve feet long, these creatures weigh half a ton and have brains significantly larger than those of humans. Toni felt a mystical rapport with the belugas, a kind of psychic connection. Her encounter with them put her into a trance, briefly transporting her to another world. From then on, she was fervently enthusiastic about human-dolphin communication research.

Later, she returned to Sea World with a wet suit so she could swim with the belugas in their chilly water. She was accompanied by her friend, photographer Paul Gaer, who snapped impressive and touching photos of Toni facing Belinda the beluga, some of which appeared in *Communication between Man and Dolphin.*

The kind of experience Toni had, that of being pulled out of ordinary, human, physical reality and taken on a journey elsewhere by the cetaceans, is not uncommon among sensitive people in the presence of dolphins and whales. Some people say dolphins offer a higher state of consciousness to those who are open to the experience. John himself had had many episodes in the Islands when it seemed as if the cetaceans were somehow generating a more potent reality than that of the ordinary human world.

Toni thus embraced the world of the dolphins in a way she did not for many of the other unusual realities to which John exposed her. She had encountered the internal reality through him, but had no desire to live there as John did. She had failed to grasp the extraterrestrial reality. She had experimented with psychedelic drugs in the 1960s, the period of history when it was fashionable for artistic members of her generation to do so, but, with occasional exceptions, she had left this pursuit behind. She was fond of quoting Alan Watts on this point: "When you get the message, hang up the phone." She summed up her overall impression of LSD as "squiggles and giggles."

But dolphins . . . they were her kind of people.

In 1978, Burgess Meredith invited John and Toni to a dinner party with Joseph E. Levine, producer of the 1973 film *The Day of the Dolphin,* and his wife Rosie.

Levine's film had infuriated John. Clearly, it was based on John's scientific work with dolphins; its promotional literature even cited his endeavors explicitly. John found that George C. Scott, in the role of the kindly scientist, was not an unattractive alter ego. But the film was an inaccurate and misleading rendition, in which dolphins, who actually vocalize in air with their blowholes, were shown talking through their mouths like humans.

John also disliked the film's portrayal of dolphins involved in espionage and violence, which he thought was exactly the wrong kind of image of dolphins to project to the public. At the time, he was not fully appreciative of the prophetic character of the movie's theme: A kindly scientist's idealistic research with dolphins is taken over by covert agencies and turned to violent ends. Years later he would discover that in this respect, *The Day of the Dolphin* really was his own story.

As John saw it at the time, the producers of the film had used his name and reputation to promote their film without his permission, and without even consulting him concerning the script. Then they had made a film that badly misrepresented his scientific work, presenting an unrealistic image of dolphin behavior. John was reasonably concerned that the realistic things he had reported about dolphin behavior might be discredited by people mixing them up with the unrealistic behavior portrayed in the movie. (Years later, in fact, John would find himself unjustly accused in the press of claiming that dolphins talk like humans!) John sued the producers on a charge of copyright infringement, and lost.

Now John was sitting down to dinner with his courtroom nemesis; predictably enough, an awkward moment ensued. Levine broke the ice by confessing, "Dr. Lilly, I realize that my movie must have caused you great distress."

"Yes, very great," John said somberly, recalling the old insult. "Very great indeed." Both John and Joe Levine then looked toward Burgess who, realizing the opportunity inherent in the occasion, promptly elicited from the Levines an offer to donate $20,000 to the Human Dolphin Foundation.

The money was used to acquire a pair of two-year-old dolphins from off the gulf coast. Named Joe and Rosie, after the Levines, the pair were transported to Marine World/Africa USA, located on the shores of San Francisco Bay at Redwood City. The Human/Dolphin Foundation moved the Dodge van containing its portable laboratory to this zoolike environment on the bayside mud flats and set up Project JANUS, whose insignia was an image of the two-faced Roman god of portals and beginnings.

JANUS (Joint Analog Numerical Understanding System) attempted to match the channels of communication of each species; the human face of JANUS was a computer screen and keyboard, while its dolphin face was composed of underwater loudspeakers and microphones. Since dolphins' brains are oriented more toward the auditory than the visual, the system allowed dolphins to communicate by sound; since human brains are more visual than auditory, the system allowed humans to communicate through the manipulation of visual symbols on the computer screen, translated into high-pitched digital signals within the dolphins' hearing range. Such a system was far less complex and less expensive than one that would have attempted to translate directly between the speech and hearing range of humans and the hearing and vocalization range of dolphins.

By the late 1970s, computers had become available that were fast enough at least to begin to perform the work required, yet small, portable, and inexpensive enough for Project JANUS. During the time of the first dolphin project in the Islands, an equivalent system would have cost several million dollars; now it cost in the neighborhood of $100,000 to take the first steps toward interspecies communication.

With the help of Mike and Patti Demetrios, the operators of Marine World/Africa USA, the new dolphin lab came together. In the back lot, past the elephant house and the giraffe barn, two large, circular pools had been set up for marine mammals. A channel was built connecting these pools into one huge aquarium. Once they were filled with 200,000 gallons of saltwater, Joe and Rosie were installed in their new home.

The JANUS truck was parked beside the channel, the hydro-phones lowered into the water, and work began on the second epoch of human-dolphin communication.

The project combined unprecedented computer translation techniques with the intensive personal interaction that John had earlier found to enhance communication and learning between the two species. As the new facilities offered only deep, relatively cool water, a sturdy breed of human participants was called for. The foundation recruited an avid crew of college-aged men and women who were adept swimmers; John called them his dolphin boys and dolphin girls.

Over the next several years, Toni often joined the dolphins in the water, floating in her wet suit in an innertube. A string of hundreds of invited guests had the opportunity to experience intensive interaction with dolphins. Tots from the Esalen Institute nursery school trooped in with their teacher, Janet Lederman, to splash with their new "dolphriends." (For these little ones, the effective depth of the water was decreased by stretching a net about two feet below the surface.) And a number of celebrities visited, including singer/songwriter John Denver, Werner Erhard, Timothy and Barbara Leary, actress Barbara Carrerra, and many others. Each had their own version of the dolphin encounter, usually ranging from exhilarating to ecstatic, and most of them went on to publicly praise the dolphins and John's work with them. In the case of the Learys, the dolphin experience helped to advance the formation of a friendly relationship with John, who had earlier rejected Timothy.

And the dolphins, Joe and Rosie, contributed to these in-teractions as only they could. They did everything in their power to educate humans in unexpected ways, including teach-ing the humans games they had invented using the large stock of oversized floating toys. Among these games was "dolphin frisbee." When the dolphins played it with one another, Joe would hook the rim of the frisbee over his chin, twirl it around, and toss it. Rosie would leap to the appropriate position, catch it on her chin, and toss it back. When humans on land beside the pool became involved, the dolphins began generating varia-tions in the rules. They turned it into fetch, with humans assum-ing the part customarily reserved for dogs. The dolphins were often inventive in this way, using such interaction to "shape" the human's behavior. The dolphins clearly proved that humans were not the only ones who could be trainers.

Following John's pioneering work at CRII, during his hiatus from dolphin research, and while he was gearing up for project JANUS, many others entered the field—most of them inspired by John's early work and its impact on our culture through the media.

By 1980, some of these numerous other players were pulling dolphin research in very different directions from those John pursued. The biggest of these players by far was the U.S. Navy and the researchers it supported. John had been asked to help the navy set up its dolphin research program at Point Mugu in the early 1960s. He had suspected then that the navy's program would be less scientific than "operational"—i.e., directed toward training dolphins to accomplish military objectives. Nevertheless, he had attempted to stay in touch, hoping to keep informed of anything the navy might be learning about dolphins but not disclosing to the public. The program was eventually moved to the Naval Oceans Systems Center at San Diego, where it was submerged under deepest secrecy.

In 1980, John found that the Naval Oceans Systems Center had organized a conference on dolphin research, to which they invited a number of prominent scientists, conspicuously excluding John Lilly. He contacted the conference's hosts and expressed his outrage at being excluded, but to no avail.

The navy's delegation to this conference was headed by Dr. Forrest G. Wood. The ostensible purpose of this meeting was to help the navy establish its priorities for funding outside scientists. From a transcript of the conference proceedings John later obtained from a colleague, he learned that Wood and another scientist, Dr. Robert Buhr, had urged their colleagues to organize a cadre among dolphin researchers to oppose John's ideas. Their complaint was that his efforts had established in the public mind a pervasive image of dolphins as intelligent beings. This perception, according to Wood and Buhr, had contributed to the enactment of federal law—Marine Mammal Protection Act (MMPA), which set limits on the number of dolphins that could be captured or killed and prescribed regulations governing their treatment in captivity. This, they noted, was already impacting the tuna fishing industry (the tuna fishermen found it inconvenient to net yellow-fin tuna without slaughtering hundreds of thousands of dolphins per year in the process). They did not specifically mention the obstacles the MMPA might pose for the navy. (In 1989, the MMPA would serve as the basis for a lawsuit against the navy, alleging abuse of the dolphins.)

According to Wood and Buhr, their objective was to establish an authoritative group that would work to counter John Lilly's position that dolphins are intelligent. It was a project that would have to be systematically carried out over many years in order to alter the public's high regard for dolphins.

When John learned what the agenda of the conference had been with respect to his own work, he reacted angrily, writing letters to various participants. A flurry of acrimonious correspondence ensued. As a result, John became aware of the entrenched opposition to his views on dolphins among some institutionally supported scientists.

Under the Reagan administration, with its penchant for channeling the public's research money through the Department of Defense, the influence of the navy-related researchers grew. Subsequent events were organized by essentially the same people who were involved in the 1980 conference. This group achieved a de facto prominence in the otherwise undersupported area of dolphin research. (Certainly, many participants were unaware of the agenda Wood and Buhr advanced; certainly there were others who, while aware, did not support it.)

In the years that followed, John noticed in the press the appearance of articles that quoted a small set of researchers who consistently made statements about John's own work that were both derogatory and inaccurate. They stated in vague, unscientific terms that Lilly's work was fanciful, and that dolphins were unlike Lilly's description of them. At the same time, these researchers were busy performing experiments whose actual results, if fully analyzed, supported John's major thesis about dolphin intelligence and language ability. But the researchers were careful not to analyze or describe their results in these terms. They avoided making explicit references to Lilly's numerous scientific publications about dolphins and of course did not make the connection to his theories, even as their own experimental work validated those theories.

The prophecy of *The Day of the Dolphin* in many respects

came true. The field John founded was largely taken over by a covert group operating under military secrecy. And beyond this inner circle, on the "public" side of dolphin research, the agenda became increasingly dominated by the side effects of the military's operational objectives, at the expense of the open, scientific pursuit of truth. John knew, however, that the scientific process is such that both individual prejudice and institutional bias eventually would be overcome by the force of nature—and the truth would come through. There were many sincere seekers of truth by the path of science who kept a low profile out of prudence.

As Project JANUS proceeded, John experimented privately with Joe and Rosie, attempting to communicate through channels which lay well outside the purview of the research program. These experiments were based on the leaky mind hypothesis, or on John's evolving ideas about the nature of the reality in which dolphins live.

He was coming to the conclusion that through their vocalizations dolphin create a three-dimensional world of sound, a virtual reality of sonic images resembling a kind of "cetacean television," constantly broadcast at one another. The dolphins, after all, live more in an environment of sound than one of sight. Since they communicate sonically, John suspected that such communications create a shared, simulated reality. The situation is somewhat analogous to what might happen if humans could communicate by creating images directly in one another's minds or, perhaps, to the world of images humans generate through electronic communication. According to John's view, by concentrating on simple verbalization, the research program was only tapping into a tiny segment of the dolphins' available communication channels.

It occurred to him that the virtual realities in which dolphins are immersed might resemble the internal realities he had explored. The internal realities are always operating at a low level in the human brain, constrained by a person's participation—John called it "interlock"—with the external reality. With techniques such as isolation, the internal reality can be "uncoupled" from the the external reality and can thus be enhanced, made more vivid and detailed, and set free.

John thought that he might be able to disconnect his internal reality from the external reality through isolation, and connect it with the virtual reality of the dolphins. To accomplish this, he had an isolation tank set up in a building next to the Project JANUS dolphin pool. This tank was equipped with underwater loud-speakers connected to receivers in the pool. He also rigged a microphone in the air above the flotation fluid in the tank. As he floated face up on the surface, he could speak into this micro-phone and be heard in the dolphin pool.

With this setup, John spoke to the dolphins, who immediately recognized his voice and responded by producing an extraordinary phenomenon for him. They emitted sounds that produced a three-dimensional holosonic space for him, as if he were in the pool with them. Then they produced a trill that systematically resonated with different parts of his body, sweeping it from head to toe. The acoustic resonance was so perfect that it tickled his skin.

Apparently the dolphins were able to effectively "visualize" the space inside John's tank, even though it was connected to their pools only by electrical wires and audio amplifiers. With this information, working through the remote audio channels, they were able to manipulate the acoustic space around John's body and present this stunning demonstration. For humans to accomplish a similar feat, they would require the most powerful computers available in the 1980s and about a year to get the programming right. But the dolphins just did it in their heads. Equally impressive was the fact that the dolphins had taken the initiative, correctly appraised this opportunity for communication, and made the required effort.

In some experiments with the poolside isolation tank, John used ketamine to enhance his ability to program his internal reality. He visited both the internal reality and the extraterrestrial reality and allowed the dolphins to program his experiences. The results were so bizarre as to be utterly indescribable in terms of human consensus reality. Even a veteran explorer such as John had difficulty assimilating them afterward.

In other experiments, John shut off the electronic link with the dolphins and, from his internal reality, invited the dolphins to program his experiences by any means available to them. This explored the assumption that dolphins could communicate with humans telepathically, which had first occurred to John in his isolation tank above the dolphin pool in the Virgin Islands lab. John conjectured that telepathic communication might use the portions of the brain's cerebral cortex that are called "silent areas," regions not apparently directly linked to any kind of physical sensation or observable muscular behavior. Since dolphins have larger silent areas than humans, John thought that they might be more readily telepathic than humans. A few humans he had met seemed to have a special rapport with dolphins that might be telepathically based. He thought that perhaps such individuals had relatively large silent areas which they could use this way.

During one of these experiments, John mentally asked Joe and Rosie certain questions. In his internal reality, they appeared to respond to his questions by linking him with what he could only describe as a dolphin group-mind, which, in turn, plugged him into the whale group-mind. Completely beyond description, this experience was overwhelming. John later described his reaction: "I'm just one human, and all I can handle is one dolphin at a time!"

There were, however, problems with JANUS from the start. The project was starved for funding; grant proposals to the National Science Foundation, made from 1978 through 1980, were favorably received by the peer review committee, but drew no funds due to funding shortages and other, higher priorities at NSF. With the exception of a grant from the Erickson Educational Foundation, which paid a part-time salary for physicist John Kert, lack of money necessitated staffing by volunteers, mostly enthusiastic youngsters selected because of the ease with which they shared the dolphins' aquatic environment. These sassy and athletic kids were bursting with energy and pride, but lacked real understanding of the requirements of documented scientific research; mature, expert scientific and technical personnel were notably scarce. The full array of talent necessary to systematically develop the computer software and advance the research agenda never arrived.

Additionally, the physical environment in which dolphins and humans could interact at Project JANUS fell short of the ideal. These facilities, thrown together with charity, luck, and "cosmic coincidence control," fell below the minimum standards for human-dolphin interaction labs that John had drawn up in the 1960s and only partially achieved in his first dolphin lab in the Virgin Islands. The climate and the water at Redwood City were too cold for humans and dolphins to comfortably hang out together. There was no access to the ocean for the benefit of the dolphins. The pool was deep, failing to provide a shallow-water interaction zone where humans could stand their ground. Thus there was not enough of a shared environment for interspecies cooperation.

Moreover, the computers the foundation had acquired in 1978 began to appear rather outdated after a few years. The PDP-11 computers at the heart of JANUS were designed in the early 1970s. Much more powerful computers were now available at the same price, but even if they could be used, the art of software design was still too primitive to do justice to the JANUS concept. John would eventually realize that his facilities and software were inadequate to demonstrate the spectrum of dolphins' communication abilities. By this time as well, the concrete results had been disappointing. John concluded that to succeed in producing the stunning interspecies breakthrough he sought, it would require a fresh start with expert personnel, ideal facilities, and the next generation of computers and software.

Project JANUS came to a close in 1985. Among various contributing factors was the fact that Marine World/Africa USA was moving. Toni Lilly's vitality was waning in the final years of her living with cancer. Also, there was the pact that John had made with Joe and Rosie when he first brought them to the dolphin pool; he had pledged to return them to the society of wild dolphins after five years of interacting with humans in captivity. It was a promise he felt they had somehow understood and accepted, one that he was not about to break.

When Project JANUS ended, Toni joined forces with Barbara Clarke (administrator of the foundation and other diverse activities whom John had brought on board in 1980) to raise $30,000 from Meredith and others in order to return Joe and Rosie to Florida. Later, the pair were transferred to the Georgia coast, where Jim Hickman, Gigi Coyle, and environmental consultant John Allen developed a program to prepare Joe and Rosie for their return to the wilds of the Atlantic Ocean. Rick O'Barry, formerly Flipper's trainer, helped to prepare them for their new life, in part by teaching them the art of catching their own fish. Their final release, late in 1987, was televised in a National Geographic/TBS special program early the next year.

Joe and Rosie have since been spotted swimming with a baby dolphin. One can only speculate what information they have been sharing with their child and with other dolphins of the Atlantic after their eight-year education among humans.

Although JANUS data has never been sufficiently analyzed to be eligible for publication in a scientific journal, the project did not terminate without some positive results. By the time it was wrapped up, Joe and Rosie, approaching sexual maturity, knew high-pitched, computerized versions of fifty human words and, more significantly, the syntax to go with them. The dolphins successfully picked up the beeps and squeaks of the JANUS computers, which, while within their normal hearing-speaking range, were unrelated to the dolphins' normal sounds. Yet they reproduced these sounds to express the same conventional meanings as those humans assigned to them. They caught on to the idea that the precise *sequence* of words conveys additional meaning in the humans' world, and they used the sounds and sequences deftly to respond to humans and control events in their environment.

Another positive result of Project JANUS was that the idea of using computers as intermediaries between humans and dolphins caught on elsewhere. It was emulated at other laboratories, including the University of Hawaii, where a form of this work continues, and at the new Marineland in Vallejo, California. At the Kewalo Basin Marine Mammal Laboratory, software expert Karl Langton and his colleagues are currently developing artificial intelligence (AI) software to sort out the torrent of sonic interaction among dolphins and human researchers. The several researchers who have tested dolphins' ability to learn languages have generally produced results that confirm John Lilly's observation that dolphins are highly language-capable.

The prolonged contact with Joe and Rosie during Project JANUS reinforced John's view that dolphins are not animals to be experimented upon, but rather genuine alien intelligences with which humans can interact in strange and marvelous ways, given the right conditions. John dreamed of human-dolphin interaction centers, where his long-term ambition of learning from and with dolphins and letting the dolphins learn human ways as well, could be pursued. His research center at Dolphin Point in the Virgin Islands had been only a first and, in many ways, an inadequate attempt. The facilities at Marine World had been even less adequate, despite the excellent intentions and better computers.

In the 1980s, many people demonstrated their interest in interactions with dolphins and a few centers for such activity came into existence, such as Dolphins Plus in Florida. John and Toni explored many avenues to establish an ideal center in a warm-water location. While others became involved in these discussions, the necessary combination of dedication and material support did not appear.

The dyadic cyclone composed of John and Toni resembled the natural phenomenon from which it took its name. There were often storms and persistent crosscurrents of conflict between them.

Individually, they attracted different sorts of people and invited different modes of contact. Thanks to Toni, the couple's work was made accessible to many who could not have maintained an interaction with John. Toni interpreted the signals emitted by her extraterrestrial husband to her friends, and to the world at large.

John sometimes took exception to the translation. Despite the obvious public-relations benefits of humanizing John's "stainless steel computer" mind, and translating his intimidatingly precise concepts into warmer, less precise, more palatable forms, John was occasionally (perhaps frequently) vexed by her packaging and popularization, which often smudged out the finer points that were vitally important to John. He hated it when she would say something like "What John really means to say is . . ." and then substitute what he considered to be a glib platitude.

This undercurrent of conflict surfaced in a television interview conducted beside the dolphin pools at Marine World/Africa USA. Toni presented their research in her own terms, which she suspected would play well in the world of television. John kept objecting and Toni persisted, even interpreting his objections, to which John in turn further objected. Neither budged from positions entrenched by years of practice.

John was fond of playing the role of an intellectual Zen Master, who meant his words to challenge, stimulate, and even perplex. Toni took on the role of a den mother, who wanted to be understood by as many cubs as possible—and she sometimes seemed to be playing the role of a mother rationalizing the prodigious words and deeds of her precocious child.

John had been visiting Alternity on the night in 1971 when he entered that house in the Hollywood Hills and was swept into the dyadic cyclone, locking in on Toni. That event had been the resolution of Alternity: in the peculiar jargon of quantum physics, "the wave function collapsed," and the outcome was a single reality, John and Toni's life together. In prosaic terms, out of all the men and women in the world, they chose each other. In more sublime terms, out of all the potential beings in each of them, their intersection selected one pair. The chemical bond was formed, and the future was fated.

Like the meeting of sperm and egg, the joining of two out of thousands of cells selecting a single genetic combination, a single being with finite limitations and definable characteristics, brought into actuality; similarly, John and Toni's meeting created a single reality and, in a sense, a third entity, the Dyad, out of all possible ways they could have paired.

Unlike Toni, John had been consciously aware of Alternity. Later, he began to feel that he had somehow lost something, even as he gained the particular world shared with Toni. He felt himself uncomfortably squeezed back into a limited identity. His adventures during the 1970s might be viewed as a series of attempts to reopen himself to Alternity without leaving the dyadic shell entirely. And now, coiled within him like a sleeping dragon, were all of the other possibilities that Alternity enfolded.

The closer he and Toni grew, and the more integrated their lives became, the less he could recall Alternity. Only by using chemicals could he fly into Alternity, leaving Toni behind in her own reality. Through such methods, he attempted to maintain contact with Alternity and with Toni as well—and that was asking a lot from a relationship!

On her 52nd birthday, John wrote Toni a thank-you note. It was typed, signed, framed, and hung on the wall:

To My Love and Best Friend on Her Birthday

Toni Lilly

25 November 1980

Malibu

The place you have transformed for our shared living is your
ten-year work of art. Everywhere I look that your artist's eye
has lingered and thought and created anew is some harmony
novel to me. I think pragmatically with some utilitarian ends
in mind for the external reality introjected. You think in ways
beyond my ken, and generate works of merit with criteria of
mystery and ancient lore. Thank you, my Love and best
friend, with a happy birthday.
        —John Lilly

Clearly, John was not unhappy with the reality they had
created together—rather, he longed for the possibilities it excluded. Ten years after leaving Alternity behind, he was sorely
missing it.

The actuality they had generated in the intervening years
was certainly positive in many ways. The dyadic cyclone had
made quite a stir in the world. There was the institute dedicated
to communication between humans and dolphins. There were
five new books in the world and more in the works. The little
ranch behind Malibu had been developed into a beautiful country
estate, where hundreds of people could be entertained at one of
the many parties they gave for people interested in their work.
Their friends included interesting, intelligent, important, wealthy,
and influential people who could support and contribute to their
projects.

All this had come about in spite of—or perhaps because
of—John's irrepressibly eccentric experimentation, death-defying
stunts, and occasionally startling public behavior. Toni did not
know what to make of this seeming paradox. It was those very
things about her man—the most startling, most unacceptable,
most *scary*—that accounted for the success that she was enjoying with him. John had things to say, and people were interested
in listening to him, precisely because he had done those things
that everyone had told him not to do. Most remarkable of all, he
was still alive.

As John began to long for Alternity, he started to feel that this scene around him was unreal, that Toni had created a mirage. Combining her outstanding social agility with the home-centered prowess of a powerful Mediterranean matriarch, she had spun a silky web of social prominence. She had gathered people whom John felt really had no idea what he was all about, but who, through Toni's intercession, could be seduced into supporting— sometimes almost worshiping—the image of Dr. Lilly, the brilliant scientist, psychoanalytic genius, patron of the lovable dolphins, and friend of humanity.

Despite its resplendent facade, the dyadic cyclone held many closed doors within it. Doors to spaces he had gone to but couldn't bring Toni were closed for John; doors to spaces for which she simply had no affinity were closed for Toni. Gradu-ally—it took years—John noticed Toni's intrinsic limitations, characterizing a creature so utterly dissimilar from himself. Slowly the illusions, the infatuation, the entrancement wore off. John recognized that once again he had projected onto an available screen what he wanted in a partner, and had clung to those projections in spite of the mounting evidence of experience. He realized that he had entered into three marriages seeing not the woman standing there, but only his desires and expecta-tions.

In Toni, John had first seen the perfect partner for the spiri-tual trajectory on which he was launched after his journey west and his initiation at Arica. But as it turned out, she was really something else. Instead of being, like John, a denizen of hyper-space, she was more of a skillful and beloved anchor to external reality. By now, they were both well aware of this situation and understood each other as well as two people could. At this point they had come to accept each other for what they were, and they were, after all, old friends. Life was for learning; on this and a few other points they tacitly agreed.

John's sixty-sixth birthday party bustles and hums around him. Toni, in a gorgeous silk outfit hand-painted with butter-flies, presides over a circle of friends. Dozens of people drift through the house, passing the three bars, spilling out onto the lawns and patios, dancing to the band outside. John settles in a recliner in the corner of the living room. He sees his image reflected in the huge mirrors covering the opposite corner of the room, among reflections of the others present. He sur-

rounds himself with a meditative aura, hoping to be left alone for awhile, and begins a journey through time.

In his mind, he moves back to last year's birthday party. It was a similarly festive occasion, featuring many of the same players. Toni was a little livelier, although not so comfortably in command; there was more of the little girl in her, less of the sophisticate. Back in the present, he notices a few guests have not reappeared. One of them, Gregory Bateson, has died in the intervening year. He sees his own reflection across the room as if across the abyss of time.

Next he superimposes the two years, the two parties—an operation which physicists call a coherent superposition. The images do not smear or blend together, but rather become transparent, overlaid on each other, with each retaining full clarity. Both images are present without mutual interference; he can tune in on each in turn, as they waver in apparent competition for both the space in the room and in his mind.

He realizes that the two images are alternating as his attention shifts back and forth from a detail of one to a detail of the other. He relaxes and takes in the whole scene without attraction and without discrimination. When both images are balanced, a remarkable new phenomenon occurs. At first a ghostly mist appears; then, as the balance becomes perfect, it transforms into a shimmering aurora borealis, connecting this year's images with last year's.

Three dimensions can no longer contain what John is seeing, and words cannot describe it. He passes from the present into the flow of time. In the billowing folds and scintillations are both the present and the past, linked to all their unrealized possibilities, and the future with its range of possibilities not yet reduced by passage through the bottleneck of immediacy. He tunes into the following year and the years beyond. Now he becomes deeply saddened, for he perceives an ever-widening chasm opening up in his reality, establishing itself finally as an irrevocable facet of the structure of his life to come.

He rises and retires to his room. There, he lies on the bed and leaves the scintillating stream of spacetime in which he has been swimming and retreats into the void beyond it. There he rests and attempts to recover from the impact of what he has seen.

Fifteen minutes later he rejoins the party.

In 1981, John accompanied Toni to Forth Worth, Texas, for cancer therapy at the institute of Dr. Carl Simonton. She had recently undergone a lumpectomy surgery in Los Angeles, performed by a conventional breast cancer specialist. He had said, "I hope we got all of it, but you never know." John was well aware that even a single cell of the tumor escaping into her circulatory system might well lodge elsewhere in the body and start growing into a malignant mass.

Dr. Simonton was among the first medical practitioners to openly state the observation that the level of a patient's immune system response is affected by mood and emotions. In view of the crucial role of the immune system in eliminating cancerous cells, he conjectured that a patient's chances for recovery could be enhanced by mental exercises that induce a sense of well-being and control over the situation. At his clinic, patients were taught to visualize their body's immune system cells making a vigorous attack on cancer cells and destroying tumors. Toni attended this program to improve her chances for full recovery.

One night, in a Fort Worth hotel room, John chose to explore alternative realities in hope of shedding light on their difficulties. He took an injection of ketamine and they lay down together on the round, king-size bed. In his internal reality, they became the yin and yang, the ancient Chinese symbol of duality in unity, and this symbol expanded in scope to the entire universe, with John and Toni the reigning god and goddess. From this vantage point, the possibility of a disease interfering with this divinity seemed absurd and insignificant. (Later, John considered this experience a symbol of the overvaluation space in which he had put Toni and their life together.)

Toni completed her therapy at the clinic, and they returned to Malibu. It seemed as if the cancer had been beaten. For some time to come, there was not a single sign of the disease.

In 1982, while psychiatrist and psychotherapeutic trailblazer Ronald D. Laing was visiting John in Malibu, John arranged a ketamine session with him. As he emerged from the alternate realities, John looked at Ronnie's face, which seemed to radiate beatitude, love, and grace at that moment.

"I love you, Ronnie," John said, "and I've never said that to a man before."

"John, the way in is not the way out," Ronnie replied.

Ronnie Laing's response referred to the directions in psychotherapy he had pioneered as an alternative to prevailing concepts based on psychoanalysis. The implicit assumption built into most schools of psychotherapy is that you work through your earlier experiences, or what you can remember of them. One attempts to get in touch with those past experiences that presumably are influencing one's current behavior. Whether through analysis, acting them out, or some other technique, the past is reconstructed and recapitulated. In theory, one works one's way out of one's psychological problem by dealing with the same material that generated the problem in the first place. In other words, "the way in *is* the way out."

Laing was among the post-Freudian pioneers who disagreed with this. According to him, the purpose of therapy is to facilitate a growth process through which one grows out of and beyond the problem. Health is fought for and won through a series of discoveries, trials, and innovations, unique to each individual, which raise a personality to a higher level of functioning. One has new experiences that supersede, in meaning and significance, the experiences of the past. This process, along with the individual path that is discovered therein, provide *the way out.*

Since his psychoanalysis with Robert Waelder, John had been aware that he had difficulty feeling positively toward other people. In analysis, he devised an explanation for this inhibition of positive feelings that was consistent with Freud's ideas: He concluded that he had cut off his love for his mother at the time of weaning. According to the underlying premise of psychoanalysis, the problem, once analyzed in this fashion, should thereby have been solved.

But it hadn't been. In the intervening years John knew that he still carried with him a basic inhibition of positive feelings, overcome only on occasion by his susceptibility to transports of infatuation or overvaluation, particularly with women.

Now, with ketamine in his system, John was able to experience and express his love for Laing, whose remark struck him with the realization that he was now functioning at a higher level. His problem of inhibited love, and whatever may have been its cause, had been left behind. The way in, whatever it might have been and however complicated it might have seemed, was a relic of the past, merely a quirk of the particular life story of the personality called John Lilly, nothing more than a biographical coincidence.

From that moment, many of the people around John began to notice that an immense burden seemed to have been lifted from him. He began to be happy most of the time, and often wore a smile that reminded some people of a beatific saint. The rubber-band effect, snapping back from extraordinarily high states to extraordinarily low states, ceased to reappear.

One afternoon in 1981 at Esalen, John held forth before a small group, expounding his latest ideas on Alternity, quantum mechanics, and the relationship to individual experience of the physical and chemical states of the brain.

One woman, an old friend of John's, interrupted to object that John was carrying on too much as a scientist, using terms and concepts she did not appreciate. He was being "too intellectual," he was "on a head trip." She wanted to hear something more "spiritual" from John. Other members of the group chimed in, complaining that John was not "going with the flow," was not "in the Tao."

John explained that he was just as interested in the Tao, or God, as they, but he also wanted to know how the Tao works, or "how God does it." John told the story of the Scottish physicist, Clerk Maxwell, who, listening to a science lecture as a schoolboy in the early nineteenth century, reportedly told the lecturer, "That's fine, sir, but I want to know the GO of it."

John frequently encountered such reactions to the manner and mode of his search for Reality. After the publication of *The Center of the Cyclone* in 1972, many people came to view him as a spiritual adventurer and teacher, a kind of guru. Some felt that his speaking and acting as a scientist somehow constituted an aberration from the spiritual path, a regression into cold, hard, mind-locked science, or "Newton's Sleep," as poet William Blake called it.

No doubt those who have so objected subscribe to the commonplace view of the scientist as one who, with arcane intellectual machinations, studies isolated parts of nature in the world outside himself. John's view of the scientist is much more inclusive. In *Programming and Metaprogramming in the Human Bio-computer,* he defined a scientist as one who includes *himself* in the subject of his research and he later elaborated as follows: "Science is finding out what God did and how He did it, using your best intelligence. You can then do some of it yourself. Unfortunately it often comes out weird; instead of creating a sun, you create a nuclear weapon."

John has long held that science is just as mysterious as mysticism; it should not be thought of as separate from the world of the spiritual. Over time, phenomena of nature previously relegated to the realms of the mystical and spiritual can fall under the scope of science, as people begin to develop scientific models for them. A favorite example of this process is the phenomenon of radio waves. In the 1700s, any description of them would doubtless have sounded quite mystical to the people of the time, because there was no way of detecting and manipulating them in those days. John is fond of saying, "In the 1700s, radio was silent." An analogous contemporary situation, ESP phenomena are at best quite controversial from a scientific point of view; at worst they are taboo. John's view is that ESP is currently "silent" in the manner of radio waves in the 1700s, because as yet we have no publicly verifiable way of detecting it.

Many of those who have tried to classify John have had difficulty deciding whether he is a believer in physics or in metaphysics. John has responded by saying:

> I take on the beliefs that people have in order to communicate with them—for example, the contained-mind belief for those who think the mind is contained in the brain. You can simulate anything I've experienced within this system. If you experience the inside of someone else's mind, then you can just say, "That was telepathy, which is something like radio." Just as easily, you can assume that the mind is not contained in the brain, and then explain the same experiences in those terms. Some people prefer it this way.
>
> The computer software model of brain/mind demystifies all the stuff about souls, spirits, psyche, etc., without taking a position either for or against the existence of these things. I realized early on that all those people trying to talk about "consciousness" were totally confused by their own language. The model of a computer clears this up. That computer in the next room has a "contained mind." The software

isn't walking around the room; it's contained in the computer. But if you run a wire from that computer to another computer, then what have you got?

In 1985, Toni weakened and became ill. For a time, it had appeared as if she had beaten the cancer; in fact the disease had been silently spreading for five years, invading tissues and wrecking bones. She chose to shun the half-hope offered to someone in her condition by the medical establishment with its knives, rays, and poisonous drugs, but she was not about to give up. Although her light was fading, her sense of her own existence waning, she wanted it back. She would not "go gently into that good night."

In the final months of the year, she went for broke, seeking with whirlwind determination the regeneration of the familiar body and the continuity of the full clarity of being Toni Lilly. She tried everything the New Age had to offer in the way of healing—herbs and wheat grass, vitamins and garlic, crystal amulets and psychic healers laying on hands.

In the final weeks, she journeyed to Mexico with her friend Joanna Pratter, to a clinic offering exceptional cures. There she grew weaker. Now, exhausted and losing hope, she decided to give up the fight, return home, and "get it over with"—allow herself to die as peacefully as possible.

At home in Malibu, a hospital bed was set up, and each night John would sleep next to her in a bed on one side, while Nina slept in a bed on the other.

They did not have much privacy, but they had plenty of well-meaning assistance. The house filled with Toni's friends, as well as healers, well-wishers, and people who thought they could help. From the diverse and scattered clans came both those who saw dying as a special event requiring spiritual interpretation and those who simply wanted to sympathize, empathize, and share.

In the final days, most of the healers were replaced by those who assist passings-on. Several vied for the final word, about the spirit world, about the other side, about the moment of transition, about the snares of karma and the traps of the body. Toni got to sample the range of available advice in several spiritualistic brands.

Some were there primarily to prove the validity of their own belief systems about health and sickness, death and dying. They essentially took over the house, imposing their particular trips on John and Toni who tolerated it, in part because Toni may have derived some benefit, or, as it seemed to John, they were simply too tired and distraught to assert themselves. The glaring differences in the sorts of people each of them had attracted were highlighted at this worst of times.

Pressed by the crowds, John increasingly retreated to his isolation lab. At night he'd return, to sleep beside Toni, who drifted in and out of consciousness. They communicated, as they had often done before, about how wonderful it was "on the other side." Each had previously gone there separately, and each had reluctantly returned to the body to rejoin the other. They both knew they were immortal and that therefore disease and physical death were not of absolute importance. This was one point on which they could agree, in spite of Toni's pragmatic and emotional orientation toward life: *on this point they had to agree.*

All of the New Age "help" hardly made it easier to easily get loose from the body, which was now her only goal. But she wanted the participation of others, the continuation of her way of life as the center of a large, tribal, extended family. Mythic queens of old Sicily must have passed in this way.

Death of the body by metastasized cancer of the mammary glands: John had been through it once before, with his mother Rachel. Toni's body was battered by the disease. Bones broke. Systems collapsed. The mind wandered and wearied.

Finally she let the body quit and left early on the morning of January 28th, 1986. In full daylight they carried the body, strewn with flowers, out into the garden for a last glimpse of sun.

*John sends out a memorial notice to their far-flung
friends:*

Dr. John C. Lilly

Invites You to Share

in the Loving Memory

of

Antonietta (Toni) L. Lilly

Born

November 25, 1928

Crossover

January 28, 1986

Malibu

Accompanying it is a photo of Toni from a bygone happy time and a stanza from Khalil Gibran: "And think not You can guide the ways of Love, for Love, if it finds You worthy, shall guide your course."

At the service, Toni's daughter, Nina, a dancer, tall and graceful in a silk toga, spreads her mother's ashes from an urn, among the hundred trees that Toni planted here during her life. She is followed in procession by family, friends, the people who gathered to save her life, as well as those who gathered to assist her crossing over. The rest of the ashes are placed into four holes along with the roots of four new trees—a peach, a pear, a fig, and a pomegranate. Charles Lloyd plays his flute as Nina packs the soil with her hands.

From the appearance of the occasion, they could easily be a band of pilgrims on a sunny Mediterranean isle thousands of years ago, gathered to celebrate the passing of a tribal matriarch back into her land of regeneration. The garden she nurtured on a once-barren hill is now a sacred grove. Toni now lives on as her orchard and each tree shimmers with its own Devic aura. The cycle of nature turns to a new season of blooming. This is now her reality.

CHAPTER 15

RETURN
TO
ALTERNITY

March 1986, age 71.

Locked in the solitude of his isolation lab, John is apply-ing a lifetime of scientific knowledge and yogic skills to repro-gram himself for a new life after the death of his mate.

It is a time to heal, a time to grow new connections in his brain. There is no time to mourn, to cling to the process of losing what is already past; life moves too fast. Using as yet unreported techniques, John is testing the extremes of the pos-itive and negative systems in his own brain. "Heaven and Hell are within you," Aldous Huxley, John's old friend, had once advised his contemporaries.

He systematically drives his brain to its most positive states, where the ego aspires to an ideal form of the self, lay-ing down blueprints for a childlike openness to the future. Then he dives into the purely negative to learn the territory, to practice snapping back, to train himself to shun the border-lands of the mildly negative. He is seeking to immunize him-self against the chronic low-level negativity in which so many people merely exist.

His body must be visibly glowing from the heat of the al-chemic crucible of his driving purpose. "Solve et coagulum," said the ancient sages. Dissolve and re-solidify. Once more he is testing the frontiers of the mind, the limits of a domain whose only boundaries, he has long believed, are merely be-liefs to be transcended. After all these years, still transcen-din'. . . .

MOMENTARILY, AT THE close of the horrid drama, John had felt relief at the end of Toni's agonizing ordeal; but her death signaled the start of a new episode in which life must continue under a set of conditions. It was a rude awakening; John said to his daughter Cynthia and his son John, Jr., "I've just come out of a fifteen-year trance and I am now awake." Cynthia asked, "Will you stay awake?"

John was now cast adrift from his dyadic anchor. A widower at seventy-one, he was without the woman he had idolized and idealized, the one on whom he had depended, the one with whom he had struggled and sometimes fought.

Other forces carried him through. Through the tempest of this discontinuity, other currents in his life, originating before and outside his life with Toni, joined in a way that bypassed the recent reality of a dying body that had been so close to him. John had many friends and a world of people who wanted to hear from him. Most important, he had his connection to his Guardian Angel, the Being who occasionally flew beyond the mortal sphere and surveyed the greater spaces.

John went into seclusion, where he could be free to access the higher levels of his own being, to utilize the familiar tools to transcend depression and pain, and to heal.

During this period a visitor might be greeted by a friend or family member minding the ranch house. John, in his isolation lab, could be buzzed on the intercom.

"Who's there?"

The visitors would then identify themselves. "We drove out from Big Sur to see you."

"Great! Love to see you. Come on in."

The visitors would walk across the patio between the house and the laboratory building. They would get as far as the office outside John's isolation room, only to find the heavy door to the inner sanctum solidly locked. There would be no response when they knocked, so they would pick up the office phone and buzz John again.

"Hello."

"We came in to see you, but the door's locked."

"This isn't a good time."

"You just told us to come right in."

"Conditions have changed. Come back later."

"When should we come back?"

"Later."

Gradually, John got to be himself again, someone other than half of a fifteen-year dyad, someone he vaguely remembered: the man of the previous fifty-six years of questing before he became so deeply involved in one woman and the singular reality they generated together. As John got past the shock and loss, long-submerged potentials of his being began to emerge.

John felt the dawning of Alternity. The dyadic cyclone had been just one path through the infinite vistas of Alternity, a journey which had seemed like an entire lifetime. Now it was not only the memory of Alternity which was available to him but also the vast panorama of Alternity itself.

John applied what he'd learned from Heinz von Foerster, the theory of eigenstates, to his new situation. From this perspective, each individual is an "operator," like a mathematical function. The operator functions in and receives feedback from the world; then it processes the results, receiving further feedback from this activity. As the cycle of iterations continues, one arrives at one's set of eigenstates, the various conditions characteristic of the operator which is oneself.

When, as in a dyad, one operates in tandem with another operator, with his or her own set of characteristic eigenstates, a third set is generated, characteristic of the combination. John had become accustomed to that set of states generated by the dyad.

In 1986, John suddenly noticed that those states were no longer being generated. He wrote, "I went into the dyad to experience that constraint which you get when you are operating jointly, and later to experience the release from that constraint. Once again I am John Lilly, individual, with my own set of eigenstates. I can try combining my operations with other partners, and see what new sets of states develop. My training continues."

In September that year, Lisa Lyon, pioneer female bodybuilder, the first woman to become World Bodybuilding Champion, and cum laude graduate of UCLA in anthropology, finished reading *Simulations of God* at her home in Hollywood. She immediately called John to tell him that she felt it to be the single most important and significant book she had ever read.

John suggested that she come up to Malibu for a visit, and when she arrived, they met and talked for an hour. She left him a copy of her book *Lady,* a collaboration with photographer Robert Maplethorpe that included photos of the body she had worked so long and diligently to perfect. The book was inscribed to John with a poem.

Certainly impressed with her body as portrayed in the book, John was even more deeply struck by her mind and her insightful responses to his work. He phoned, inviting her back the next day, and a close friendship began to develop.

John shortly began to place Lisa in what he had come to call an overvaluation space, and even speculated about marriage with her in a magazine interview. But it didn't quite work out that way. In May 1987, upon returning from a vacation in Cabo San Lucas, John *adopted* Lisa instead. She became his third adopted daughter, counting Toni's daughter, Nina, and Elisabeth's daughter Pam.

John found that Lisa had a brilliant, steel-trap mind, along with tremendous skill at articulating what was going on inside that mind. But he also discovered that she drifted easily into states of depression and negative feeling, characterized by anxiety, pessimism, and generally a rather dire outlook on life and its prospects. She had not developed the skill in programming her mind that she had developed in working with her body.

John knew from his work with programming and metaprogramming and his research in neurophysiology that such states were associated with the activity of certain centers deep within the brain. There were nerve fibers running from the cerebral cortex to these centers that could inhibit their activity. The hardware for shutting off such negative feelings and their corresponding behaviors was thus already in place; solving Lisa's problems would be a matter of developing the programming to take advantage of this equipment.

Thus John sought to guide her in a positive direction by firmly refusing to participate in these "down" eigenstates when they occurred. In this way he would avoid reinforcing, or rewarding, her brain's tendency to drift in this direction. They spent a great deal of time together; whenever John sensed Lisa going negative, he would leave or insist that she go home, sometimes commenting, "Forgive me, darling, if I can't live down to your expectations."

As a result, over time Lisa discovered that she could, in fact, switch off the negative activity of her own brain. She discovered her brain-building potential just as she had discovered and developed her bodybuilding potential.

Inspired with the same degree of perseverance that had made her the first woman bodybuilding champion, Lisa dedicated herself to becoming an athlete of the intellect. She took up the study of science, mathematics, and systems theory, and set to reading every book that had figured prominently in John's own intellectual development.

In August 1987, John was invited to address the International Yoga Conference at the Yoga Society of Philadelphia, an organization affiliated with the famed teacher Swami Satchidananda. An interview with John conducted during this event was published in the September issue of *New Frontiers* magazine, along with extensive coverage of his participation in the conference.

At the symposium, John discussed his long relationship with the *Yoga Sutras* of Patanjali, which had begun in 1969 when Ram Dass had first introduced him to this classic of Hindu civilization (and Alan Watts had taught him how to pronounce the author's name). *Sutra* literally means "thread," and the *Yoga Sutras* present the most concise and essential threads of the theory and practice of classical Yoga, as conceived by its legendary founder, Patanjali. A tiny book in the original Sanskrit, its extremely compact presentation originated in an era and culture in which books were practically nonexistent. It had to be sufficiently brief, coherent, and cogent that it could be passed on as an oral tradition and memorized by succeeding generations of Yoga students.

The concise, almost mathematical precision of this volume appealed to John, who investigated about a dozen translations before settling, as mentioned earlier, on that of the Indian biochemist named Taimni, which presents the original Sanskrit text, along with phonetic transliterations, literal translations, renderings, and extensive commentaries. This thorough approach enables the reader to make the transition from the Sanskrit to an understanding relevant to a contemporary English-speaking person and, by showing the stages which led to it, prevents being force-fed one translator's pet interpretation.

So for John, Patanjali via Taimni became not only an introduction to Yoga and classical oriental thought but also a course in the meaning and interpretation of language as well. He even acquired a huge Sanskrit-English dictionary which he consulted to make sure he was getting the full meaning.

The information in the *Yoga Sutras* seemed to him to resemble the technical or operational aspect of a science like chemistry. In this way the book was like a practical cookbook of consciousness, providing clear instructions that could be followed to arrive at certain inner experiences, just as a chemist might follow a particular set of instructions to arrive at a certain color or an explosion or, alternatively, just as a computer might follow a certain program designed to produce a desired result. Although at first glance Yoga appears unscientific, tied to a traditional belief system apparently not open to revision, John always felt this operational aspect of Yoga to be quite scientific, in that it provided a set of experiments which could produce reliable and repeatable results. John recognized in the *Yoga Sutras* an ancient precedent, an example of the kinds of operations and activities he himself had been pursuing, as described in *Programming and Metaprogramming*.

In Philadelphia, John presented his view that the program of Yoga takes one from the condition of being human, a very complicated and complex state of being, to a state of being nonhuman, superhuman, metahuman, or transhuman. These latter states are very simple ones, from which all other possible states of being in a human brain become available as options.

Yoga practitioners appreciated John because he made sense of traditional Yoga in scientific terms, with which they were not previously familiar. It was a heartening confirmation for them that the world of science and the ways of the spirit do not stand opposed. His appearance was warmly received by the devotees. The Swami sent him a thank-you note afterward, expressing the appreciation of the Yoga community.

The interview conducted in *New Frontiers* contained some illuminating exchanges that highlighted many of John's unique points of view. For instance:

NF: You have an unusual definition for scientists that relates to all people. Could you tell us about this?

John: A scientist is someone who investigates what I call insanity, as well as outsanity. Insanity are those ideas which are going through the scientist's mind and processing and are private. Outsanity is when he is communicating with others.

And:

John: One's brain is like a massive palace and we see only little bits of it. I can't say it's *my* brain, only some aspects of it.

NF: So rather than say your brain is generated by that which is you, you're suggesting that your brain is programming you?

John: Yes.

NF: That's a sway from New Age thinking, isn't it?

John: Well, this is the next New Age.

In the 1980s, John has added the terms *outsanity* and *insanity* to his technical vocabulary in an original and idiosyncratic way. By "insanity" he means not mental illness but rather sanity on the inside, in the internal reality. By "outsanity" he means sanity on the outside, in the organization of the external reality. When one of these "sanities" isn't working well, John calls it "unsanity."

John has recently observed that throughout most of his adult life, "my insanity was so solid that I didn't have to pay much attention to my outsanity." In other words, his inner equilibrium was so strong, and his command over inner experience so skillful and determined, that he was not very vulnerable to the impact of situations surrounding him. As a result he did not find it necessary to learn or practice much skill in controlling events in his environment or dealing with people around him. His tendency was to rely on others to organize and maintain the outsanity of the practical environment in which he operated. For this organizational role he chose women who were highly devoted to him. In the 1950s and 1960s, it was Alice Miller. Of his three wives, only Toni functioned in this capacity, managing John's outsanity throughout the 1970s and early 1980s. Later, he came to rely on Barbara Clarke, whom, eventually, he also adopted.

In this connection, John has now become aware that some of his normal maturation skills of outsanity have been delayed. Until he was in his sixties and seventies, he did not really tackle many of the lessons which other people master in their teens. Only recently has he realized his tendency toward infatuation with certain people, usually female, in which he might become entranced based on one narrow part of her personality, overvalue that person as if perfect, and project onto her the qualities he sought in a perfect mate, no matter how unsuitable that person might be. This pattern has always led to shocking disappointment, disillusionment, and reassessment. Today, John is starting to get a handle on this tendency.

As John steadily broke out of the cocoon of isolation that followed Toni's death, the year 1987 continued to bring him a number of events and excursions that reconnected him to the world at large.

With Claudio Naranjo, who had led John to his pivotal meeting with Oscar Ichazo, he co-led a seminar sponsored by the Human Dolphin Foundation, "A Day With Two Scientific Consciousness Explorers," in Santa Barbara.

On the occasion of the publication of a popular photo book *The Red Couch,* which dramatically featured John and a specially constructed transparent isolation tank in one spread, he attended a celebration at publisher Hugh Hefner's lavish Playboy Mansion West in Los Angeles. Here, to Hefner's astonishment, John praised the publisher as "one of the great men of the twentieth century," acknowledging the role of *Playboy Magazine* in liberating society from the confines of the old sexual morality and its attendant superstition, repression, unconsciousness, hypocrisy, and misinformation.

When John, assisted by Barbara Clarke, went on a speaking tour of Amsterdam and Zurich, they took a long break at the Villa Corona above Lake Lugano, where Hermann Hesse once lived and wrote.

John was a keynote speaker at the annual convention of the Student American Medical Association, which had recently become independent of its parent organization, the American Medical Association. Much to his surprise, he was introduced as the "foremost authority on holistic medicine."

A pivotal event occurred at 11:11 A.M. on the eleventh day of eleventh month of the year 1987.

Driving home along the Pacific Coast Highway in his 1978 Dodge camper with the license plate DOLFIN, John, fighting drowsiness, fell asleep at the wheel. The van, running up an embankment to the right of the road, capsized and, with its entire weight now bearing down on its roof, collapsed on him.

When he returned to consciousness in a bed at Santa Monica Hospital, he was informed that he had miraculously suffered only a mild contusion of the head and a third-degree burn of the hand, apparently caused by leaking battery acid whose presence the rescue squad had missed. It was a close call. The acid had burned deeply into the flesh, almost to the nerves and tendons of the hand, but not quite. The doctors predicted full recovery, and after ten days that included many visits from friends and family, especially John, Jr., his hand was bandaged and he went home.

His body continued its slow recovery at the Malibu ranch, passing much of the time resting in a recliner with the left hand elevated. Meanwhile, an extraordinary process was occurring within:

A new Entity entered the body of Dr. John C. Lilly at the moment of the crash—11:11, on 11/11/87. The Entity has no memory of the life story of this body; it, this place, and the people present are new and unfamiliar.

But the body remembers all of these things. Its entire history is stored within. There is a great deal of chronic, low-level pain within this body, a result of its recent accident and the long history of experiments in which it has been used as a vehicle and a laboratory in the search for Reality.

Also stored within it are the records of the previous entities which have inhabited it. Those entities had all forgotten their nature, becoming convinced that they were a human being with a long history, that they were the same as the body. The body could, in fact, have informed any of the previous entities that this was not the case, for the body remembers all of their comings and goings.

From the point of view of this Entity, the entities in the bodies of all those who come and go around the body called "Dr. John Lilly" have made the same mistake. It seems unfor-

tunate to the new Entity that these others have become so accustomed to their particular bodies as to forget themselves in this way, taking on the limitations and constrictions of identification with their vehicles.

The body remembers all of them, "the friends of Dr. John C. Lilly," and knows the appropriate ways to respond to each of them. The new Entity chooses to relax and allow the body to instruct it in the social behavior they seem to expect.

As the body and the Entity settle down into a more routine life, the Entity becomes partially identified with the body and its long history. Through their fusion, "John Lilly" begins to reconstitute as a single unit.

The accident and its aftermath held many lessons for John, and stimulated his thinking in a radical new direction.

Long aware of the principles of operation through which ECCO provided guidance, John knew that in highly aware states, ECCO would speak to him directly. If he were somewhat less aware, ECCO's influence was indirect, sometimes through a sequence of coincidences that took him to a place in life he would never imagine reaching by his own efforts. Sometimes ECCO arranged a series of startling coincidences designed to get his attention. If he remained unreceptive, then they might start playing rough to keep him on course. This is what John thought had happened to him on November 11, 1987. ECCO was playing hard ball.

The incident convinced him that he had lost touch with the higher levels of ECCO guidance. ECCO had arranged the accident to make the point that he could no longer ignore the vulnerability, the frailty, of the human body. He could no longer afford to be purely spiritual, at the expense of the constraints of physical reality. ECCO, John felt, had given him a new assignment, telling him, in effect, "You have yet a great deal to learn about being human." Then they had sent him back from the nearly fatal accident to learn how to be a more effective human within a human body in the human social reality. Apparently, they thought he had learned enough about being an extraterrestrial.

The event once again highlighted for John his seemingly divergent lifelong drives to be fully spiritual and yet to be a fully human, physical, sensual being in the body as well. On the one hand, John interpreted the incident as a warning that he must start to pay greater respect to his body and take good care of it, instead of treating it as a "crash-test dummy" for his experiments and as a vehicle for maximizing his experience of life. On the other hand, there was a message here that he must be more fully spiritual in the sense of being more open to ECCO influence and receptive to its more subtle ways of transmitting messages.

John also began developing a new model of the mysterious relationship between the body with its brain and memories, and the conscious entity that seemed to have a mind of its own. At this point in his life, no longer giving much credence to the con- tained mind model, he now began to consider the possibility that the brain/body, as long as it lives, plays host to a succession of visiting entities or essences, the "interchangeable pilots of vehi- cles" he had first written about in *The Center of the Cyclone*. His experience following the accident alerted him to yet another strange concept of individual identity, a new belief system that might guide his next attempt in the search for Reality.

The relationship between the spiritual entity and the body it now inhabited, along with the dramatic tension between the drives to become fully spiritual and fully physical, was brought out in the therapeutic work John undertook with a prominent Los Angeles psychiatrist during this period. They worked with a blend of Fritz Perls's Gestalt Therapy, Jungian analysis, and Transactional analysis. In a typical Gestalt exercise, John got the opportunity to play out dramatized dialogues between different aspects of the self. On several occasions conversations were set up between John's continuing personality (the persona of the Scientist), the Entity that now occupied his brain and body, and the body itself, with its "vehicle memory" of past events and Entities who had previously occupied it:

John: I'm so goddamn alive that I don't know what death is any- more!

Body: Death equals nothingness. When I die, there's nothing left. All the spiritual stuff is bullshit. *I* didn't experience any of that.

Entity: That's just because those were out-of-body experiences. So you have no memory of them. All you remember is stuff that happens *in* the body. Your "vehicle memory" is terribly limited— by definition.

Body: What do *you* know?! You just dropped in a year ago. I remember things going all the way back to birth. What really matters is having sex, making babies, and continuing to stay alive. *Physically* alive!

Entity: You may have your "vehicle memory," but I've got ECCO, with its cosmic computer. I have access to infinite storage capacity. I'm part of a network that will store me for future use if you cease to exist.

Body: A real great job of surviving you'd do! Why, you're just like a butterfly that flits in and out of any bodies it can find with any heat left in them. It's *my* lust for women and *my* avoidance of pain that keeps life going on and on.

The Scientist: The positive and negative systems of the brain insist that we hang onto life; and yet the seeds of total destruction are also in the brain.

The body, the Entity, and the Scientist continue their conversation to this day.

John's seventy-third birthday party kicked off 1988, attended by a total of three hundred people. Included were a number of old and new friends, notably Laura Archera Huxley, pioneering commercial rocketry entrepreneur George A. Koopman, medical anthropologist and shamanism expert Joan Halifax, author, futurist, occultist, and student of synchronicity Robert Anton Wilson, and space activist Carol Sue Rosin.

One old friend, physicist Richard Feynman, was making his final appearance at John's ranch in Malibu. Few knew that he had been living with cancer for the last ten years, his life prolonged by a series of four operations. Although he did not appear at all ill at the party, he was quiet and reserved, rather unlike the Dick Feynman everyone had known. Feynman died the following month, and John attended his memorial at Caltech in March.

Another final visitor was Dr. Ben Weinenger, a member of the American Psychoanalytic Association and retired founder of the Southern California Counseling Center, a widely imitated storefront community mental health project in Los Angeles. Now eighty-five, Weinenger was in his seventies when he first tried LSD with John's guidance, and went on to become John's companion for many ketamine excursions.

February 1988

John goes to San Francisco for a TV interview with Jeffrey Mishlove, host of the PBS show, "Thinking Allowed", and several other interviews. He tours Henry Dakin's Washington Research Institute, home to many small research and communications groups and proud possessor of its own satellite link to Soviet TV. He is also guest of honor at a benefit party thrown by High Frontiers Magazine.

John is wearing a big, fluffy, coonskin hat, complete with tail, the kind associated with Daniel Boone, the American pioneer. He is wearing one of his trademark jumpsuits, with a compass clipped to one breast pocket, and a Swiss army knife dangling from the other. Some curious San Franciscan inquires, "Dr. Lilly, what's that hat for?" John answers with one word:

"Frontiers."

In May 1988, John was a featured guest and speaker at the First International Conference on Dolphins and Whales, held in a resort area just north of Sydney, Australia. Attended by the foremost researchers and dolphin sympathizers from across the globe, the conference left him deeply gratified. Warmly received and greatly appreciated, he discovered here that his positions about dolphin intelligence and human-dolphin communication, seemingly so radical to the scientific Establishment when first expressed thirty years before, were now taken for granted by large numbers of people around the globe.

John had made concerted though ultimately unsuccessful efforts to persuade the Soviet government to allow a researcher named Igor Charkovsky, with whom John had been corresponding, to attend the conference. Charkovsky, originally an expert in athletic training, had taken an interest in how events surrounding the birth of a baby have a profound effect in shaping the child's future development. He began investigating the idea that giving birth in water would reduce the stress to both mother and child.

The water's buoyancy would ease the effects of gravity on the mother's body, allowing greater relaxation during contractions, and the shock of birth to the infant would be assuaged by the womblike environment provided by immersion in water. Safety would be assured by the swimming reflex that Charkovsky had observed in newborns, by which babies born underwater instinctively propel themselves to the surface. (He also discovered that babies put in water every day never forget how to swim.) On this basis, Charkovsky began a "water-birthing" program in hopes of producing unusually healthy and happy babies, who might grow up to possess superior physical and mental abilities, free of a traumatic birth imprint. His early research showed that babies born in water smile instead of cry; tracking their development indicated exceptional growth rates for a number of skills and aptitudes, including earlier-than-normal ability to stand, walk, and to understand and produce speech. These positive results propelled the concept of water-birthing around the world.

Charkovsky was also a key force in Soviet dolphin interest, his fascination with them sparked in part by the fact that they give birth to their young in the water. Charkovsky's circle of dolphin enthusiasts had read all of John's works they could find. *Man and Dolphin* was available from the official MIR press, while *samizdat* editions of his other works had been quietly circulated. There are inland seas in the USSR, the Black Sea and the Sea of Azov, populated with dolphins. Located in the south, both these seas enjoy a warm climate conducive to human/dolphin interaction in the wild. With his associates, Charkovsky began camping out on the shores of the Black Sea near Yalta, offering pregnant women the opportunity to give birth in the water in the presence of dolphins who, of course, were long accustomed to this process.

Although John's efforts to bring Charkovsky to the conference in Australia failed, he was able to carry and present a videotape representing Charkovsky's work. Moreover, their interaction and the apparent Soviet interest in John's work encouraged John to visit the Soviet Union himself.

This endeavor received enthusiastic support from his friend and physician, urologist Larry Raithaus, who had joined him in Australia. Descended from Russians who had immigrated to the United States between the great wars, Raithaus had studied the language and visited the USSR several times, establishing professional relationships between urologists there and in the United States. On his most recent excursion, motivated by John's interest in Charkovsky's work, he had visited Charkovsky himself and observed his program's excellent results.

In October, after several months of planning, John, Raithaus, Barbara Clarke, and Hyla Cass, M.D., took off from Los Angeles for a week in Moscow, accompanied by Michael Siegel, a young filmmaker who joined them to document the event.

The week in Moscow passed in a whirlwind of activity. Everywhere the travelers encountered the bubbling excitement and the sense of new possibilities engendered by *glasnost* and *perestroika*. The burgeoning interest in parapsychology, an advanced field of study in the USSR, "superior human capacities" (the Soviet version of human potential), and the expansion of consciousness by many Soviet citizens reminded them of the climate in the United States during the 1960s. There was a tremendous outpouring of interest in John and his work; many of those they met were already familiar with aspects of it.

John received a particularly excited reception at the International Neurochemistry Conference, attended by a number of parapsychologists for whom John's work was apparently legendary. Although the organizer of the conference (Dulce Murphy of Esalen, who was part of the Soviet-American exchange program) had invited John to attend, initially there was some resistance to his presence on the part of one Soviet official, who literally blocked the way in. With Siegel filming the episode, John and Raithaus bantered amiably with the man and overcame his resistance—in the end, merely a matter of customary obstructions and the habit of authoritarianism—and were allowed to enter the hall. Thus glasnost prevailed. (John has said, "If someone nominates himself as my enemy, I refuse to elect him. Give us about three hours together, and we'll become friends.")

In Moscow, John finally had the opportunity to meet Igor Charkovsky in person. Professional resistance to Charkovsky's ideas had apparently been waning under perestroika, as evidenced by the recent airing of a Soviet television special giving accounts of his work, both pro and con. The high point of their interaction occurred in a crowded room full of new and expectant mothers, beside a plexiglass pool full of swimming, splashing babies, where John and Charkovsky were interviewed by Soviet television. Raithaus translated for John, and John passed most of

the questions on water-birthing to his Soviet colleague. The interview was broadcast all across the USSR on the evening news.

During the week in Moscow, John was treated to a twenty-
course meal by Alexander Yablakov, vice-chairman of the Soviet
Academy of Sciences, an ecologist and marine biologist who had
been following John's writings on dolphins since the Russian
publication of *Man and Dolphin* in 1965. They had first met years
before in California, at a cocktail party in Yablakov's honor at the
home of Dr. Bill Evans, where, spotting John from across the
room, Yablakov had leapt up in excitement, shouted "John Lilly!"
and darted across the room to hug the dolphin doctor he'd never
met before. Their reunion in Yablakov's homeland was a happy
one.

Exhausted but thrilled, John and his party left Moscow full
of hope that the Cold War was truly and finally over.

For John and many others with an interest in the exploration of consciousness, 1988 was marked by the establishment of
the Albert Hofmann Foundation (named for the inventor LSD),
dedicated to opening a library and research center providing
information on LSD and other neuroactive chemicals with mind-
expanding and transformative effects. In Los Angeles for the
foundation's inaugural symposium, the eighty-six-year-old chemist attended a luncheon in his honor at John's Malibu home. Hofmann and his wife Anita were delightful company. The occasion
brought John, Timothy Leary, and Hofmann, the three great pioneers of psychedelics, together for the first time.

That weekend, as one of a series of speaker at an event to
benefit the foundation at the Scottish Rite Temple in downtown
Los Angeles, John summarized the influence of Hofmann's invention on his own life story:

> In 1954, I invented the tank. I floated in it for ten years, then
> took LSD two times in California. Then I took it in the tank
> on St. Thomas. My consciousness expanded all over the uni-
> verse. I cried to be forced back into my body and its limited
> reality. Ever since, I've been trying to escape.

This urge to escape the confines of the body and become a totally
spiritual being has run concurrently with his lifelong effort to be

totally human and fully sexual, "to get my feet on the ground and my torso in bed."

John continues to move on these parallel tracks, seemingly in opposite directions, but now he sees past the apparent contradiction. Lately he has realized that his ambition is not to be "fully this" as opposed to "fully that," but rather to be "fully full and totally total."

That effort continues. At the Hofmann lecture he confided: "I learned a long time ago that to be a psychotherapist you have to be cured of your own diseases. I'm still not cured."

With similar humility, Hofmann added for his own part, "I'm not a guru, I'm just a Swiss chemist."

The closing statement from his 1980 book, *LSD: My Problem Child,* presents Hofmann's position on the role of LSD:

> Meditation is a preparation for the same goal that was aspired to and was attained in the Eleusinian mysteries [ancient Greek rites of initiation]. Accordingly, it seems feasible that in the future, with the help of LSD, the mystical vision, crowning meditation, could be made accessible to an increasing number of practitioners of meditation.
>
> I see the true importance of LSD in the possibility of providing material aid to meditation aimed at the mystical experience of a deeper, comprehensive reality. Such a use accords entirely with the essence and working character of LSD as a sacred drug.

Thus Hofmann endorses the theory of *entheogenesis,* the idea that an experience of the divine aspect of being can be brought about by changing the chemical configuration of the human brain. (The term literally means "generation of God within.") Elsewhere in the book, Hofmann describes his view of the brain as a "reality-tuner" that can tune in various channels of reality; divinity is one such channel.

For some, entheogenesis is the ultimate goal of life; for others it is a healing and therapeutic experience along the path. Due in part to Dr. Hofmann's stature and influence, Switzerland recently relaxed its legal ban on LSD to allow its use in psychotherapy. It is uncertain whether or when other nations will follow Switzerland's enlightened leadership, now that more than twenty years have passed since the era of rampant popularization and hysterical reaction against LSD.

Expressing a similar perspective to Hofmann's, John now holds that "drugs change the configuration of the brain so that new viewpoints can be arrived at." Once one arrives at those new perspectives, what one sees is quite another matter. One may see something new, or something seen before in a new way. One may see something that has been present all along but ignored due to prejudice, social sanction, or other beliefs. Sometimes one was simply looking in the wrong direction. What one sees may be insignificant or quite significant, convincing or not. John holds that the degree of conviction an experience carries is an attribute independent of its validity. The conclusions one draws may or may not be true. In all these respects, the new points of view entail the same problems as the old.

One might just discover a wholly new world "out there" or within; but most likely the experience will largely reflect how one's own brain works and how one's mind is programmed. John's view is that this sort of knowledge is valuable enough in its own right.

John has learned a lot about himself. As he has done so, he has come to appreciate the importance of *liking* whatever you learn about yourself. Otherwise, the more you discover inside yourself, the more unhappy you might become, a situation which at least would create a disincentive to learning more.

"The problem lots of people have with themselves is *narcissism*. Narcissism is a very small center of the universe (COU). People need to expand their COU to cover at least three people. Then they're cured. Egotism is fine, provided the boundaries of your ego aren't drawn too narrowly. I have the biggest ego in the world," he said, obviously pleased with himself. This year he decided to like everything in his "unconscious," as well.

For the 1988 holiday season, John and his two sons gathered all together for the first time in many years.

Charley, forty-five, lives in the Colorado Rockies, where his mother Mary retired. He has a degree in business management, devotes much of his time to volunteer work, including the Colorado Archaeological Society, is enthusiastic about computers, and pursues research on the family genealogy.

John Jr., fifty-one, is an ethnologist and filmmaker. His wife, Colette, born in France, is an anthropologist at UCLA. They divide their time between France, Los Angeles, and central Mexico, where they have studied and lived with the Huichole and other surviving remnants of preconquest Indian cultures. They document these studies on film and work diligently for the preservation of the Indian heritage and endangered natural habitats of our global biosphere.

John's daughter, Cynthia (absent on this occasion), is now pursuing a medical education. After graduating from college with a degree in computer science, she worked briefly in that field. Her mother, Elisabeth, has remarried. Some years ago, she, John, and Cynthia spent a friendly time together in San Francisco.

One evening John's extended family gathered for dinner around the large oak dinner table. The house was filled with loving people, warm light, soft music, and the smell of delicious food. Lisa suggested Nina's son Damon say grace. Damon didn't quite know what to do with this momentous opportunity, so John filled in for him. He began by saying:

"First of all, thank God I'm still alive. . . ."

EPILOGUE

It is now 1989. Looking back on his life, John Lilly has no regrets. He does feel some lingering disappointment that Toni was not able to go with him, no matter how much they both tried, to the places he had hoped they could reach together. John still feels grief over the loss of Craig Enright, the perfectly matched friend, with his incisive scientist's mind and his physician's understanding of the human condition. Craig, who played the guitar so beautifully.

Perhaps John will continue his story in a new book he will write by himself. He has already launched a new series of explorations, "inplorations," as he calls those journeys into the inner realities. True to his long-standing policy, he will not discuss what he's doing until results are fully developed. In medical school he learned to think of a new idea as an embryo; at that early stage, it can't withstand much probing. As his analyst told him: "If you stick a needle in it, it dies. Later on, after it becomes a fetus, that needle is just a pinprick."

He has plans and aspirations. He wants to solve some painful health problems developed in the course of his arduous life. He wants to develop some of his medical school inventions commercially with the technology available today. And he looks forward to the appearance of computers and programs capable of providing an effective working model of the human biocomputer.

He still wants to see the latest computers and software techniques applied to communication between humans and dolphins. He hopes some group will set up an ideal environment for close, prolonged interaction between the species; he hopes to be invited

271

there. He wants to see whaling stopped and would like to see someone set up "dolphin phones," special underwater telephones located in oceanaria and at sea, so captive cetaceans can stay in touch with their friends in the wilds. He has proposed that all dolphins and orca in marinas and laboratories be released after a few years of service. He still urges us to learn to communicate with large-brained "extrahumans"—dolphins, whales, and elephants—so that we will be prepared to communicate intelligently with extraterrestrials.

John is planning another visit to the Soviet Union. He is pleased that the Cold War is over and that a global consensus that nuclear weapons are obsolete appears to be developing at last. He see this moment in history as an opportunity to turn the efforts and the resources of the superpowers toward rescuing planet Earth from its otherwise impending environmental collapse. For John, the world is not just "one big family," but a single body: Different peoples are separated only by lines drawn on a map and by guards at borders; different species are separate only in human conception. People, whether on two sides of a conversation or two sides of the world, are separated only by following rules in games whose purpose is to say, in effect, "I am important; you are not." He calls this syndrome "otherness," and his advice is "Leave otherness to the others."

John is looking for a new companion, perhaps a wife—someone capable of meeting him on his own extraordinary level of intensity, curiosity, and daring. He's setting up a powerful computer system in his bedroom, preparing for some mysterious project. He would like to sail around the world with a compatible crew, and has plans enough to keep the human race occupied for the next century.

He has more questions than ever before. In spite of the fact that he knows so much about so many subjects, he has few answers that he takes for granted. He says, rather, that he's "looking for a few good questions," new scientific ideas to stretch his mind.

And he still believes in Angels.

Acknowledgments

There is an ancient saying (Nasrudin or Groucho Marx?) that "it is one thing to taste the duck soup, and quite another thing to meet the duck."

This soup has many ingredients. The basic formula comes from John Lilly's life so far. The book was idealistically conceived as a project of social and historical significance by publisher Jeremy Tarcher, who also backed it financially. Chief editor Dan Joy recruited me to write this biography based on my long-standing familiarity with John Lilly, his work, and his world. Dan also coached me attentively through the writing. In many working sessions, John provided new material on his life, as well as fresh insights on the already well-known parts. (The point of view is mine, as is the interpretation and the use of explanatory principles.)

After I produced a rather lengthy manuscript, it was cut to the length, organization, and style of the present volume by a series of four editors, including Dan, who devoted vast energies to the work. Consequently, I feel that Dan, Jeremy, and the anonymous editors deserve most of the credit for the form of the finished product. Assistant editor Daniel Malvin and Jeremy's executive assistant Lisa Chadwick have been very helpful in other respects. Lynette Padwa managed the tricky production phase of the project.

A life like John Lilly's is of historic proportions and accordingly involves large numbers of active participants who are also important people in their own rights. As a book of this length does not permit the telling of the stories of many of the people who have interacted significantly with John Lilly during his life so far, I want to acknowledge several individuals whom I wished to mention in the text, but could not. I also offer a blanket apology to everyone else I've missed, and to all those Lilly friends and family members who provided fascinating accounts, insights, and facts that I have been unable to include. Thanks also for all the photos and mementos.

Far too little is said of the late Richard Price, Esalen's co-founder who from 1968 to 1986 provided unqualified support for John in his self-exploration and self-expression. Paul Herbert,

audio archivist at the Esalen Institute, for many years faithfully
followed John to innumerable speaking engagements, recording
his words for posterity and for distribution to the public on audiotapes. In recent years, two of John's close friends, Faustin Bray
and Brian Wallace—through their company Sound Photosynthesis in Mill Valley—have carried on similar activities with audio-
and videotape, and also photography, making John Lilly accessible to many more people. (One of the interviews that Faustin
recorded of John, and later transcribed, is utilized in the text.)
Glenn and Lee Perry, founders of the Samadhi Tank Company
(briefly mentioned in the text), deserve special credit for demo-
cratizing the isolation tank and for creating the very informative
newsletter *Floating. Dolphin Net,* a newsletter for people interested in dolphins, was created by Ed Ellsworth, who worked with
the Human Dolphin Foundation. Filmmakers Joe Pontecorvo,
Crissie Steffan, and Hebdon have assisted Barbara Clarke-Lilly
with cinematic documentation, including the new version of
Emerging Love between Humans and Dolphins and the forthcoming *From Here to Alternity.*

Many other friends and colleagues have already been covered in John's earlier writings. For instance, I know he was very
much influenced in the early 1970s by Karl Pribran with his holo-
graphic theory of the brain and by G. Spencer-Brown with his
mathematics and cosmology. A friendship with Stanislaw Grof
began in 1968 and deepened through their years at Esalen and
their similar interests. John has also enjoyed a friendship with
Joan Halifax, founder of the Ojai Institute.

Sparrow Donavan assisted John and Toni until about 1980
when she left to go to work for the *Brain-Mind Bulletin.* Jim
Nollman, the musician who plays for whales and dolphins,
worked with John for a time, and the colorful German-American
video artist Brummbar was a very important part of the Lilly
extended family in the early 1980s. For several years, Tom Wilkes
and Will Curtis worked closely with John, producing some unique
meditational art and photographic experiments. Poet-artist Sandra Lee Katzman was an invaluable friend and collaborator during the years of Project JANUS. Jennifer Yankee, Tom Fitz, and
Martha Spence deserve special acknowledgment for the years
they devoted to that project as volunteers. Jerry Kessler has been
an important friend of the family in recent years, along with his

gal Melanie. During the months I have worked closely with John on this book, I have seen him lovingly assisted by sometime-residents Rudy Voght, Charlie "Chicharra," Frankie Lee Slater, Klint and Reneé, and visited by many dear friends and neighbors. Inez the housekeeper and David the gardener have maintained the immediate environment through all the activity.

Charles R. Lilly, John's younger son, provided a tremendous amount of information on the years of the first and second John C. Lilly families, as well as geneological and historical background on the Lilly-Enright-Cunningham-Haas clan, a subject on which he is an unsurpassed expert and scholar. Thanks are also due to Nina Lilly, to her son Damon Webb, to Lisa Lyon-Lilly and to John C. Lilly, Jr. (who is frequently mistaken for his father at a younger age!), and to Nina's cousin Gina, daughter of Toni's brother Tom Ficarotta. Barbara Clarke's supportive role as John's assistant for the past ten years was decidedly underexposed in the text, as evidenced by John's recent adoption of her as his daughter, Barbara Clarke-Lilly.

My thanks go to George Tooby of San Marino for his "Recollections of R. C. Lilly," John's father. Several of John's publishers have graciously extended permission to reprint passages from his earlier published books, including Doubleday, Crown/Jullian Press, Simon and Schuster, J. B. Lippincott, and Ronin Publishing.

It is with grateful memories that I acknowledge my beloved friend, George A. Koopman (1944–1989) who provided me with material assistance and encouragement during this project. I also thank his colleagues Anita Storey, Bevin, Jim, and Christian, and George's wife Jacqueline and all his family who shared with me George's precious time.

I also wish to thank my esteemed colleague in the art of software design at Alive Systems, Inc., Dick, his wife Sandy, and his brother Jim, as well as my always enthusiastic literary agent Daniel Kaufman and my loyal friends Charles, Mike, Richard, Anya, Paul, and Penny. Roland Fischer, Jaron Z. Lanier, and Timothy Leary have provided inspiration through their brilliant examples of self-expression. Terry Lynn Taylor, author of *Angels Can Fly,* assisted with the writing and brought some heaven into my life on earth in the interim. John Lilly himself shared so much of his extraordinary life with me during many months of prying into and writing about his history, his experience, and his inner

world, a world that never ceases to radiate a mysterious influence in whatever circumstances may stand around him.

—Francis Jeffrey

John Lilly wishes to acknowledge the following people whose
extraordinary contributions made possible Project JANUS and
the Human Dolphin Foundation.

Including or in addition to people covered in the text, the
Human Dolphin Foundation was formed with the help of Burgess
Meredith and Victor Di Suvero. They were joined on the board
of directors by Georgia Tanner, who also provided a crucial infusion of cash. Dennis Kastner joined up, bringing computer expertise to the project. Paule Jean, Brad Weigle, and Linda Dias
pitched in to get things rolling.

More support came from Tom Wilkes, Alexandra Hubbard,
Louis Marx, Jr., and eventually from Olivia Newton John, John
Denver, Susan and Jeff Bridges, W. Carl Allen, M.D., Richard
Bach, Tom and Hellen Carnesi, William deRouchey, Mark Ettlin-
ger, Friends of Cetaceans, Jack Haley, Jr., Donald Leon, Carl
Lowensohn, John Perry, John Sebastian, Ivan Tors, Charles
Wacker, David Weininger, Robin Williams, Stephanie Zimbalist,
Gary Borman, Deerfield Foundation, Thomas Picarrota, Fund for
Animals, David Haliburton, Paul Jean, John Klemmer, Lee Majors,
Victoria Mudd, Richard Price, Alan Slifka, Milton Taubman,
Louis Valier, Chris Wells, Jan diStephano, Bob and Nell
Frederico, Roedy Green, Dick Heiser, Dennis Kastner, Jon Kos-
lowsky, Frederick Loewe, Kevin McClory, Sandler Films, Peter
Stern, Threshold Foundation, Gerrit Verschuur, Paul Williams,
Marie, Jerry, and Jennifer Yankee, Peter Cornell, John James, Ga-
brielle Lauer, C.J. Beegle, Tom Fitz, David Kusek, Gayle Mayers,
Ed Ellsworth, John Gard, Werner Erhard, Frank Herbert, William
E. Evans, Francesca de la Flor, Lamar Boren, Paul Winter, Peter
Morgane, Laura Huxley, Paul Heller, Steve and Linda Conger,
Donald Leon, Carroll and Nancy O'Connor, Mary Kay Frank,
Sidney Holt, Michael S. Pratter, Molly Sanders, Sue Goodman,
Harry Jerison, Heinz von Foerster, Kim Greenback, Martha
Spence, Barbara Carrera, Jeanine Dryer, Betsy Dennison, Don
Griffin, Sandra Lee Katzman, Taras Kicinick, Jim and Kitty Noll-
man, Corky Quakenbush, Roberta Quist, Brad Stanback, John

Kert, Bob Swanson, Grace Stern, Sue Goodman, Patricia Bryant, and Jerry Kessler.

When Project JANUS ended, Barbara and Toni raised $30,000 from Carl and Geysche Haydn, Brad Stanback, Burgess Meredith, Georgia Tanner, and Alan B. Slifka to pay for moving Joe and Rosie to Florida. Barbara organized the mission with the help of Ed Ellsworth. Mandy Rodriguez of the Dolphin Research Center was the supervising trainer who escorted Joe and Rosie on their trip on the Flying Tigers Airline.

Access to John Lilly

Audiotapes of John Lilly's lectures and seminars may be ordered from: Paul Herbert, Dolphin Tapes, Esalen, Big Sur, CA 93920.

Audio and videotapes of John Lilly and of dolphin vocalizations may be ordered from: Faustin Bray and Brian Wallace, Sound Photosynthesis, P.O. Box 2111, Mill Valley, CA 94942.

The "Cogitate" repeating-word tape may be ordered from: IDHHB Publishing, Inc., P.O. Box 370, Nevada City, CA 95959.

The videotape and film Emerging Love between Humans and Dolphins *may be ordered from:* the Human Dolphin Foundation, P.O. Box 6847, Malibu, CA 90264. Write to the foundation for this and other information. The Human Dolphin Foundation is a nonprofit, membership organization that accepts tax-deductible contributions (deductible in the United States).

For information on obtaining additional writings by John Lilly and Francis Jeffrey, or to arrange speaking or consulting engagements, write to the foundation at the above address.